Business Negotiations in China

Business Negotiations in China provides a holistic overview of the institutional, organizational and cultural issues that underpin successful business negotiations in China.

Good negotiation strategies and management are essential for establishing successful business deals and new ventures in China. The author addresses the current key issues and risks, high-level business management, planning, innovative approaches and modern negotiation strategies. The text opens with a review of the evolution of key negotiation models that have been used in China right up to the most current. This is followed by an analysis of the various negotiation frameworks and processes being undertaken in China and their similarities and differences with other global negotiation processes. Alongside the negotiation itself, the author provides advice on: the selection of the negotiation team and the various strategic roles within it; the detailed preparation and analysis required prior to starting negotiations in China; the effective management strategies for each of the various stages of negotiation to achieve successful, sustainable outcomes.

Business Negotiations in China is supported by examples and analysis drawn from actual high-level business negotiations by leading international companies with Chinese State-Owned Enterprises. It also explores the fierce competition between multinationals and China state-owned companies and their respective different negotiation strategies. This book is an important, indispensable insider's guide to the strategy and practice of negotiating in China and is relevant to professionals, academics, researchers and students alike.

Henry K. H. Wang is a senior executive and an international adviser, author and speaker with extensive global business experience. He is President of Gate International Ltd and director of various companies. He is a former director of Shell China and SABIC in Riyadh. He has been invited to advise leading international agencies, companies and universities globally and speaks regularly at international conferences, leading universities and business schools. He is a Fellow of the Royal Society of Arts FRSA and a Fellow of Institute of Chemical Engineering, UK. His first book, *Successful Business Dealings & Management with China Oil, Gas & Chemical Giants*, was published in 2013 and his second book, *Energy Markets in Emerging Economies: Strategies for Growth*, was published in 2016.

Business Negotiations in China
Strategy, Planning and Management

Henry K. H. Wang

Routledge
Taylor & Francis Group

LONDON AND NEW YORK

First published in paperback 2024

First published 2018
by Routledge
4 Park Square, Milton Park, Abingdon, Oxon OX14 4RN

and by Routledge
605 Third Avenue, New York, NY 10158

Routledge is an imprint of the Taylor & Francis Group, an informa business

British Library Cataloguing-in-Publication Data
A catalogue record for this book is available from the British Library

Library of Congress Cataloging-in-Publication Data

Names: Wang, Henry K. H., author.
Title: Business negotiations in China: strategy, planning and management /
Henry K. H. Wang.
Description: 1 Edition. | New York: Routledge, 2018. | Includes
bibliographical references and index.
Identifiers: LCCN 2017031426 (print) | LCCN 2017047493 (ebook) |
ISBN 9781315467092 (eBook) | ISBN 9781138205420 (hardback: alk. paper) |
ISBN 9781315467092 (ebk)
Subjects: LCSH: Negotiation in business–China. | Strategic planning–China.
Classification: LCC HD58.6 (ebook) | LCC HD58.6 .W36 2018 (print) |
DDC 658.4/0520951–dc23
LC record available at https://lccn.loc.gov/2017031426

ISBN: 978-1-138-20542-0 (hbk)
ISBN: 978-1-03-283880-9 (pbk)
ISBN: 978-1-315-46709-2 (ebk)

DOI: 10.4324/9781315467092

Typeset in Times New Roman
by Deanta Global Publishing Services, Chennai, India

Contents

PART IV
Chinese joint venture negotiations and establishment 159

Notes

This book is based on the author's research, literature surveys, high-level business experience and learning accumulated over some 40 years of successful international business and negotiations in China and globally. He has worked as a senior executive and international adviser, author and speaker, plus as a director and board member of several leading companies. He has also been invited to advise various international organizations and leading companies, plus universities and business schools.

The views expressed in this book are results of the research insights, personal learning and high-level business experiences of the author. This book represents a contribution by the author, as part of his global corporate social responsibilities together with his strong interest, to support the development of future thought leaders plus outstanding youths from various countries globally. We hope that this book will help executives and negotiators to negotiate more effectively. The book also aims to help academics, researchers and students in their studies and research into business negotiations theories and practices in China and globally.

About the author

Henry K. H. Wang is an international adviser, author and speaker with extensive high-level business experience globally. He is President of Gate International Ltd, a Hong Kong-based boutique advisory and investment firm. He is director of various companies and has held board roles in public companies and joint ventures globally. He is a former director of Shell China and then SABIC in Riyadh. He has been invited to advise leading international agencies, companies and universities globally. He is invited to speak regularly at international conferences and media interviews. Leading universities and business schools frequently invite him to speak and lecture.

He is a Fellow of the Royal Society of Arts FRSA and a Fellow of the Institute of Chemical Engineering, UK. He has been invited to join the UK Climate Change Advisory Committee and the Imperial College London Grantham Institute Stakeholder Committee. He is former Vice Chairman of the OECD Business Energy & Environment Committee, plus former Vice President of the EU and British Chambers of Commerce of China. He is a graduate of Imperial College London and University College London. He has also undertaken advanced management courses at Wharton and Tsinghua.

He has published books and technical and management papers globally and held various international patents on new inventions. His first book, *Successful Business Dealings and Management with China Oil, Gas & Chemical Giants*, was published in 2013 and recommended by leading institutes. His second book on *Energy Markets in Emerging Economies: Strategies for Growth* was published in 2016 and he has been invited to speak about it at leading institutes globally. His negotiation management paper was selected as one of the Top Five UK Management Papers of the Year 2015 and published by UK Chartered Management Institute globally.

Preface

This new book aims to provide a holistic overview of the institutional, organizational and cultural issues that underpin successful business negotiations in China, covering the critical areas of negotiation management, planning and strategies.

There are currently high levels of business and academic interest in China's business negotiation management and strategies. Good negotiation strategies and management are essential for establishing successful business deals and new ventures in China. This new book addresses the current key negotiation issues and risks, plus negotiation planning and strategies relating to current Chinese business negotiations. It first reviews the evolution of key negotiation models that have been used in both China and worldwide, and then it looks at the latest business negotiation models. It analyses the various negotiation frameworks and processes being undertaken in China and its compatibility with global negotiation processes. The importance of selecting the right China negotiation team with appropriate members together with their different strategic roles is reviewed. The detailed preparation and analysis required by the team before starting negotiations in China is discussed together with the latest tools. The effective management of the various stages of negotiation to achieve successful win–win outcomes is examined. Proven negotiation tactics to drive finalisation and closure of negotiation in China are also reviewed. The various joint venture agreements and contracts required for finalisation are discussed. The key processes in China for joint venture implementation post negotiation are reviewed. Real life high-level business negotiations by leading international companies with Chinese State-Owned Enterprises (SOEs), are analysed and supported by relevant business case examples.

This book also looks at the difficult negotiations between multinationals and Chinese SOEs and their respective negotiation strategies. This book analyses the new business negotiation strategies and new strategic approaches being adopted by leading international and Chinese companies to establish successful joint ventures in China and globally.

This book aims to provide practical and theoretical perspectives with relevant, up-to-date commercial business context to help practitioners and business executives to better understand Chinese business negotiation strategies and tactics which should help them undertake their negotiations more effectively. The book also aims to help academics, researchers and students to support their studies and research into business negotiations theories and practices with a situational and contextual bound nature. This book complements the two Taylor & Francis books already published by the author globally, *Successful Business Dealings & Management with China Oil, Gas & Chemical Giants*, published in 2013, and *Energy Markets in Emerging Economies: Strategies for Growth*, published in 2016.

Acknowledgements

I would like to thank the valuable input, support and encouragement that I have received from many senior executives, thought leaders, and key stakeholders in leading companies, international agencies, universities and business schools in China and globally on this book.

My sincere thanks to Taylor & Francis, who commissioned and published this book. I would like to thank all the editorial and production staff at the Taylor & Francis Informa Group who have contributed to the successful design, editing, copywriting, typesetting, proof-reading, publication and marketing of this book.

I would also like to thank the UK Chartered Management Institute and its members for selecting my management paper on 'China Business Negotiation Strategies' as one of their 'Top Five Management Papers of the Year 2015'. This has motivated and inspired me to write this book to share my China and international business negotiation experience with negotiators and academics globally.

I would like to sincerely thank my loving wife and two wonderful children for all their great support, love, understanding and encouragement, which are much appreciated and treasured every day. Their strong support and encouragement were essential to keep me going to complete the book, considering the large amount of personal time and effort required for the extensive research, writing and editing. I also would like to thank my mother, sisters and their families, plus our close friends globally for their valuable advice and support.

I would like to dedicate this book to my Mother for all her support and remarkable strength, after the passing of my dear Father, whom I sadly miss every day.

Part I

The context of negotiations in China

1 Chinese negotiation models

十年树木,百年树人

shí nián shù mù, bǎi nián shù rén

Ten years for a sapling to grow into a tree and a hundred years to develop enterprises.

Good wine takes time to mature.

Executive overviews

Global and Chinese business negotiations have become very complex and can take on many different facets. International business negotiations have evolved from the traditional distributive negotiation model to the more modern integrative negotiation model. Chinese business negotiation models have also been evolving in line with international trends. These changes have been driven by the increasingly complex business environments and modern business practices in China. Literature surveys and analyses of relevant business negotiation models show that whilst there are many similarities between international and Chinese business negotiations, there are also important Chinese characteristics and specifics that negotiators need to understand for successful negotiations in China.

International business negotiation definitions and models

Literature surveys and analysis of international business negotiation definitions show that business negotiations have commonly been defined as a discussion between two or more business parties to reach new, sustainable, joint business agreements, which are commercially acceptable plus mutually beneficial for all the business parties involved in the negotiations.

International business negotiations would normally involve various negotiation models and processes comprising different negotiation stages and phases. Normally the different business parties involved agree to sit together to discuss and negotiate all their key business issues and differences, rather than sue each other in courts or have ugly, open disputes.

The different negotiators from the various business parties would normally evaluate the pros and cons for each key negotiation issue and identify their target objectives, prior to starting negotiations. They would also develop appropriate negotiation strategies in order to achieve their negotiation objectives. After appropriate negotiation preparations, the negotiators from the different parties would then sit together and start to negotiate the various key issues to try to reach jointly acceptable agreements. In modern international business negotiations, the different business parties would normally try their best to negotiate new joint agreements which should be mutually acceptable and win–win for all parties.

With the constantly changing global business environment, international business negotiations have been evolving fast with increasing complexities. Literature surveys and analyses of the different business negotiation models being applied in international business negotiations show that there are three main generic classes of negotiation model. These include the distributive business negotiation model, the integrative business negotiation model and the zero-sum negotiation model. The key characteristics and applicability of each of these negotiation models will be discussed in more detail below.

The distributive business negotiation model represents the older, more traditional business negotiation model. The distributive negotiation model is also called the positional or confrontational negotiation model as the negotiators would normally be arguing hard against each other over some key negotiation positions, such as the issue of distribution of benefits to the parties. A gain by one party would then normally lead to a loss or concession to the opposite party. It would often not be possible to make trade-offs based on different preferences as there would be only one major issue at stake. Neither party would like to concede or give up easily or lose their profit and position. Hence the negotiation would often be restrictive and difficult. There would also be little room for expanding the scope of the negotiations to include other important issues. The agreements reached would normally be win-loss agreements which would often be unsustainable for the longer term in the modern business world. The losing party would normally try their best to get out of these win-loss deals as soon as possible.

The late US President John F. Kennedy gave good advice on the distributive or positional negotiation model in his White House radio and television address to the American people on 25 July 1961: "We cannot negotiate with people who say what's mine is mine and what's yours is negotiable." What he has said some 56 years ago is still very much relevant today regarding the distributive or positional business negotiation models.

The integrative business negotiation models are more representative of the newer, more modern business negotiations. Integrative negotiations are also called collaborative negotiations as the negotiators from the different parties would normally try their best to negotiate the different issues on a collaborative basis. The negotiators would be trying to make appropriate compromises and concessions. They would also be trying their best to negotiate and combine their various interests into new mutually acceptable agreements which would maximize values and benefits for all parties. The common objective of the negotiations would be to create maximum lasting value for all parties. This would normally be achieved during negotiations by all the parties by making some important strategic trade-offs and compromises on their different key business issues. These trade-offs would normally be made based on the overall holistic benefits for the new joint venture. The different negotiating parties would normally be negotiating hard to achieve their most valuable business objectives whilst being prepared to compromise on their less important business issues. These would help the negotiators to develop new joint agreements which were acceptable and win–win for all the parties. These win–win agreements would likely be more sustainable on the longer-term basis.

Analysis of modern, high-level business negotiation cases shows that they have been evolving from the older, traditional distributive negotiation model to the more complex, integrative negotiation models. These negotiation changes are in line with the modern, complex international business environments and requirements. In the past, most companies were driven primarily to maximize their profit positions and their negotiations were mostly based on the distributive negotiation models. These negotiations would then result in win-loss agreements which would normally be unsustainable in the longer term. The business parties who felt they had lost out in the distributive or confrontational negotiations would normally try their best to get out of the win-loss deals as soon as possible after getting what they wanted.

With the growing complexity of the international business environment, modern business negotiations generally follow the newer integrative or collaborative negotiation models. The negotiators would normally be trying to trade off different positions during negotiations and make compromises on the different key business issues. These would help to develop new, mutually acceptable agreements which should be win–win for all the parties involved.

A good example of an international and Chinese integrative business negotiation is the Sinopec Apache negotiations on Egypt oil and gas. On 15 November 2013, Apache Corp agreed to sell its 33 per cent stake in its Egypt oil and gas business for US $3.1 billion to the Sinopec Group after long negotiations. Apache agreed to sell their upstream oil and gas assets in Egypt to Sinopec as part of their new global strategy after long, difficult Sino-foreign negotiations. Apache's new strategic thrusts were to rebalance their global portfolio and to reduce their exposure in Egypt amidst the rising political unrest. Sinopec agreed to purchase the upstream assets from Apache under the Chinese government's 'Go Abroad Investment Policy' which encouraged Chinese companies to purchase foreign oil and gas assets to secure extra equity in oil and gas exports to China. These assets would help to support the rising oil and gas imports to China. Apache reported gross oil production of 198,000 barrels per day and gross natural gas production of 912 million cubic feet (MMcf) per day in 2013 from its upstream oil and gas operations in Egypt. Apache and Sinopec negotiated hard on the various key business issues along the integrative model approaches. They were finally able to agree a mutually acceptable win–win deal in 2013, which met both the strategic objectives of Sinopec and Apache.

The zero-sum negotiation models and strategies would normally be applied by companies when they have little common ground for negotiations but have been instructed to carry on negotiating for various special political and business reasons. These bilateral deals would typically be driven by state or national priorities such as international bilateral energy supply deals between countries. With the growth of State-Owned Enterprises (SOEs) in international business, the zero-sum negotiation models would often be applied by some leading SOEs in negotiating difficult, bilateral mega deals, such as major energy deals, which would often be driven by different governments.

Good examples of zero-sum business negotiations would be the international oil or gas supply deals between different producing nations and consuming countries. These bilateral oil and gas supply deals would normally involve complex political and business aspects which would all have to be negotiated. The various state oil and gas companies from the producing and consuming countries involved in these international supply deals would have to go through the complex negotiation process to demonstrate to their key government sponsors the various major business issues and negotiation hurdles. Based on these, the SOE government sponsors would then be able to re-evaluate and weigh up the different political options and costs. They would then try to work with the different political parties and interest groups within their country to develop new, compromised negotiation positions which are acceptable to all the powerful stakeholders. The government leaders would then convert these compromises into appropriate new negotiation mandates for their SOEs. Then the SOE management and negotiator would use these in their next rounds of business negotiations with other international SOEs. Hopefully the SOE negotiators would then be able to, using the new negotiation mandates, undertake integrative constructive negotiations with the negotiators from the other SOEs. These should then generate new joint agreements which would be win–win for all parties and the governments involved. Otherwise the SOE negotiators would have to continue these difficult zero-sum negotiations over long periods. These would then normally result in disappointing lose-lose negotiation outcomes for all the parties involved.

An example of a good business negotiation case is the gas supply negotiations between Russia and China. Gazprom and China National Oil Petroleum Company (CNPC) have negotiated for many years the possibility of a gas supply agreement from Russia to China. These bilateral negotiations were very difficult and proceeded in line with the zero-sum negotiation model with little progress made. Then the international sanctions on Russian gas exports to Europe motivated the Russian government and its gas companies to open up new gas export markets to China and Asia. These new international developments enabled Gazprom and CNPC to make breakthroughs in their negotiations. CNPC and Gazprom were finally able, with their new negotiation mandates from their respective government sponsors, to negotiate and agree a major new joint gas supply agreement for the delivery of 38 BCM of Russian gas by Gazprom over the next 30 years to CNPC in China. The new joint gas supply agreement was a win–win deal for both Russia and China. It helped Russia to diversify its gas customer base from Europe to the fast-growing gas markets in China and Asia. For China and Asia, Russian gas imports would help to diversify their gas supply sources globally which would help to improve the energy security of China and Asia.

High-level businesses negotiations in China have also been evolving in line with international business negotiations. The key drivers influencing Chinese business negotiations, particularly from the Chinese business environment and key industrial sectors, will be discussed in more detail in this chapter.

Chinese business negotiation models and tactics

In Chinese, the word for negotiation is 'tan-pan', which literally means a combination of discussions and judgements. In Chinese business negotiations, it would usually be considered very important for both parties to first build trust with each other before they get into serious negotiations. The build-up of trust between the Chinese and international negotiators would also take time and would normally involve detailed dialogues between the two parties. Each party could then judge and evaluate the other partner's capabilities and relative values. The Chinese negotiators would normally only start to negotiate with the international negotiators after they have decided that the international company could be a trustworthy long-term partner to the Chinese company. Then the negotiators from two parties would start to negotiate the required agreements over many negotiation rounds. The Chinese negotiators would also stress that the negotiation should be along the key principle of 'equality and mutual benefit' for both parties.

The Chinese negotiation process would also support the idea that both negotiating parties can negotiate and reach mutual understanding on specific business issues in a way that both parties feel is 'a mutually beneficial, win–win deal'. The primary objective of Chinese business negotiations would usually focus more on creating a lasting framework for long term co-operations rather than rushing to draft a one-time agreement quickly.

Business negotiations in China are often considered to be a dynamic, ongoing process which have to take into account the actual ongoing business situation with various changes. Many traditional Chinese negotiators would also prefer the dynamic, ongoing negotiation approach to the Western negotiation approach, which would normally focus more on agreeing and drafting written contracts and agreements. Many Chinese negotiators would perceive negotiations that would focus primarily on developing written contracts quickly as more in line with the Western style of negotiations. International negotiators undertaking major business negotiations in China should understand and master these key differences in negotiation culture and negotiation models in order to achieve successful negotiations in China.

Literature surveys and analyses of the different Chinese business negotiation processes and models show that these have also been evolving quickly in response to the changes in international and Chinese business environments. In addition, the rapid economic growth of China and its integration with the global economy have also contributed to more alignment of the Chinese negotiation styles and processes with international negotiation developments.

In the early days of business negotiations in China during the 1960s and 1970s, high-level business negotiations between Chinese and international companies have initially followed the traditional distributive or positional negotiation models.

These negotiations have focused primarily on the key issue of profit and benefit distributions. This was seen to be the most important commercial co-operation issue between Chinese and international companies in the early days of international trade. These negotiations have often resulted in win-loss agreements, as neither the Chinese nor the international partner would like to give up their position and share of the profits or benefits. Many of these contracts have also shown to be unsustainable for the longer term as the partner who felt that they have a losing agreement would want to terminate these agreements as quickly as possible.

Analyses of recent, modern high-level Chinese business negotiation cases show that the modern business negotiation models currently used in China have evolved more in line with international business negotiations. In high-level business negotiations between Chinese and international companies, the traditional distributive negotiation models, which would focus primarily on the key single issue of profit and benefit distribution, have been gradually phased out. One key reason was that these negotiations had usually resulted in win-loss agreements which were unsustainable for the longer term. In addition, there would also be many different business issues that would need to be negotiated in the bigger business deals being negotiated in China at present.

Modern business negotiations in China have been using the integrative or collaborative negotiation models more and more. As China integrated more into the global economy, it has also been adopting more international business and commercial practices. The majority of modern business negotiations in China between Chinese and international companies have also became more complex and multifaceted. The business negotiations in China have been developing in line with the increasingly complex business environments and requirements in China and worldwide. These negotiations would normally involve many complex legal and commercial issues which the Chinese and international negotiators would need to consider, discuss and negotiate. The key business issues would no longer be just profit and benefit distribution, which were the key business issues in the early days of international trade many years ago.

The Chinese and international partners now need to negotiate and consider many other important commercial and legal issues, such as joint venture organization, human resources, staff nomination, talent development, management control, board composition, corporate social responsibility and sustainable development, etc. It is also very important for the Chinese and international business partners and their negotiators to identify their critical 'win–win cooperative issues' which they could compromise upon and to share values with their partners during negotiations.

A good example of a successful Chinese and international partner integrative negotiation is the petrochemical joint venture negotiations between Sinopec and SABIC on their major Tianjin petrochemical joint venture. The Chinese and international partners discussed and successfully negotiated the various joint venture agreements and associated contracts for their major new joint venture in Tianjin, the Sinopec SABIC Tianjin Petrochemical Company (SSTPC) Limited. They agreed, after long, complex, integrative negotiations, that the final shareholding ratio would be 50:50 between Sinopec and SABIC. They also negotiated and agreed the sensitive issues of feedstock pricing, board composition plus joint venture staff nomination and planning. After government approvals, the joint venture was established in Tianjin, China with a joint investment of US \$2.7 billion. The joint venture successfully constructed and operated a new, world-class petrochemical complex with one million tonnes per annum Ethylene Cracker complex plus associated chemical plants. After successful plant commissioning and start-ups, the joint venture has been successfully producing over three million tonnes of petrochemical products per annum, including Ethylene, Polyethylene, Ethylene Glycol, Polypropylene, Butadiene, Phenol and Butene-1.

Many high-level business negotiations in China for major Sino-foreign business deals and joint ventures in China also involve 'multiple negotiation parties'. In addition to the main Chinese partner, these negotiations could also include the local government or leading local companies. These local Chinese entities might eventually become minority shareholders in the future joint venture due to the importance of these new joint ventures to the local economies. During negotiations, new strategic alliances may also develop between the different Chinese parties involved in the negotiations. Hence the international negotiators would have to be very vigilant on the ongoing developing relations of the different Chinese parties during their negotiations. New coalitions could form between the different Chinese partners during negotiations. These new coalitions would normally be quite powerful and could seriously influence the negotiation directions.

The famous Chinese military philosopher, Sun Tzu, gave very good advice on Chinese negotiation hundreds of years ago in his famous book, *The Art of War*. He said, "if you do not seek out allies and helpers, then you will be isolated and weak." These ancient sayings from hundreds of years ago are still very much valid today on the requirements for strong Chinese partner coalitions in negotiation with international companies in China.

A strong example of successful, multi-partner, Sino-foreign joint venture negotiations, involving different Chinese and international partners in the downstream refinery and petrochemicals sectors in China, is the ExxonMobil, Saudi Aramco, Sinopec and Fujian Province Joint Venture. The four Chinese and international partners negotiated and successfully formed a fully integrated refining and petrochemicals joint venture together with an oil fuels marketing joint venture in China. The manufacturing joint venture was agreed to be jointly owned by ExxonMobil at 25 per cent, Saudi Aramco at 25 per cent and Fujian Petrochemical Company Limited at 50 per cent. The partners agreed to build a new world-scale refinery integrated with an 800,000-tonnes-per-year ethylene steam cracker with integrated polyethylene, polypropylene, paraxylene and chemicals units. They also agreed to establish a separate marketing joint venture (JV), owned jointly by Sinopec at 55 per cent, ExxonMobil at 22.5 per cent and Saudi Aramco at 22.5 per cent. The marketing JV would be responsible for marketing the oil fuel products, diesel and motor gasoline, produced by the JV refinery. The marketing JV established a network of oil product distribution terminals with more than 750 oil retail service stations in Fujian and neighboring provinces in southeast China.

Analysis of Chinese SOEs' business negotiations with other international SOEs have also shown that the zero-sum negotiation models have sometimes been applied to difficult complex international negotiations. The zero-sum negotiation models and strategies would normally be applied by China and overseas SOEs when they have little grounds for common agreements but have to undertake negotiations for various special political and business reasons. These massive deals would often be driven by higher state, government or country requirements and aspirations.

The zero-sum negotiation model has been widely used by negotiators from Chinese Energy SOEs in their high-level international negotiations of oil and gas supply agreements with various major oil and gas exporting countries, such as Russia and Middle Eastern countries. These oil and gas supply deals would normally include high-level government to government negotiations. These would involve complex political and business aspects which have all to be negotiated and agreed. The various SOEs and energy companies involved in these deals would have to go through long, complex negotiation processes to demonstrate and highlight to their state and government sponsors the various key negotiation problems and issues. The SOEs would then use these negotiation barriers to ask for new guidance and negotiation mandates from their government sponsors. Based on these initial negotiations, their government sponsors would re-evaluate and weigh up the different political options and costs to the state. The governments would then work with the different interested parties and powerful internal stakeholders in their country to try to develop new, compromised negotiation mandates for their SOEs. The SOEs' negotiators would hopefully, with the new mandates, be able to undertake the more constructive integrative negotiations with other SOEs so as to negotiate new joint agreements which would be win–win for the SOEs and the governments involved. Otherwise the SOEs would have to continue their difficult zero-sum negotiations, which would normally result in disappointing lose-lose negotiation outcomes for all parties.

A good example of a high-level international business negotiation case is the lengthy, but ultimately successful, China Russia Gas Supply Agreement negotiations. For years, CNPC and Gazprom have been trying to negotiate a new gas supply agreement from Russia to China. They have made little progress even after long, hard negotiations. Their difficult negotiations, in line with the zero-sum negotiation model, showed that there were big gaps on many key commercial and political issues. In particular, there were big differences on the gas pricing formulas and gas availability aspects which both China and Russia were unwilling to compromise on. The SOE negotiators also did not have appropriate mandates from their government sponsors to negotiate any compromises until recently.

In 2014, the international and European sanctions enforced upon Russia motivated Russia and Gazprom to actively explore alternative gas export markets and negotiate new gas export contracts for markets outside Europe. Gazprom renewed their gas supply negotiations with CNPC with new mandates from the Russian government. The Gazprom negotiators followed a new, integrative negotiation model approach with CNPC as they were keen to reach a new gas supply deal with

China quickly so as to offset the restrictive effects of the international sanctions on Russian gas exports.

After long and hard business negotiations, CNPC and Gazprom finally agreed and signed a preliminary Gas Purchase and Sales Contract for Russian gas imports to China via the eastern route in May 2014. CNPC and Gazprom then continued tough negotiation on the commercial details and managed to finalize their gas supply deal. There were also high-level political supports and guidance for this very important bilateral negotiation, particularly on the difficult negotiations on the final pricing formula for the Russian gas export to China for the next 30 years. In the end, the Chinese and Russian negotiators were able to make win–win compromises which helped the finalization of the key agreements and closure of the major deal.

On 9 November 2014, CNPC and Gazprom signed a Gas Supply Agreement, during the APEC summit in Beijing, in the presence of Chinese President Xi Jinping and Russian President Vladimir Putin. CNPC Chairman Zhou Jiping and Alexey Miller, Chairman of the Gazprom Management Committee, also signed the Framework Agreement for gas imports from Russia to China via the western route. Under the agreement, Gazprom would transport Russian natural gas to China for 30 years with the gas delivery rates gradually increasing to 30 BCM per year over a period of four to six years.

The analyses of many high-level business negotiations in China to date show that in practice the majority of business negotiations do not strictly follow either the distributive or the integrative model. Most business negotiations between Chinese and foreign business partners would normally be a combination of both the distributive and integrative negotiation models with a complex, non-linear, negotiation process. There would normally be many complex business issues which the Chinese and international negotiators would need to negotiate to create maximum value for both parties as part of their final win–win agreements.

The many complex business issues at stake for these major deals would normally make it very difficult for the Chinese and international negotiators to agree these issues quickly. Many rounds of negotiation would often be required over long periods to reach mutually acceptable and beneficial agreements. In these negotiations, it would be very important for the Chinese and international negotiators to identify the potential 'win–win cooperative issues' where they could make compromises and share values effectively at different stages of the negotiations. Then, during the negotiations, the chief negotiators on both sides could decide the right time to offer concessions to the other side on some of the non-key negotiation issues. These compromises during negotiations would help to build good relations and *guanxi* between the negotiators as well as promoting good negotiation progress. These good relations and *guanxi* would also support future partnership and good co-operations by the partners in the new joint venture.

Looking ahead, the future economic growth of China should continue to create new business opportunities for international and Chinese companies to cooperate and form new joint ventures. Good negotiations between Chinese and international negotiators on these major deals are important for their materialization in the future.

Chinese economic growth and business negotiations

China's economic growth and international trade developments have generated many new potential business opportunities for international companies to cooperate with Chinese companies in China and globally. Good business negotiations between Chinese and international companies would be critical for the successful realization of these new business opportunities in China and globally.

Looking back, China's economy grew rapidly during 2001–2008. The economic growth was characterized by continuous high Gross Domestic Product (GDP) growth rates until the first half of 2008. In the second half of 2008, as the global economy began to weaken, China's economic growth was also seriously affected. In the second half of 2008, there was a significant downturn in China's GDP growth along with reducing investment and exports. However, with the economic counter measures implemented by the Chinese government, China's economy recovered quickly. In 2012, China's nominal GDP reached US $8.2 trillion, making it the second largest economy in the world, after the USA.

Looking ahead, the new norm for China's future economic growth is likely to be single-digit GDP economic growth rates, rather than the high, unsustainable double-digit growth rates recorded during 2003–2007. China's economic growth in the coming years is still likely to remain comfortably higher than other major economies. This should allow China to keep its position as one of the world's key growth leaders, but on a more sustainable basis. China has also made good progress in transforming its economic and industrial growth models and its economic structures. Rising domestic demands and consumption play significantly larger roles in driving China's future economic growth.

China has been able to effectively deal with the challenges of the global economic environment so as to maintain its stable and rapid economic development. China has been working towards achieving most of the economic and industrial goals laid out in the government's 'Five Year Plans'. A good example is how China's Twelfth Five-Year Plan had set a national GDP growth target of 7 per cent, which was slightly lower than the 7.5 per cent target set in the Eleventh Five-Year Plan. With the new Thirteenth Five-Year Plan, which covered the period 2016–2020, China planned to accelerate the pace of economic restructuring and to upgrade its industrial sectors plus improving sustainable environmental developments.

Looking ahead, most analysts have been predicting that China's GDP growth rates would likely decrease to around 6–7 per cent from 2016–2020, within the Thirteenth Five-Year Plan period. For 2021–2025, China's GDP growth rates are likely to further reduce to 5–6 per cent from the highs of 7–8 per cent. The actual GDP growth rates in China will be subjected to future markets and business environment conditions at the time. Taking into account the varying economic and social requirements of employment creation and improving standards of living,

China would need to maintain national GDP growth rates which would be neither too high nor too low and be sustainable in the longer term.

The future economic growth in China would also be more focused on the quality and sustainability of economic growth, rather than just on achieving high economic growth rates. China would also be pushing ahead with economic reforms to shift their growth model from their previous export and manufacturing-driven models to a more domestic consumer and service-driven model. Most economists have been forecasting that these reforms would help China to achieve lower but more sustainable economic growth in the future. The eastern coastal region, which has become one of the most industrialized areas in China, would likely experience slower economic growth as it would have to reform and upgrade its industrial sector structures. The central and western regions will likely grow more rapidly with the Chinese government's 'Go West Policy' which promote investments and growth in these regions.

Looking ahead, China's economy will likely overtake the US economy to become the largest global economy during the Thirteenth Five-Year Plan period of 2016–2020. China's national GDP growth rates are likely to grow steadily at slower and more sustainable rates. Many economists have been forecasting that China's national GDP is likely to grow to over US $19 trillion by 2020 and become the largest global economy. The continued economic growth in China will generate many new business opportunities for international companies. These opportunities will require good Chinese and international negotiations to realize and materialize.

The main key risks and challenges to China's economy reforms and growth will involve managing the various economic imbalances on a sustainable basis, such as containing the real-estate bubbles whilst keeping the economic recovery going. These will be especially important given that China could not rely much on monetary policy reforms with their asset price inflations. To stabilize future economic growth, China will likely need to employ more appropriate fiscal measures.

The global demands for China's exports in the coming years is likely to become lower and much more subdued than during the boom years of the 2000s. If the demands for China's exports would continue to decline, then these would have severe repercussions for China's export-led economy. These would be major potential future risks to China's future economic growth, though more of a medium- to long-term risk nature. Similar risks would also apply to other rapidly emerging economies in Asia and globally, as these have also been relying heavily on rising external demands and exports to power much of their economic growth.

In addition, China's investment-heavy, export-oriented model of economic growth is likely to be reaching its limits. Increases in future domestic consumer spending is an essential part of the economic transformation that China needs to promote internally so as to shift its economic growth model away from its heavy reliance on investments and exports, towards more domestic consumptions. The Chinese government has recognized the importance of this re-balancing act. They have been pushing ahead with appropriate reforms on income redistribution and social welfare to encourage more domestic private consumption in China.

If the PRC Government can implement all their planned reforms successfully, then China should be able to successfully engineer a shift from their current economic growth model to a more sustainable consumption-driven model. This should then be able to generate self-perpetuating, long-term, sustainable economic growth for China. In addition, if China's new massive urbanization drives are successful, they could also trigger structural shifts conducive to productivity gains and long-term, sustainable growth. Rising household incomes and benefits would also add help to increase domestic private consumption in China and the growth of the middle class across China.

If China's economic reforms are successful, then these would support more sustainable future economic growth. Economic growth should continue to generate many potential new business opportunities for international companies to cooperate with Chinese companies and partners. Good and effective business negotiations in China are critical for the successful realization of these new business opportunities in China and globally.

With the planned, new, key developments, the negotiation of good manufacturing and supply contracts by Chinese manufacturers with their customers inside and outside China would also become more complex and important. They would have to take into consideration the current demands and pricing trends as well as potential future demands and pricing scenarios. They would also have to consider the possible risks of future trade blocks and their commercial implications.

Energy growth and development opportunities in China

China's energy and industrial sectors have been one of the key drivers for China's economic growth. These sectors have also generated a lot of Sino-foreign co-operations and joint ventures, such as oil and gas exploration and production, petrochemical and chemical manufacturing, etc. Many high-level business negotiations have taken place between international and Chinese companies on the successful establishment of new joint ventures to realize and capture many of these major new business opportunities in different regions of China.

China's energy consumption has been growing fast, in line with its GDP. China has become one of the leading oil and gas importing nations globally. By 2020, many energy planners are forecasting that China could account for 15–20 per cent of the world's total primary energy demands. China would also likely account for almost half of the energy consumptions in the entire Asia-Pacific Region.

China has also been a net importer of oil since 1993. In 2003, China's crude oil imports were only one third (33 per cent) of its total crude consumption. In 2012, China consumed over six million barrels of oil per day, with imports accounting for over half of this. By 2020, it is expected that China's crude consumption will rise by another 33 per cent to over eight million barrels of oil per day. China's crude oil import dependency, which has already grown to be above 50 per cent, is likely to increase further to above 60–70 per cent in the future.

To meet this increased demand for energy, China has been actively diversifying its energy supply sources and types. China has also been accelerating their exploration and development of conventional and unconventional oil and gas resources, including shale gas, in different regions of China. These new oil and gas exploration and production opportunities present new cooperation opportunities between Chinese state oil and gas enterprises with the international oil and gas companies. A good business case example is the PetroChina and Chevron joint venture for gas exploration and production in China. More details of this successful Sino-foreign joint venture will be given later in this chapter.

Coal has been a major part of China's overall energy mix but has also contributed to environmental pollution. China has been actively developing new, clean coal technologies and shutting down poor quality coal mines. These have led to new, Sino-foreign, clean coal joint ventures, such as the Shell Sinopec Coal Gasification Joint Venture in Henan. Details of this joint venture and its negotiations will be given later in this chapter.

Looking ahead, China will also be actively developing new, cleaner sources of energy, particularly gas and renewable energy sources. These will all be important elements of China's continual commitment to environmental improvement and sustainable development. These will generate many new clean energy and green financing business opportunities for international companies to cooperate with Chinese companies.

Clean energy investments opportunities in China

In China's new Thirteenth Five-Year Plan, covering the period 2016–2020, new clean energy developments and investments have been identified to be one of the new, key energy growth sectors. These will be important to support China's global climate change efforts and Paris Agreement commitments.

Key Chinese government authorities have recently announced plans for more than US $360 billion of new investment into the clean energy and renewable sectors in the future. These will lead to many new business opportunities for cooperation between international and Chinese renewable and clean energy companies. Good business negotiations between Chinese and international energy companies will be required to realize these ambitious clean energy investment growth targets.

China has also been actively promoting the development of clean and renewable energy resources across the country in their new Thirteenth Five-Year Plan. The Chinese government National Energy Agency (NEA) has announced that China is planning to invest 2.5 trillion yuan or over US $360 billion into China's renewable sector. They also announced that China, which has become the world's largest energy market, will continue to shift away from coal power generation towards cleaner fuels and renewable power generation. They also forecasted that these clean energy investments in China would help to create more than 13 million new jobs in China. They predicted that the total installed renewable power generation capacity in China, comprising wind, hydro, solar and nuclear power together, would be contributing to about half of the new electricity generation capacities in China by 2020–2030.

The China National Development and Reform Commission said that solar power would receive 1 trillion yuan or over US $140 billion of new investment. China is planning to increase its solar power capacity by five times, the equivalent to about 1,000 major solar power plants across China. In addition, some 700 billion yuan or US $100 billion of new investment is planned to go into new wind farms across China. Another 500 billion yuan or over US $70 billion of new investment is planned to go into new hydro power stations across China. Major investment from China into new tidal and geothermal power generations is also planned in the future.

These massive planned investments into the various clean energy sectors in China will generate many new clean energy financing business opportunities for international companies to cooperate with Chinese companies. In addition, these huge planned investments will generate many green financing opportunities for international banks and finance houses to work with Chinese banks and finance institutions.

Clean coal joint ventures negotiations in China

Coal has been a major part of China's overall energy mix but has also contributed to environmental pollution. China's long, high dependency on coal as a primary energy resource has contributed to serious environmental pollution with associated direct and indirect financial costs. These problems have been recognized by the government who has issued plans to reform and improve the coal sector in China. Looking ahead, coal is likely to continue to be a major contributor to the primary energy mix in China but with stronger controls.

The future challenges for China on coal cover two strategic aspects. First, China needs to improve coal industry management and introduce effective regulatory mechanisms. China has been shutting down poor quality coal mines and reforming their coal companies. Second, China has also been actively developing new clean coal technologies with new research and developments domestically and with international companies. These should help to improve the environmental performance and impact of coal in China as coal currently still makes up almost two-thirds of the country's primary energy mix. These have also led to successful negotiations of new Sino-foreign joint ventures on clean coal technologies.

A good clean coal business case example is the Shell Sinopec coal gasification joint venture. After long, tough negotiations, Sinopec has agreed to license the Shell Advanced Coal Gasification technology to convert coal into syngas. Then Sinopec would use the clean syngas to produce fertilizers. Shell and Sinopec had long and tough negotiations on the different terms of technology licence and technical service agreements. They were able to negotiate and agree a mutually acceptable Licence Agreement and Technical Service Agreement for Sinopec to apply the Shell Advanced Coal Gasification technology at their chemical complex in Henan, China. Their new joint venture successfully constructed and commissioned the new clean coal gasification plant in Henan. Sinopec have been using the clean syngas to successfully produce fertilizers in their downstream chemical complex in Henan.

Chinese oil and gas negotiations

The rising international activities by China's top SOEs in oil and gas, such as PetroChina, Sinopec and CNOOC, in acquiring overseas oil and gas resources is in line with the government's 'Go Abroad Investment Policy'. In addition, these expansions are also in line with their new strategy to globalize and expand onto the international stage.

Energy security has also become a critical high-level policy concern for the government and energy planners in China. China's growing energy needs mean that it has to actively look outside its borders to ensure that its future growth is sustainable with adequate, secure energy supplies. Since the mid-1990s, China has been a net importer of oil, with strong dependency on Middle East crude imports. China has recognized the strategically important requirement to diversify its energy supplies globally, especially crude and gas import sources. China has been implementing its new global oil and gas supply diversification strategy to balance their oil and gas imports from different oil- and gas-producing countries.

A good example is the successful negotiation of the new oil and gas import agreements from Russia to China. The international sanctions on Russia have motivated the Russian government and state energy companies to actively broaden their customer base into the fast-growing Chinese and Asian markets. Negotiations between Chinese and Russian energy companies have resulted in major oil and gas supply agreements. These new Russian oil and gas imports into China will help China to diversify its oil and gas imports away from the Middle East which has traditionally been the largest oil and gas importer into China.

The leading Chinese SOEs, with support from the People's Republic of China (PRC) Government, have also successfully negotiated various complex oil and gas supply agreements with different leading oil- and gas-producing countries, including the Middle East, Africa, Central Asia, Russia and Latin America. These oil and gas supply agreements negotiations would normally be very complex and involve large financial commitments. The Chinese and international negotiators have also to take into account the current and future demand and pricing trends as well as different pricing scenarios. In addition, these agreements would often involve major investments by Chinese SOEs into the overseas oil and gas fields in the various producing countries. Many of these major bilateral deals would also involve major investment from China into new infrastructure and other related support areas in the various oil- and gas-producing countries.

A good, high-level example of a successful Chinese and international oil business negotiation is the Sinopec Kazakh oil purchase agreement. In August 2015, Sinopec completed the purchase of a 50 per cent stake in a Kazakh oil producer from the Lukoil PJSC for an agreed payment of US $1.09 billion. This allowed Sinopec to gain full control of an overseas oil and gas venture with stakes in five big oil and gas fields. The sale of the Caspian Investments Resources Ltd. received the required approval and permits from the Kazakhstan state authorities in late July 2015. The deal was concluded after more than a year of hard business negotiations. After good integrative and collaborative negotiations by the Chinese and Kazakh negotiators, the different partners agreed a final sales price of US $1.09 billion, which was less than the US $1.2 billion initially discussed in April 2014.

The final Sinopec Kazakh oil purchase agreement was a win–win, integrative, non-linear negotiation outcome for the various international and Chinese parties. Sinopec agreed and signed the accord with Lukoil as the deal would help them to secure access to good overseas oil resources. These were in line with the Chinese government's national Go Abroad strategy to diversify energy supply sources abroad to meet the rising domestic energy demands. Sinopec already own, since 2010, the other half of the Caspian Investments Resources, which holds stakes in fields with more than 200 million barrels of proven oil and gas reserves.

Lukoil also achieved its strategic objective of retaining strategic stakes in the Tengiz, Karachaganak and Kumkol oil and gas fields in Kazakhstan and the Caspian Pipeline Consortium. These made Lukoil the largest Russian investor in Kazakhstan. Its share of oil and gas productions in the Central Asian nation was about 4.3 million tonnes of oil and 1.5 billion cubic meters of commercial gas in 2014.

Foreign international companies have also been playing major roles in China's oil and gas sectors developments with large investments. In the oil and gas sectors, foreign companies are actively working with Chinese partners on upstream oil and gas exploration and production, downstream oil product retails, gas infrastructures, plus liquefied natural gas (LNG) imports.

The setting up of successful joint ventures by international companies and Chinese SOEs in the oil, gas and petrochemical sectors would normally involve long, complex business negotiations as these would be massive deals involving major investment by both the Chinese and international partners. These negotiations would in many cases also involve the Chinese and international companies negotiating with the relevant central and local government authorities on these major Sino-foreign cooperations.

An important business negotiation example of Chinese and foreign gas company negotiations and co-operations in the upstream gas sector is the Chevron and PetroChina Joint Venture. In upstream onshore gas, Chevron and PetroChina have been jointly developing the Chuandongbei gas field in Sichuan. After long, complex, high-level business negotiations, PetroChina and Chevron reached agreement on Chevron taking 49 per cent interest and operating the large 487,000-acre (1,969 square kilometer) Chuandongbei natural gas area in the onshore Sichuan Basin. The Chinese and international negotiators also agreed a total investment cost of US $4.7 billion by both PeroChina and Chevron. In addition, Chevron and PetroChina have also been jointly developing the Luojiazhai and Gunziping natural gas fields in China. Construction of the first natural gas processing plant and development of the Luojiazhai and Gunziping natural gas fields have been progressing. Site preparation at the second natural gas processing plant, well pads and gathering system locations were undertaken. The planned maximum total daily natural gas production will be over 550 million cubic feet per day.

Chinese gas and LNG negotiations

Natural gas is central to China's future in terms of sustainable economic growth and environmental improvement. Meeting the anticipated threefold increase in gas consumption in China in the next 10 years will be a major undertaking. This will involve harnessing indigenous conventional and unconventional gas resources, including shale gas resources, in China. They will also need to develop and improve the gas infrastructure and gas pipeline systems across the different provinces in China. China's natural gas and unconventional gas reserves have been relatively underdeveloped. Most of the gas resources in China are located far from the vast gas consumption markets on the east coast. Hence, China would need to, in the foreseeable future, continue to import gas and LNG from different overseas producing countries, particularly from Qatar and Australia, etc.

An important example of an international China LNG business negotiation would be the successful Australia China LNG supply purchase agreements for the large LNG imports from Australia to the Guangdong LNG Terminal in Southeast China. The LNG supply agreements were very complex and it took a long time to negotiate the various key terms so they would be mutually acceptable. The supply period covered a long time period of some 20 years. The financial commitments have been massive for both the Chinese and Australian parties. Hence the LNG agreements have involved long, complex business negotiations between the China SOE buyers and the Australian LNG producers. After long, hard negotiations, they were able to agree mutually acceptable LNG pricing formulae, plus win–win LNG supply contracts which were acceptable to China and Australia. There was also strong support and guidance from both the PRC and Australian governments for the major bilateral LNG supply deal and its negotiations.

China petrochemical and chemical negotiations

There has been rapid growth of petrochemicals and chemicals in domestic Chinese chemical companies, suppliers and new manufacturing facilities. China has already overtaken the USA to become the largest petrochemical and chemical market in the world. Looking ahead, China is likely to remain import dependent on petrochemical feedstocks, especially olefins, plus key chemical products for the foreseeable future. This is likely to be the case, even when taking into account all the planned new major domestic petrochemical and chemical manufacturing projects which should be coming on stream in the near future.

China has also become a major exporter for petrochemical finished products to the global consumer market. The various petrochemical products manufactured from the imported chemical feedstocks have been exported by China to different markets globally, including some going back to the feedstock supply countries. A good business example of this is that the exports of finished products and chemicals by China to the Middle East has been rising steadily to over US $60 billion per year. The details will be discussed further in the next section.

A good Chinese international trade case example is that Saudi Arabia and the Middle East have been the leading oil and petrochemical feedstock suppliers to

China, especially in crude and olefin feedstocks. However Saudi Arabia and the Gulf Cooperation Council (GCC) countries have also been the leading importers of Chinese manufactured products and finished petrochemical products including plastics and chemical products. The accumulated annual value of the Chinese exports to Saudi Arabia and the Middle East have grown to over US $60 billion recently. Looking ahead, the Chinese and Middle East governments have also announced, in recent Sino-Middle East bilateral investment forums, that they are planning to boost their bilateral trade significantly by over three times in the near future. These large bilateral international trades between China and the Middle East involve long important negotiations on all the relevant import and export agreements.

In particular, the petrochemical supply, import and export contracts would normally involve complex business negotiations by the Chinese SOEs and leading Chinese private chemical companies with the overseas international petrochemical companies. In these complex business negotiations, they would have to take into consideration current petrochemical demands and pricings plus future pricing and consumption scenarios. In addition, the negotiators must also take into account the various international trade considerations, including potential future trade blocks and new bilateral Free Trade Agreement implications.

A good example of high level international trade contract negotiations is the China and Middle East international trades and investments. Companies and SOEs in China, Saudi Arabia and GCC countries have been playing important roles in global trade, particularly in oil, gas and petrochemicals. The GCC international trade of oil and gas, plus petrochemical and chemicals feedstocks exports to China have been particularly important and largely handled by the leading regional SOEs, such as Saudi Aramco and SABIC, i.e. Saudi Basic Industry Corporation. Saudi Arabia and GCC countries have been some of the largest suppliers of crude oil to China in recent years. In 2013, KSA supplied 20 per cent of China's total oil imports with a total value of over US $45 billion. China imported around 1,064 thousand barrels of oil per day from Saudi Arabia.

In 2013, Saudi Arabia and GCC countries collectively supplied over 35 per cent of China's crude oil imports with a total value of over US $85 billion. GCC countries supplied over 1,960 thousand barrels of oil per day to China. In addition to oil and gas trades, the SOEs in China and GCC countries also have strong bilateral trades in a wide range of manufactured goods and chemicals. In 2013, China imported from GCC SOEs, in addition to oil and gas, a large variety of feedstocks and goods, including chemicals, metals, salts and Sulphur, with a total value of US $112 billion. Crude imports contributed US $85 billion which represented the bulk of the bilateral trade between China and GCC. However petrochemical and chemicals have also contributed around US $14 billion. Other feedstocks, products and minerals imports from GCC to China have accounted for US $12 billion.

On the other hand, in 2013 China has also exported a large variety of finished chemical products to GCC and Saudi Arabia, including machinery, tires, electrical, plastics, furniture and ceramics with a total value of some US $54 billion.

Chemical products exports contributed US $2 billion and other products contributed US $52 billion.

The associated supply, import and export contracts for these massive bilateral trades between China and GCC countries have involved long, complex business negotiations between Chinese state companies with leading Saudi and GCC companies. There have also been strong supports by the China and GCC governments on fostering good bilateral relationships. These helped to provide the appropriate open international trade environment to support the relevant business negotiations and contracts. In addition, proper governance, integrity and anti-corruption measures were also discussed, negotiated and agreed by the various Chinese and GCC companies and their negotiators in these important bilateral agreements. These will help to ensure higher standards of integrity, transparency and efficiency in the different international trade supply chains and value chains involved in these massive international supply and exports between China and GCC countries.

Foreign international companies have also been playing major roles in China's petrochemical and chemical manufacturing growth. In the petrochemical and chemicals sectors, foreign companies have been actively involved in base, fine and specialty chemicals manufacturing and marketing, plus research and developments with leading Chinese Partners and Institutes.

Setting up successful joint ventures by international companies and Chinese SOEs in the petrochemical and chemical sectors would normally involve long, complex business negotiations as these are massive deals involving major investment by both the Chinese and international partners. These negotiations would, in many cases, also involve the Chinese and international companies negotiating with the relevant central and local government authorities on these major Sino-foreign agreements.

An important and successful example of China and international petrochemical and chemical joint venture negotiations is the Sinopec and BASF Petrochemical Joint Venture in Nanjing. Details of this joint venture will be discussed later in this chapter.

China international trade and investment negotiations

International trade and investment have been major drivers for Chinese economic growth. Long, complex business negotiations involving Chinese and international partners would normally be required to negotiate and agree the major agreements and contracts for the various major deals and investments.

Since 2001, after China had joined the World Trade Organization (WTO) and implemented its WTO commitments, China has been experiencing rapid economic growth. China's nominal GDP values have grown by 6 times from US $1.3 trillion in 2001 to US $7.3 trillion in 2011 and then US $8.2 trillion in 2012. These accounted for over 11 per cent of the world's GDP of US $71.7 trillion, as estimated by the International Monetary Fund (IMF).

China's international trade policies have also become more liberal in a bid to boost its international trade and investments. Since its entrance into the WTO,

China has taken several major steps to liberalize its trade policy. China has also expanded its 'open-door policy' to make its investment environment more friendly and simple for multinational companies (MNCs) and other prospective investors.

China has witnessed considerable returns in its international trade and investment growth resulting from their 'open door policy'. China has successfully attracted high amounts of Foreign Direct Investments (FDI) into China. Many Foreign Investment Enterprises (FIE) and joint ventures have also been established, taking advantage of the preferential foreign investment policies in China. The establishments of FIEs and Sino-foreign joint ventures in China would normally involve complex and intense business negotiations between the Chinese and international negotiators. These negotiations will be discussed in detailed in the various chapters of this book.

A good business negotiation case example of a major Sino-foreign petrochemical joint venture is the Sinopec and BASF petrochemical joint venture near Nanjing in China. BASF and Sinopec have agreed to jointly invest and build a new major petrochemical base near Nanjing. The deal has involved over three years of long, complex business negotiations by BASF and Sinopec negotiators. They managed to agree the required joint venture agreement and associated contracts for their Yangtze Petrochemical Company Joint Venture. After approval by the Chinese Central Government, they then successfully established their Yangtze Petrochemical Co. joint venture near Nanjing of Jiangsu Province of China. The joint venture has successfully constructed and started up a world class petrochemical complex near Nanjing. After some years of successful operations, Sinopec and BASF then negotiated and signed new agreements for the BASF and Yangtze Petrochemical YPC Joint Venture Phase II expansions. The expansion projects included the construction of nine new chemical production plants, including a 60 KTPA NIS plant, a 130 KTPA butadiene plant, a 50 KTPA IB plant, a 50 KTPA PIB plant, an 80 KTPA 2-PH plant, an 80 KTPA BG plant and a 60 KTPA SAP plant. BASF and Sinopec have agreed to invest about US $1 billion together for the new expansions.

China has also acted quickly to counter-balance the negative impacts of tough international factors, such as global trade declines, global financial crisis and pressures from foreign exchange rate changes.. The growth in international trade, which has been a key pillar of support for the global economy until the 2008–2009 financial crisis, has also been declining. Looking ahead, international trade growth will likely increase by 5–6 per cent in the next few years. Experts generally agree that the growth is unlikely to return to its pre-crisis peaks of around 10 per cent due to a mixture of different external factors. These include moderate global economic growth, particularly in advanced economies, reduced trade financing availability from banks, plus moderately rising global trade protectionism in different countries.

Chinese Free Trade Agreement negotiations

Internationally, China has also been active in negotiating different international economic co-operation agreements, such as Free Trade Agreements (FTA), with various strategic trading countries. China has also liberalized their international trade with many key countries and trading partners globally. China has successfully negotiated and agreed many new FTAs with key trading countries and partners.

Good examples of the successful FTA negotiations include the China–ASEAN FTA from January 2010, China–New Zealand FTA from April 2008, China–Singapore FTA from October 2008 and China Thailand FTA from October 2003.

China is also in the process of signing bilateral FTAs with several key countries, including Australia, Gulf Cooperation Council (GCC), Iceland, India, Norway, South Korea and Switzerland. These 'Free Trade Agreements' signed with the different countries have helped to increase China's foreign and international trades. These have also helped to boost the foreign trade of different countries with China.

An important international FTA negotiation case example is the successful China and New Zealand Free Trade Agreement. After long, complex negotiations by both the Chinese and New Zealand governments' negotiators, together with key inputs from their major companies, China and New Zealand agreed and signed their new FTA in April 2008. Since the FTA signing, there have been large increases in New Zealand's foreign trade with China. The value of the bilateral trade between China and New Zealand has grown by over three times. China has now overtaken Australia to be New Zealand's largest foreign trade partner internationally.

2 Chinese business negotiation processes

逆境出人才
Nì jìng chū rén cá
Difficult situations force people to rise to the challenges.
Crisis breeds wisdom.

Executive overview

Business negotiation processes globally and in China have become very complex. The Chinese and international negotiators need to manage their negotiation processes well to achieve successful negotiation outcomes. Literature surveys and analysis of business negotiation processes show that the negotiation processes globally and in China have been shifting away from the traditional, linear negotiation processes which would normally involve single or few issues, to the modern, more complex, multi-issues non-linear business negotiation processes. In some complex business negotiations in China, the actual negotiation process could also involve multiple negotiation channels and might include multiple negotiation partners.

International business negotiation processes analysis

International business negotiation processes have been changing fast with increasing complexities. Literature surveys and analysis of high-level international business negotiation processes show that they have been evolving quickly and in line with the complex, international business environment and commercial requirements. Many high-level business negotiation processes have been shifting from the traditional linear negotiation process to the more modern non-linear negotiation processes. The various changes in the international negotiation processes have mainly resulted from the rising complexity and demands of modern international commercial negotiations.

In the older, linear business negotiation processes, the negotiators would concentrate on negotiating a limited number of key negotiation issues such as profit and losses or the distribution of benefits between the partners in their negotiations. The negotiators on the two sides would be arguing hard against each other over these limited number of issues until they could reach agreement on them.

Linear negotiation processes would also often be applied with the traditional distributive negotiation models. These negotiations would often result in win-loss agreements in which a gain by one party would often result in a loss to the other party. Often it would not be possible to make trade-offs across different negotiation issues as both parties would be concentrating their negotiations on a limited number of key issues. Typically, the business negotiations would be concentrating on the key issue of profit and loss, plus the distribution of benefits which neither party would like to give up easily. The negotiation process would often be restricted and narrow. There would also be little room for the negotiators from both parties to expand the scope of their negotiations to include other important issues. The agreements reached under these older, linear negotiation processes, which would normally also involve the distributive negotiation model, would normally be win-loss agreements and would often be unsustainable in the longer term in the modern business world. Hence the older, simpler, linear negotiation process would really only be applicable to simple business negotiations involving a few key business issues to date.

In the more modern non-linear negotiation processes, the negotiation parties would normally try to negotiate a basket of different business issues which would be important for the parties and the success of their business deal. The negotiators would also normally be negotiating the different issues using the integrative negotiation model together with the non-linear negotiation process. These would then allow them to make trade-offs and compromises over the different key business issues during negotiations. The negotiators from the different sides would normally try to achieve their most valuable business objectives whilst being prepared to compromise on the less important business issues during negotiation. This should help the negotiators to make good negotiation progress and to integrate their different interests into a new joint agreement which should be win–win and create maximum values for all the parties in the negotiations.

Analysis of high-level international business negotiations shows that the parties would normally start their first round of negotiations after extensive preparations. Negotiations of many related issues would likely follow the non-linear negotiation process together with the integrative negotiation model during the various negotiation rounds. It would be quite normal during these negotiations that there would be different trade-offs and compromises over a basket of the various key business issues being negotiated. As a result of different concessions, new demands and new negotiation issues might be created which would have to be further negotiated.

It would often not be possible in high-level business negotiation for the parties to reach full agreement over all the issues quickly, in the initial rounds of negotiations. Hence it would be normal that the parties would agree to adjourn after the initial negotiation rounds. Then the negotiators on both sides would take some time to review their negotiation progress and evaluate the pros and cons of the latest negotiation issues. Then they could develop suitable revisions to their negotiation strategies plus seek new negotiation mandates. The chief negotiator and their team could then discuss these with their top management and seek their support of the new negotiation mandates including revisions in negotiation strategies, prior to the start of new negotiations in China.

It would also be very important for the negotiation teams to review their negotiation learnings and integrate these after each negotiation round. The negotiator could then develop suitable revisions to their overall negotiation strategies. In this way, the overall negotiation strategy would be kept updated and could evolve in line with the ongoing business negotiations. The negotiators would normally continue their negotiations until all the key business principles are negotiated and agreed. This would enable the negotiators on both parties to develop their final win–win agreement for both parties in the negotiations.

Analysis of business negotiation cases also shows that the negotiators from both partners would be applying the modern non-linear negotiation processes together with the involvement of multiple, local and international partners. These changes would be in line with requirements of the complex, international business environment. With the growing complex business environment, business negotiations could involve multiple partners and not just the traditional two parties, especially for some of the mega international deals. These could involve leading SOEs, private companies and multinational companies.

Good business examples of international non-linear negotiations involving multiple parties are the major international oil and energy supply agreements. These major agreements would normally involve various SOEs, private companies and international companies in different consortiums. There might also be additional, multiple minority partners involved in these major deals. These could include leading local companies, key government bodies and supply chain companies. They would all have their own specific interest in the overall deal and would be tabling their various negotiation issues in the complex multi-party negotiations. These would make the negotiations become more complex, difficult and mutli-faceted.

A successful case example of a non-linear, integrative, international, Chinese business negotiation would be the China Russia CNPC Rosneft Tianjin Oil Refinery agreement. On 27 May 2014, CNPC and Rosneft signed a joint agreement on the design and construction planning of the new Tianjin Refinery and Petrochemical project after long, complex integrative non-linear business negotiations. They negotiated and agreed that the mega oil downstream project would be built by their new joint venture PetroChina-Rosneft Orient Petrochemical Tianjin Company in Tianjin, China. After hard negotiation on the sensitive issue of shareholding ratios, they agreed that Petrochina would hold 51 per cent shareholding whilst Rosneft would hold 49 per cent interest in their new joint venture in China. The new Tianjin Refinery would be designed to process the Russian crude oil being imported into China under the new CNPC and Rosneft international oil supply agreement.

The Chinese and Russian negotiators have also negotiated hard on the sensitive issues of downstream oil product sales and marketing. After long negotiations, they agreed to supply the oil products from the new refinery to the fast-growing eastern China markets. In follow-up to site selection negotiations with the central and local government agencies, PetroChina and Rosneft have selected a site in the Tianjin Nangan Industrial zone to build the new PetroChina-Rosneft Orient Petrochemical Tianjin integrated refinery. The new refinery was to be designed to have a refining capacity of 13 million tonnes per year (260,000 BPD) of crude oil out of which 9.1 million tonnes would be sourced from Russia. In addition to the new oil refinery, the partners agreed to construct a simple, new petrochemical complex which would include aromatics production units and pyrolysis plants. In addition, they have also negotiated hard on oil product retail and sales. After long negotiations, they agreed that there would be 300 new oil retail stations for the sale and distribution of the oil transportation fuels from the new refinery. The new Tianjin refinery total capital investment was estimated to be large at US $4.6 billion. The new refinery would likely start commercial operations in 2020.

China business negotiation processes

Literature surveys and analysis of China business negotiations show that the negotiation processes in China have also been evolving fast, in line with international negotiation practices and developments. The majority of modern business negotiation processes in China have been shifting away from the simple, traditional, linear process to the more complex, modern, multi-issue, non-linear process. These changes in Chinese negotiation processes have been driven by the increasing complexity of the Chinese business environment and modern commercial requirements.

In the past, the older linear business negotiation processes were used in China when business negotiations were simpler and involving only a limited number of business issues to be negotiated. Then the Chinese and foreign negotiators would normally concentrate on negotiating a small number of key business issues. Typically, these would focus on profit and losses, distribution of benefits plus management control and shareholder ratios between the Chinese and foreign partners. The linear negotiation processes have often been applied with the traditional distributive negotiation model. These linear, distributive, business negotiations would often result in win-loss agreements between the Chinese and foreign partners.

A good example of the linear business negotiation process would be the negotiations on joint venture management control and shareholding ratios between Chinese and international negotiators. Normally neither the Chinese nor foreign negotiators would be willing to give up management control or lower their shareholding ratios in their new joint venture in their negotiations in China. Hence the negotiation process on these issues would often be linear, restricted and narrow. In many cases, the Chinese and foreign partners would not be able to reach agreement, even after long, hard negotiations. Then they would normally agree to have an equal shareholding ratio of 50 to 50, i.e. each partner holding 50 per cent of the shareholding of the joint venture. This would then result in the Chinese and foreign partner being able to each nominate an equal number of directors to the new joint venture board. If there is no serious disagreement in the board on joint venture operations, then the board should generally be able to function well. However, if there are serious disagreements between the partners on some key, strategic issues, then this could result in a split board with a stale-mate board situation.

Typical good business examples on issues which could lead to serious board disagreements in China would include discussions on possible future expansions, capital injections or introductions of future partners. These sensitive issues have often led to serious board disputes in many joint ventures. In the worst cases, they could even lead to the termination of the joint ventures if there were serious disagreements between the partners.

As the business environment and commercial requirements in China have become more complex, the business negotiation processes have also been shifting to the more modern non-linear, multi-issue negotiation process. The Chinese and foreign partners would normally try to negotiate a basket of different business issues which would be critical for the success of their business deal or joint venture in China. The Chinese and foreign negotiators would normally be negotiating the different issues along the non-linear negotiation process together with the integrative negotiation model approach. This would then allow the Chinese and foreign partners to make the necessary trade-offs and compromises across the different key business issues in a holistic way during negotiations. This should help the negotiators on both sides to integrate their different business interests plus make the necessary compromises and concessions. These should help the negotiators on both sides to develop a new joint venture agreement which should be win–win for all the parties in the joint venture.

Analysis of modern business negotiations in China shows that the Chinese and foreign partners following the non-linear multi-issue negotiation process would normally only start their first round of negotiations after sufficient preparation by the negotiation teams. During the initial negotiation rounds, they would negotiate multiple business issues in a non-linear negotiation process together with the integrative negotiation model approach. These negotiations would normally involve the negotiators on each side making some concessions on different business issues on the negotiation table.

After the initial negotiation rounds, both the Chinese and foreign negotiators would normally agree to adjourn. Then the negotiators for each side could review their negotiation progress and the changing negotiation positions. The chief negotiators would discuss these with their corporate sponsors and seek new negotiation mandates from their senior management before starting the next round of negotiations. The negotiations would then continue with different negotiation rounds following the non-linear process until the negotiators have negotiated all the key business issues and reached a win–win agreement acceptable to both sides.

The late US President John F. Kennedy in his US President Inaugural Address on 20 January 1961 gave very good advice on negotiation processes and preparation. He said, "Let us never negotiate out of fear. But let us never fear to negotiate." What he had said over 56 years ago is still very much true today in that if the negotiators really understand the different negotiation processes and have prepared well for their negotiations, then there should be no fear for them when approaching negotiations with the opposing negotiators.

Multiple Chinese partner negotiations

Analysis of modern business negotiation cases in China also shows that in many major deals there might also be multiple Chinese partners involved in the non-linear negotiation processes. Typically, these would include the Chinese SOEs plus key local companies linked to the provincial governments. These local companies could also become minority shareholders in the joint venture due to the significant impact of the future joint venture on the local economy. During the business negotiation process, new strategic alliances might also be negotiated and agreed between the different Chinese parties. These new alliances could become quite powerful and might influence the future course of the negotiations.

In China, if there are more than one Chinese party negotiating with the foreign partner, then eventually a strategic alliance would be negotiated and formed between the different Chinese parties involved in the negotiations. The various Chinese parties would normally negotiate and agree amongst themselves to nominate one of the Chinese partners to be the 'Lead Chinese Partner'. The Lead Chinese Partner would then represent all the Chinese partners in the negotiations with the foreign partner. The international negotiators should be very vigilant and watch out for these new strategic alliances. These alliances could create new coalitions amongst the Chinese partners which could be quite powerful. These new alliances could then seriously influence the negotiation process as well as the possible negotiation outcomes.

In China, good examples of high-level business negotiations involving multiple Chinese and foreign partner partners are the large, complex oil and gas, petrochemical and chemical projects in the different provinces of China. For these large multi-billion projects, there would normally be involvement with multiple Chinese partners. These would normally include the large Chinese SOEs, such as Sinopec, Petrochina or CNOOC, together with some leading local companies which have strong links to the local government of the province where the large project would be situated.

A good business example of a successful multi-partner, Sino-foreign, joint venture is the ExxonMobil, Saudi Aramco, Sinopec and Fujian Province Joint Venture in Fujian. The four Chinese and international partners undertook long and complex negotiations over a number of years on their proposed joint venture in Fujian. The new joint venture aimed to set up a complex refinery and petrochemical joint venture in Fujian Province, China. After long, integrative non-linear negotiations, they finally agreed and successfully established a fully integrated refining and petrochemicals joint venture together with an oil fuels marketing joint venture in Fujian, China. They negotiated and agreed the ownership structure and shareholder ratio of the manufacturing joint venture. The joint venture would be jointly owned by ExxonMobil at 25 per cent, Saudi Aramco at 25 per cent and Fujian Petrochemical Company Limited at 50 per cent shareholding.

The Fujian Petrochemical Company was a Chinese company which was specially established by the various multiple Chinese partners involved in the massive deal. The multiple Chinese partners were comprised of Sinopec plus key Fujian local companies which each held an interest in the Sino-foreign joint venture. They agreed that Sinopec should be the lead Chinese partner holding the majority share whilst the other Fujian local companies would be minority partners.

China's business negotiation process: initial stages

Literature surveys and analysis of successful high-level business negotiations in China by leading Chinese and foreign companies show that modern business negotiations have normally followed the non-linear negotiation process with key issues being negotiated along the integrative negotiation model. These would help the negotiation teams to negotiate and eventually develop a win–win agreement acceptable to both sides. The negotiation process in China would also include different key phases including negotiation team selection, negotiation preparations, negotiation opening, middle stages of negotiation, plus finalization and closure of negotiations.

The negotiation process in China would normally start with the negotiation team selection by both the management of the Chinese and foreign companies. After selection, the negotiation teams would typically undertake extensive negotiation preparation prior to starting their business negotiations in China. When both the negotiation teams have completed their negotiation preparation, they would open their business negotiations in line with Chinese government and business requirements. The subsequent business negotiations might involve many rounds of negotiation lasting up to several years depending on the complexity and size of the deal. When all the key issues have been negotiated and agreed, then this would lead to the final stage of negotiation for deal closure. Both negotiation teams would then focus on the closure and finalization of the new joint venture agreement and associated contracts so that these contracts would be ready for presentation and signing by the top management of both the Chinese and foreign partners at the joint signing ceremony in China.

Analysis of successful business negotiation team selections shows that both Chinese and foreign partners should undertake the selection of their negotiation team carefully. They should start by carefully selecting their chief negotiator who should have a lot of business and negotiating experience relevant to the deal. The Chinese chief negotiator would normally be appointed by the Chinese top management and would be given an official letter of appointment with appropriate authorities. Senior management should select other negotiation team members carefully from different corporate and business functions relevant to the deal being negotiated in China. The Chinese negotiators would normally be experienced and have undertaken negotiation training within the company and with relevant government authorities.

For effective business negotiation in China, it would also be essential to include one or two good, competent translators in the negotiation team. During negotiations, the translators would have to make clear and accurate translations of the negotiation proposals and arguments to the negotiators on the other side. It would also be advisable to include the translators in the negotiation team preparation sessions. This would help them to build up their basic understanding of the technicality of the business and negotiation processes so that they could make better translations during the negotiations. In China, a lot of foreign companies might employ local or agency translators for their negotiations and business meeting as they would not have suitable experienced translation staff internally. If external translators from a local agency were to be hired for important confidential business negotiations, then it would be very important to require the external translators to sign the necessary secrecy or confidentiality agreements, prior to the start of the confidential business negotiations.

After the negotiation team selection phase, the selected negotiation teams would then normally work together in the negotiation preparation phase to undertake extensive preparations prior to the start of negotiations in China. The Chinese negotiation teams would normally undertake extensive negotiation preparation before starting negotiations with their foreign partners in China. They would normally develop detailed negotiation strategies and scenarios for the various potential negotiation cases. They would also seek appropriate negotiation mandates from their corporate sponsors. In some cases, the Chinese negotiators would also have to seek guidance and support from relevant government authorities.

International negotiating teams have generally found that the Chinese negotiators would be very knowledgeable about the foreign company's businesses. The key reason is that the Chinese negotiators would have undertaken detailed competitor analysis and research on the foreign companies as part of their negotiation preparations. This research would normally include systematic competitor analysis together with detailed strength and weakness analysis. These negotiation preparations would also help the negotiators to better identify potential areas of conflict and compromise during negotiation. These would then help them to develop better win–win negotiation solutions between the two sides. Negotiation compromises and concessions would also help to build trust and guanxi between the negotiators on both sides during negotiations.

In addition, many international negotiators have found that the Chinese negotiation teams would normally have a unique negotiation advantage during negotiations in China. In China, all Sino-foreign contracts agreed between the Chinese and international partners would have to be submitted to the relevant Chinese government ministries, such as the China Ministry of Commerce (MOFCOM), for final approval after negotiation between the business parties. These agreements and contracts would all be collated into the extensive Sino-foreign contracts database in the Ministry of Commerce. The Chinese negotiators could have access to the extensive Sino-foreign contract database in the Chinese Ministry of Commerce. In preparation for their negotiations with the international negotiators, the Chinese negotiators would normally access the Sino-foreign contract database to review all the relevant contracts that the foreign company have already signed in China with other partners. They would be able to examine the various terms and conditions agreed in different contracts that the international company have previously signed in China. During negotiations in China, the Chinese negotiators could then challenge the international negotiators by quoting specific terms and conditions that the international company have already negotiated and agreed in China with other Chinese companies.

On major Sino-foreign deals and negotiations, the Chinese negotiator would normally have to seek support from relevant government agencies in addition to mandates from their own senior management. To seek negotiation support from the various relevant senior corporate and government stakeholders, the Chinese negotiation team would normally have to prepare confidential negotiation reports detailing their negotiation objectives, strategy and plans. These would also describe their planned negotiation process plus what they want to achieve from the negotiations. The chief negotiator would then discuss these with their senior management plus relevant government stakeholders to agree the appropriate negotiation mandates. They would also consider different potential 'negotiation scenarios', including the possible arguments from the international partner and their likely demands. These would help them to better develop their counter arguments to achieve the desired negotiation outcomes.

One important analysis for both sides to do in their negotiation preparation and during actual negotiations would be to analyze and determine the 'relative negotiating power' of the other party. This would include detailed negotiation scenario analysis on what would happen if no agreement was reachable during negotiations including the potential implications. These would help the negotiators to develop their specific negotiation strategies and assess how far they would need to negotiate to reach a suitable joint agreement. The negotiation scenario analysis would also help the negotiators to better understand what could be the 'Best Alternatives to a Negotiated Agreement' (BATNA) that the opposing negotiators might have. These in turn would help the negotiators to develop better negotiation strategies to deal with these negotiation situations together with appropriate proposals and counter-arguments.

The international negotiation team representing the foreign partner must also prepare well before their negotiations in China. They should agree realistic negotiation schedules and mandates with their top management in advance of their negotiations in China. Realistic negotiation bottom lines and mandates should also be discussed and agreed with their senior overseas management to avoid unrealistically high expectations on the negotiation outcomes from China. In particular, business negotiations in China would normally take a long time with complex hard negotiations resulting in unforeseeable outcomes. So, the international negotiators should try to identify, during their negotiation preparations, potential areas of compromise which they could use to create 'win–win alternatives'. Then the negotiators should decide how best to table and use these during the negotiations to get the best negotiation outcomes. In addition, these would help to create good *guanxi* between the two sides and improve the final negotiation outcomes.

During negotiation preparations, it would also be important for the negotiation teams to find time to rehearse and practise their negotiations prior to actual negotiations in China. Clear roles and responsibilities should be assigned by the Chief Negotiator to each member of the negotiation team so that they know what they need to do during the intensive negotiations. They also require good backup and support from the corporate head office during their negotiations in China as many questions and new queries could surface during these negotiations.

When both negotiation teams have completed their negotiation preparation, they could commence the opening of the negotiations phase in China. It would be important to realize that the first phase of business negotiations in China, prior to the start of formal negotiations, would be the negotiation opening meeting. It would normally cover introductions of negotiators and for the negotiation teams to get to know each other. This might occur over an informal welcome dinner or lunch hosted by the Chinese partner. During the event, there would often be long, informal social discussions over their family, career, home countries, education and interests. These social engagements might cause some of the inexperienced foreign negotiators, who are unfamiliar with Chinese culture and customs, to become quite impatient and wonder what all these discussions have to do with the formal business negotiations.

However, it would be very important to realize the importance and value of these informal social exchanges. First, the Chinese negotiators would actually be using these informal gatherings as a valuable opportunity to get more detailed, first-hand information on the foreign partner negotiation team and its negotiators. Different Chinese negotiators would normally be trying to collect detailed personal information about each of the foreign negotiators, especially their chief negotiator. These might include trying to get first-hand information on the international negotiator's background, taste, style, family, interests and ways of thinking. These could become very important background data in the later stages of intensive negotiations. Second, these initial engagements would also help to build trust and contribute to the development of good *guanxi* or relationships between the Chinese and foreign negotiation teams. Good *guanxi* could be very useful in the later stages of tough business negotiations.

At the start of formal high-level business negotiations in China, both the Chinese and foreign party negotiation teams would normally be led by their respective chief negotiators, who should have been formally appointed by their respective management. In many major, formal, high-level business negotiations in China, it would be a normal custom at the first formal negotiation meeting that the chief negotiators from both sides would show each other their respective 'Letter of Appointment' from their head office. It would be important that the letter of appointment from the foreign partner was not only signed by the CEO or a suitable top executive but it must also be stamped with the official company chop of the international company. The Chinese partner would normally ask their lawyers to check and verify the Letter of Appointment of the international chief negotiator. They would normally also ask the international chief negotiator to supply a copy for the Chinese company's files. The international chief negotiator could also ask to see the Chinese chief negotiator's appointment letter and get an official copy.

These formal exchanges and confirmation of Appointment Letters should also be minuted and noted in the first set of the Joint Negotiation Minutes by both parties.

At the opening of negotiations and during the different rounds of negotiations, the Chinese negotiators would normally highlight the importance of the 'key principle of equity and mutual benefits'. This is an important negotiation principle in China which both the Chinese and foreign negotiation teams would need to bear in mind in order to negotiate win–win agreements which would be mutually acceptable and beneficial to both sides.

China business negotiation process stages and finalization

After the completion of the required negotiation opening formalities, then the negotiation teams would normally start the formal negotiations which could involve many negotiation rounds lasting over a couple of months to a number of years. Modern business negotiations in China would normally follow the non-linear negotiation process together with the integrative negotiation model. These would normally involve many rounds of integrative negotiations with the team negotiating hard over many different rounds of negotiations. These would also involve the negotiators on both sides offering concessions on different issues and compromising on various strategic issues during the negotiations.

In the older days of business negotiation, there would normally be fewer negotiation rounds as the negotiators would have concentrated on fewer issues. The international and Chinese negotiators would then follow the simpler, linear negotiation process with the distributive negotiation model. These would normally lead to fewer rounds of negotiations as the negotiators would be negotiating a limited number of key business issues.

Analysis of high-level business negotiations in China shows that the majority of major business negotiations would neither be just win-loss distributive nor purely win–win integrative. Most high-level business negotiations between the Chinese and international negotiators would comprise a combination of both distributive and integrative negotiations together with a complex combination of the linear and non-linear negotiation processes.

Depending on the complexity and size of the deals involved, there would normally be many complex issues which the Chinese and foreign Partners would need to negotiate and agree so as to develop the final win–win agreement. In these cases, it would be important to identify what might be the potential 'win–win cooperative issues' which the negotiators could cooperate and share values on these at different stages of the negotiations. There would normally be many complex business issues at stake which would make it very difficult for the Chinese and foreign partners to agree these straight away in the initial negotiation rounds. Normally many rounds of negotiations would be required over long periods which could take a number of months or years.

For successful business negotiations in China, the chief negotiator should assign different roles and responsibilities to various negotiators on the team. These could include primary negotiation roles which would be based on the functional expertise of the negotiators, such as financial, technical, commercial or marketing. In addition, the chief negotiators should assign secondary negotiation roles to the negotiators. The key secondary roles could include speaker, note taker, intermediary, observer, etc.

The chief negotiator should assign different negotiators to be the speaker or presenter for the negotiation team on different topics. This could also be the chief negotiator or it could be another senior negotiator of the negotiation team depending on the subject being negotiated. It would not be desirable to have the chief negotiator as the main speaker all the time. This would then allow the chief negotiator to have more room and flexibility in the later stages of negotiations to negotiate and trade different options and make the necessary compromises with the other negotiation team in order to arrive at a win–win agreement.

The chief negotiator should appoint one of the negotiators the important role of being the official note taker and minutes preparer for the team. During negotiations, the note taker should make accurate detailed notes of the negotiations. After the negotiation round, the appointed note takers should work with their own negotiators to prepare a set of joint minutes of the negotiation. The joint negotiation minutes should highlight the key areas discussed, main points agreed and other key areas still to be negotiated in future rounds. The note takers on both teams should discuss the draft minutes to agree a set of joint negotiation minutes. These could involve some clarifications of what had been discussed in the negotiations. After both the note takers have agreed the draft joint minutes, the chief negotiators of both teams should then review, agree and sign the joint negotiation minutes. Each negotiation team could then use the agreed joint minutes to update their respective corporate sponsor and top management after each negotiation round. They could then also discuss any revisions in their negotiation strategies. The negotiators should also get the necessary new mandates from their senior management, prior to the next round of negotiations.

Depending on the size and complexity of the deal, many rounds of high-level business negotiations could take place between the negotiators from the Chinese and international partners over several months or years. The negotiations might take place in both China and overseas. It would often be normal for the foreign partner to invite and arrange for the Chinese partner to visit their overseas manufacturing locations for the required site visits and inspections as part of the negotiations. These visits could also be valuable opportunities to build up guanxi and relations with the Chinese negotiators.

After each round of negotiations, it would be normal that all the new concessions gained plus new demands tabled would have to be reported to senior management by each of the negotiation teams. In addition, each of the negotiation teams would also have to evaluate and undertake detailed analysis of the new requests and discuss these with relevant businesses plus senior management. After detailed internal discussions and reviews, suitable new negotiation strategies and mandates should then be agreed with management for the next round of negotiation.

At the same time, the Chinese partners' negotiators would also have to report and discuss with their senior management about the negotiation progress and to get new mandates. In some major projects involving strategic sectors, the Chinese negotiators would also have to update relevant central or local government authorities on the progress of the negotiations and seek their support on negotiation strategies and mandates.

The complex business negotiation process between the Chinese and foreign partners could continue over a period of several years depending on the complexity and size of the agreement. Normally the negotiation would continue over several months or years until the negotiators on both sides have negotiated all the key issues so that both parties would consider these to be win–win and mutually beneficial. It would be very important for both the negotiation teams to be patient and maintain their commitments over the long negotiation periods.

It would also be important for the Chinese and international senior management to recognise the importance of long-term commitment and support for their negotiation team negotiating in China. In particular, senior management should try to avoid making changes to the negotiation team, unless it was absolutely unavoidable. Any changes of negotiation team members should be notified to the other side together with good reasons supporting the changes. It is important to ensure that the opposite negotiation team should not misunderstand that changes to some negotiators could mean that there would be changes in negotiation positions or commitments to the deal.

The final stage of negotiation closing should only be reached after all the key issues have been negotiated and agreed by the international and Chinese negotiators. Both negotiation teams should then focus on the development and finalization of the new joint venture agreement and supplementary contracts. The negotiators should work closely with their lawyers to ensure that all the key business principles agreed are included accurately into the final agreements and contracts. During drafting of the final agreements, there might be some discussions required to clarify the key principles and terms agreed during the negotiations. In some cases, these might lead to some final negotiations being required to agree the finer points.

Alternatively, some negotiation teams have chosen in the past to negotiate and agree changes to relevant key clauses in their joint agreement after each negotiation round. However, this might take time and would generally be more applicable to simpler negotiation where both the Chinese and foreign partners would agree to use standard contracts in China. In these negotiations, as the key issues being negotiated would be limited, then the teams could also discuss and agree the revisions to the clauses in the standard contracts during each negotiation round. In these cases, the negotiations would also be more likely to follow the linear negotiation process with distributive negotiation models being applied.

When the Chinese and international negotiation teams have prepared and agreed all the relevant agreements, they could present these agreements and contracts to their respective top management and seek their approval. In large projects, there might be many agreements including the joint venture agreement plus many supporting supplementary contracts and local contracts. The supplementary contracts would normally involve licensing, technology transfer, management services and marketing, etc. In some mega projects, there might also be additional agreements which need to be agreed with the local and provincial government including local contracts on land use, water supply, electricity supply and resettlement.

When all the agreements have been approved by the Chinese and foreign partners, they are then required to submit all the proposed agreements and contracts to relevant ministries in the Chinese government for approval. These would normally include the Ministry of Commercial, National Development and Reform Commission, etc. The relevant central and local government ministries and authorities would then review these agreements in detail with relevant Chinese experts. After relevant reviews and if there are no objections or questions, then the appropriate China government approvals would be granted. If there are serious questions or objections from the various government experts, then these would have to be answered and dealt with before final government approval could be granted.

After approval, it would be normal for both the Chinese and foreign partners to plan and hold a big signing ceremony in China to celebrate the signing of the major contracts and agreements. The formal signing ceremonies for important high-level agreements can be held in the government state guest house in Beijing or the provincial guest houses in the province where the project is located. These would normally be attended by senior government leaders together with the top management of the Chinese and international partners.

A good example of successful Sino-foreign joint venture business negotiations involving leading China and an international company in the petrochemical and chemicals sector is the CNOOC and Shell Joint Venture in China. Shell and CNOOC have successfully negotiated and established a successful joint venture in Huizhou called the CNOOC Shell Petrochemical Co Ltd, which was also known as the Nanhai Project. This was Shell's largest single investment in China and China's largest Sino-Foreign Petrochemical Joint Venture. CNOOC and Shell started discussing the potential joint venture and project scopes in 1990s. The project scope changed several times over a number of years due to changing requirements and business needs. The Chinese and foreign partners finally agreed to focus on a world-scale petrochemical complex in 1996. They prepared and submitted their joint Project Feasibility Study Report for government approval in 1996. The National Development and Reform Commission organized detailed reviews of proposals in the joint Feasibility Report by different Chinese experts. After satisfactory reviews, the Chinese government granted approval to the joint Feasibility Study Report in 1997. After government approval of the joint project Feasibility Report, then the negotiators from CNOOC and Shell spent over three years to negotiate the joint venture contract and supplementary contracts, including the licensing, marketing and service contracts. In addition, CNOOC and Shell also formed a joint local contract negotiation team to negotiate with the various Chinese central and local governments agencies plus state utilities companies on the key local contracts. These included the land grant contract, electricity supply contract, water supply contract, the resettlement agreement and the channel contract.

After over three years of hard integrative, non-linear negotiations, the CNOOC and Shell negotiation teams finally agreed their joint venture agreement, supplementary contracts and local contracts in 2000. They then submitted all the negotiated agreements and contracts for central and local government approval in 2000. The CNOOC and Shell Petrochemical Joint Venture was approved in 2000 by the Chinese Central Government with a 50:50 shareholding ratio between Shell and CNOOC. A large signing ceremony was then held in the state guest house in Beijing and attended by top government officials and company executives. A second large signing ceremony for the agreed local contracts was also held in Huizhou, attended by key local government leaders and top management from Shell and CNOOC.

After approval, CNOOC and Shell established their joint venture in line with their various negotiated agreements. The joint venture successfully invested US $4.2 billion in constructing a world-scale Ethylene Cracker and Petrochemical complex at Daya Bay, Huizhou, Guangdong Province. The plants were commissioned in early 2006 on time and within budget. In April 2010, they completed their first turnaround and de-bottlenecking project safely, within budget and ahead of schedule. Its ethylene capacity has been raised from 800,000 TPA to 950,000 TPA. The total petrochemical production capacity at the site has also been increased from 2.3 million to 2.7 million tonnes per annum.

3   Chinese business negotiation culture

不入虎穴，焉得虎子
bù rù hǔ xuè , yān dé hǔ zǐ
If you do not enter the lion's den, how can you get the lion's cubs?
Nothing ventured, nothing gained.

Executive overview

An important criterion for successful Chinese business negotiations is for the negotiators to understand the required negotiation culture and customs in China. The negotiators should adhere to the appropriate negotiation formalities and customs during business negotiations in China. The key characteristics of Chinese negotiation customs and culture will be discussed in detail together with their implications on the business negotiation process plus negotiation strategies in China. The importance of good relationship management and proven tactics for building up good 'guanxi' during negotiations in China will be discussed together with the appropriate best practices.

Chinese business negotiation culture

One of the most important criteria for successful business negotiations in China is that the international negotiators have to be very sensitive to the Chinese negotiation culture and customs. For the international negotiators, it is important for them to take into consideration the Chinese negotiation cultural sensitivities, requirements and customs during their negotiation planning and actual negotiations. These will help them to negotiate more effectively and to reach win–win agreements more easily. If the international negotiators ignore these Chinese negotiation culture and practices, then they normally have some very difficult negotiations with uncertain outcomes.

In important business negotiations and dealings with the Chinese negotiators, great care should be given to 'giving face' and building trust and 'guangxi' with the Chinese negotiators. These are complicated forms of Chinese behaviour and relationship management. However, if the negotiators manage these well, these could help contribute significantly to the building of respect and trust between the international and Chinese negotiators. These would then help to smooth the negotiation process and promote the chances of achieving mutually beneficial negotiation outcomes. Alternatively, if negotiation relations or guanxi were not handled correctly then these could seriously derail the smooth running of the negotiation process and adversely influence the negotiation outcomes.

In particular, the international negotiators should take into consideration three key aspects of the Chinese negotiation culture which would normally be critical for effective business negotiations in China. These are the three main Chinese cultural concepts and relationship management skills of 'guanxi', 'mianzi' and 'keqi', which will be described in more detail below.

First, 'guanxi', which literally means 'relationships' in Chinese, is one of the central concepts of Chinese relationship management culture. The key objective for building good guanxi in China is to establish a good, trusting relationship based on mutual respect between the Chinese and international negotiators. The Chinese negotiators normally spend time trying to build good guanxi and a trusting relationship with the foreign negotiators at the start of negotiations as it is part of their normal negotiation customs and practice. The international negotiators should also reciprocate these approaches with good efforts to also try to build good negotiation relations and guanxi with the Chinese negotiators.

A good business negotiation case example is that the Chinese negotiators would normally, prior to the start of formal negotiations and during breaks in negotiations or during negotiation dinners or lunches, try to engage the international negotiators socially by talking about their family, education, travels, etc. These could take place during the informal welcome meeting or over lunches, dinner or tea breaks during the negotiations. It is important that the international negotiators should also use these opportunities to engage the Chinese negotiation team socially and build up guanxi with them.

A common mistake amongst the inexperienced international negotiators would be that they might misunderstand or misconceive these initial attempts on building up trust and social engagements as a waste of time and a barrier to the negotiations. In the worst case, the inexperienced international negotiators might misunderstand these to be time wasting negotiation tactics by the Chinese negotiators. This serious mistake would then lead to poor guanxi and mistrust between the Chinese and international negotiators right from the start of negotiations which could be hard to repair. Then these would normally lead to difficult negotiations with uncertain outcomes.

Second, 'mianzi', which literally means 'face' in Chinese, is a critically important behavioural concept in China. It would be very important for the foreign partner negotiation team to understand this key behavioural concept and manage it appropriately. In particular, there would be two important aspects of face management in the Chinese business culture, i.e. 'giving face' and 'losing face'.

'Giving face' would literally mean 'Gei ni mian zi' in Chinese. This is one of the most important engagement arts or skills for international negotiators to master. The negotiators should understand and master these important skills which they can then use during negotiations in China. These skills would normally be complex arts for international negotiators to master well but are very worthwhile to learn. If properly applied, these engagement skills can help the international negotiators to build trust and good relationships quickly with the Chinese negotiators. These in turn would help in the smooth running of the negotiations and promote win–win negotiation outcomes.

A simple but proven negotiation tactic in China for the international negotiators to 'give face' to the Chinese negotiation team is to speak highly of the achievements of the Chinese negotiator or their company. A good example is that the international chief negotiator make some polite, positive comments on the Chinese company's achievements and international recognition in front of the whole Chinese and international negotiation teams during the negotiation opening meeting or in one of their initial formal negotiation rounds. Such a gesture would normally help to give face to whole the Chinese negotiation team, which they would appreciate. This would also help the international negotiators to build good guanxi quickly with the Chinese negotiators. Good guanxi would be helpful during the subsequent, tough, later stages of negotiations.

The opposite of giving face in Chinese is 'Diu-lian' or 'Diu mian zi'. Both of these Chinese phrases literally mean 'losing face' in Chinese. These could be very powerful negotiation tactics and tools during negotiations in China. However, they should be used very carefully and by very experienced negotiators who have been trained in using these complex negotiation techniques. If the international negotiator applies these well, then they could help deliver very powerful messages directly to the Chinese negotiator during complex negotiations in China. However, if it was applied incorrectly, then it could cause great harm and create bad guanxi with the Chinese negotiators. These might then adversely affect the negotiation process and lead to uncertain outcomes.

A simple but effective 'diu-lian' negotiation tactic is commonly used by experienced negotiators to deal with an inexperienced negotiator who might be boasting too much. A good business example is when an inexperienced negotiator might become very boastful during initial negotiations by trying to show off his past negotiation achievements to try to impress the opposing negotiators. The experienced negotiators normally listen and wait patiently until the inexperienced negotiator has finished his boastful delivery. Then the experienced negotiator would engineer a situation during negotiations which would lead to the inexperienced negotiator losing a lot of face in front of the others. A commonly used and effective negotiation technique applied by experienced negotiators is to patiently listen to the long, boring lecture from the inexperienced negotiator, then at the right moment, highlight significant past failures of the inexperienced negotiator in front of the negotiation teams present at the negotiation table. This would be equivalent to a 'virtual public disgrace' and would normally cause serious loss of face and embarrassment to the inexperienced negotiator. However, it must be appreciated that the individual who has suffered the public loss of face might then react very strongly to save some face publicly. Hence the experienced negotiator should also be trained to handle any strong adverse reactions to minimize any potential damage and defuse the tense situation after achieving their negotiation intention.

Third, 'keqi' which literally means in Chinese courteous and refined behaviour, is a social refinement quality which is normally very respected in China. In the Chinese business culture, a negotiator considered to be 'keqi' should behave courteously and modestly, speak softly and show great humility in their dealings with the other negotiators. The international negotiators should understand that for them to behave modestly and humbly in China does not necessarily mean that they would be conceived to be weak negotiators by the Chinese negotiators. In fact, it will make it easier for them to be accepted by their Chinese negotiators and build up better guanxi.

There are many proven negotiation techniques for assertiveness in China which negotiators should be trained to use during negotiations in China whilst they still be considered 'keqi' by the Chinese negotiators. These negotiation tactics which would help negotiators to be assertive whilst being keqi are important skills to learn during negotiation training prior to the start of negotiations in China. These will be described in more detail during the chapter on negotiation preparations.

A simple and effective negotiation tactic for being a good keqi negotiator in China would be for the international negotiator not to talk too long or boost too much during negotiations. Many inexperienced Western negotiators tend to boast too much about their international negotiation successes in front of the Chinese negotiators when they first meet. For most inexperienced international negotiators, they would frequently make the common mistake of trying to talk at length about their various international negotiation successes and achievements in front of their Chinese negotiators. Whilst this might be normal behaviour during Western business negotiations, it is not really appreciated in China. If the international negotiators talk too much about their overseas negotiation successes, then these could be considered to be boasting and not keqi behaviour in China. Whilst the Chinese negotiators might appear to be listening politely, in reality they could be somewhat upset and not appreciative of the boasting from the international negotiators. In fact, if the negotiation teams have done their negotiation research properly during the negotiation preparation stage, then they should have already found out all the relevant details of previous negotiations undertaken by the opposing negotiators and their negotiation team, including all their past negotiation successes and failures.

In many negotiations in China, inexperienced international negotiators could be unwittingly putting themselves into a poor negotiation position by giving the Chinese negotiators a good opportunity to challenge them and leading to serious loss of face situations. A good typical business negotiation case example is when the inexperienced international negotiators make the mistake of boasting too much about their various international negotiation successes and experiences in front of their Chinese negotiators. Trying to impress the Chinese negotiators with their negotiation experience could seriously backfire. Some experienced Chinese negotiators could then take the opportunity to highlight at the right moment some previous negotiation failures or mistakes made by the international negotiators.

The Chinese negotiators would usually have unearthed these as part of their negotiation preparation and searches. Such a blow, if delivered correctly during negotiation, would then seriously undermine the credibility of the international negotiator as well as causing him serious loss of face in front of both the negotiation teams. Hence it would normally be recommended that the international negotiators should be very careful and succinct in their descriptions of their international negotiation experiences and successes in front of the Chinese negotiation teams. This would help to reduce the chances of creating a negotiation situation when they could be challenged by the opposing negotiator and suffer serious loss of face.

Very good advice was given to negotiators over 2,500 years ago by the famous Chinese scholar and philosopher, Confucius (551–479 BC), in his famous *First Ten Books*, in which he said, "At fifteen I set my heart on learning; at thirty I took my stand, at forty I came to be free from doubts; at fifty I understood the Decree of Heaven; at sixty my ears were attuned; at seventy I followed my heart's desire without overstepping the line". Whilst these famous sayings by Confucius were made some two thousand years ago, they are still very relevant today on the important Chinese cultural concept of keqi.

Negotiation cultural differences and skills

Business negotiations in China would normally involve negotiators from different nationalities and cultural backgrounds. The cultural differences amongst negotiators from various countries would normally create cultural negotiation barriers which could impede the negotiation process. Hence it would be important for negotiators to learn and master the appropriate negotiation skills to handle the cultural differences during negotiations in China. These would also help them to better understand the behaviour of their opposing negotiators which should then help to make their negotiations more effective.

One of the very important cultural skills during negotiations is to have the skills to observe how the Chinese negotiators are behaving and acting during negotiations. This would involve the correct observation of both verbal and non-verbal communication from the Chinese negotiators during negotiations. This would also help to better understand the real messages that the Chinese negotiators might be trying to communicate during negotiations as these would normally involve both verbal and non-verbal communications. In addition, this would also help the international negotiators to better analyze and understand the organization of the Chinese negotiation team plus identify who in their negotiation team would have the real authority to make commitments and decisions during negotiations in China.

Negotiation team organizations would also normally be heavily influenced by the cultural backgrounds of the negotiation team members plus their corporate culture and organization. Some cultures would favour the team consensus approach whilst other cultures would prefer the individualist approach. In addition, some of the large multi-billion Sino-foreign deals that have been recently be successfully negotiated have also changed the way that leading international companies organize the roles of their senior corporate sponsor plus the chief negotiator and negotiation team in China.

In many traditional Western negotiation teams, such as American and European negotiation teams, the chief negotiator would normally be empowered by the senior management of the international company to lead the negotiation team. The chief negotiator would then have important input on the selection of the other negotiators who would normally be subordinate or of lower ranks to the chief negotiator.

However, in recent business negotiations for major multi-billion Sino-foreign deals in China, some leading international companies have also made significant changes in the roles of their senior corporate sponsor, international chief negotiator and negotiation team to mirror the Chinese negotiation organizational situations and characteristics. In these large, modern international, negotiation teams, the chief negotiator would be empowered by the senior management of the international company to lead the negotiation team in China, but he would not be the final decision maker for the entire negotiation in China.

The top management of many international companies would normally appoint a C-level, senior executive in the international company to be the senior corporate sponsor for the entire negotiation in China. The top corporate sponsor would normally invite other senior executives from different divisions of the multinational company to join him in a top-level, corporate, negotiation steering committee. The chief negotiator and his negotiation team would then have to report their negotiation progress after each major round of negotiations in China to this top-level, corporate China negotiation steering committee. They would then need to seek their support for any revisions in negotiation strategies and new mandates required prior to starting the next round of negotiations in China.

The organization of the Chinese negotiation teams might be more complex inside the Chinese systems. In many cases, the Chinese chief negotiator might just be the chief spokesman and nominated figure head for the Chinese negotiation team. He might often not be the real decision maker for the whole negotiation in China. In most major business negotiations in China, the Chinese decision makers would not normally join the negotiations. The real Chinese decision makers would normally be the CEO or top executives in the Chinese SOE or leading, private company. The Chinese chief negotiator and the negotiation team would have to report back to them after each negotiation round to discuss the negotiation progress and to get new negotiation mandates.

Analysis of international business negotiation team organization structures shows that many Western and American negotiation teams would normally be led by a strong chief negotiator who would normally be empowered by the senior management of the Western company to lead the negotiation team plus to make appropriate decisions during negotiations. These would be in line with the normal Western and American corporate culture and customs. These negotiation teams also tend to be smaller with a few experienced negotiators selected by the chief negotiator. During negotiations, they would tend to push quite hard for quick negotiation outcomes and decisions. These smaller negotiation team structures would also be in line with the fact that the international team would have to work away from their corporate head office and undertake their negotiations in China.

However, it is very important to recognize that in most Asian cultures, especially in Chinese and Japanese negotiation teams, they would normally prefer the team-based negotiation approach together with consensus decision making involving the whole negotiation team. These negotiation teams would normally tend to be larger as they would include representatives from different stakeholders and interest groups in the Chinese company. During negotiations, it might often not be clear to the international negotiators who would be the ultimate Chinese negotiator leader with the authority to make the key decisions during the negotiations. In many important negotiations in China, it would be quite normal that the actual high-level decision makers would in fact not be present during the negotiations at the negotiation table. They would normally be based in the Chinese corporate head office. The Chinese chief negotiator and the negotiation team would then update them after each negotiation round so they could give new instructions and mandates for the next round of negotiations. As a result, decision making could take more time and would involve more parties in China.

Hence it would be very important during negotiations in China that the Western international negotiators should be trained to recognize and understand the different Chinese negotiation team organizations. Then they could adjust their negotiation approaches and plans accordingly. If the international negotiators try to push too hard for quick decisions from the Chinese negotiators during negotiations in China, then they normally find that they are not forthcoming. The common reason would be that the Chinese negotiators would first have to update their corporate decision makers on the negotiation progress and discuss with them the appropriate negotiation responses to any new requests from the international negotiators.

Some of the inexperienced international negotiators might become quite frustrated about the slower pace of negotiation and longer periods required for decision making in China. However, they should understand that negotiation decisions in China take time and allow time for the Chinese negotiators to brief their senior executives. In addition, if they push too hard, this could let the opposing negotiators to apply negotiation tactics on time delays or come under undue pressures to give early concessions to the other side.

In addition, the negotiators from different cultures and countries should also try to understand the influence of culture on the different negotiation objectives of the Chinese negotiators. For many international negotiators, especially those from the United States and Europe, the primary goal of business negotiations would be to secure a signed business agreement or contract between the different parties as quickly as possible. They would normally also have been given tight negotiation deadlines by their senior management who would want their team to develop the agreements quickly. Western management would normally be stressing to the negotiators that time is money and they should try to accelerate the negotiations in China.

On the other hand, it would be important for the international negotiators to recognize that the negotiators from China and Asia would normally consider that the most important objective for successful negotiations would be first to create good guanxi and a trusting relationship between the negotiators on both sides. Normally only after the Chinese negotiators have become confident that they trust the foreign negotiators will they want to start serious negotiations with them. Hence initial negotiations in China could take much longer in the beginning stages as the Chinese negotiators would normally prefer to take more time to get to know the international negotiators. However, after they have built good guanxi and a trusting relationship with the international negotiators, then the negotiations on the various key issues can move along faster.

A good business negotiation example of the differences in negotiation styles can normally be seen during the negotiation opening and initial negotiation stages in China. The Chinese negotiation team would normally like to spend more time and effort at the start of negotiation to first create good relationship and guanxi with the foreign negotiation team. However, the foreign negotiating team, particularly those from North America, would often like to rush through this first phase of negotiation and get into the serious business negotiations quickly.

The international negotiators should understand that it would be important for them to comply with and follow the appropriate customs for negotiation opening and the initial negotiation preliminaries in China. These can take time, but if managed well, the effects could be quite beneficial for the subsequent negotiations. The international negotiators should be trained to have the necessary skills and patience to engage with their Chinese negotiators at the start of negotiations. They should use the valuable opportunities at the start of negotiation to build good relationships and guanxi with the Chinese negotiators before getting into serious negotiations.

If the international negotiators do not have the right cultural skills and patience, then they might quickly become frustrated with the slower pace of initial negotiations in China. Inexperienced international negotiators often try hard to push to start serious negotiations on their key business issues. However, they will find that the Chinese negotiators like to spend more time on understanding the international negotiators and building up guanxi and trust first. If the international negotiator does not understand these important requirements during initial negotiations in China, then this could lead to difficult negotiations, plus poor business relationships and guanxi with the Chinese negotiators. This could then seriously impede future negotiation progress and might adversely affect the negotiation outcomes. Hence it would be highly recommended that the international negotiators should be trained to have the appropriate social engagement skills to enable them to build up the required trust levels and guanxi with the Chinese negotiators, during the initial negotiation opening and preliminary stages, prior to the start of serious negotiations.

Great advice was given to Chinese negotiators over 2,500 years ago by the famous Chinese scholar and philosopher Confucius (551–479BC) in his famous *First Ten Books*, in which he said that "I do not see how a man can be acceptable who is untrustworthy in word. When a pin is missing in the yoke bar of a large cart or in the collar bar of a small bar, how can the cart be expected to go?" Whilst these famous sayings by Confucius were made over two thousand years ago, these are still very relevant today on the important Chinese cultural concept of trust and guanxi.

Chinese negotiation emotionalism and tactics

The cultural background of negotiators could also seriously influence the way they display and control emotions during business negotiations in China. Some international negotiators from certain cultures have higher cultural tendencies to act more emotionally during negotiations. Negotiation surveys and research have shown that some Western negotiators, especially those from Latin America and Spain, might tend to display their emotions more openly during business negotiations. However, other European negotiators, especially the German and English negotiators, would often be found to be less emotional during negotiations. Asian negotiators, especially Chinese and Japanese, are generally considered to be less emotional during negotiations.

It is important that international negotiators, prior to starting negotiations in China, are trained to observe and analyze emotions during negotiations. They should also be trained to adapt and change their negotiation approach and style depending on the emotions of the Chinese negotiators that they are dealing with in China.

Generally, the Chinese negotiators would be unlikely to show much emotion during business negotiations in China. However, if they do display strong emotions on some key negotiation issues, then this would show that this is a very important bottom line issue for them.

Taking different negotiation cultural differences into consideration, it is generally recommended that international negotiators, in preparing their negotiation process for China, should seriously consider a step-by-step negotiation approach with a series of linear increments. This might work better within the Chinese negotiation culture and process than trying to negotiate a lot of issues all at once, in a typical non-linear negotiation approach. Together with the above stepwise negotiation process, it is also recommended that the international negotiators should focus their efforts on building good relationships and guanxi, during the initial negotiation stages with the Chinese negotiators. This will help foster trust between the parties and might make them more comfortable with the international negotiators. This will then help make the negotiation process smoother and more likely to lead to win–win negotiation outcomes.

Negotiation finalization and contracts cultural differences

Analysis of cultural differences in negotiation shows that negotiators from different countries might also have different cultural approaches to finalizing their negotiations and developing their final negotiation agreements and contracts.

Whilst all negotiators would agree that written agreements and contracts are required to encapsulate and capture the details of their negotiation outcomes, there might be substantial cultural differences in the desired format and complexity of the agreements. Negotiators should take into consideration the different contract requirements from different countries and cultures. Normally different countries and governments would also have different legal requirements regarding contract details, especially on the complexity of the contracts and the format of the written agreements. The negotiators should ensure that all the finalized contracts meet the legal requirements of their host countries. In China, all the agreements and contracts negotiated by the Chinese and international negotiators should be submitted to the relevant Chinese government authorities for final review and approval. If these proposed agreements and contracts do not comply with Chinese law and regulations, then it would be very difficult for the Chinese government to grant approval.

In addition, international negotiators must also recognize that in China, there are different standard Chinese contract forms issued by the key ministries of the Chinese Central Government, such as the China Ministry of Commerce MOFCOM. Normally all the Chinese companies would have to use and comply with standard Chinese contract forms. These standard Chinese contract forms in many cases would also be different from the international contract forms and terms, which the international negotiators are more familiar with. So, if the Chinese and international negotiators could understand the various backgrounds and their different requirements, then they might better negotiate and agree a suitable contract form which is mutually acceptable to all parties. However, if the international negotiators choose not to understand or disregard these specific requirements and insist on having their specific international contract formats and terms, this can lead to very difficult and lengthy negotiations in China with entrenched positions on both sides.

A good negotiation example is that some inexperienced Western negotiators, especially the American and European lawyers, would often prefer very detailed, international contract forms which include many detailed legal and boiler plate clauses covering all possible business situations in the future. These legal and boiler plate clauses can often attempt to anticipate all potential negative situations and eventualities, no matter how unlikely these may be, such as joint venture termination and partnership disputes.

Good business negotiation examples of boiler plate clauses include long and complex clauses on sensitive business issues such as dispute resolution, joint venture termination, expansion and introduction of new partners, etc. These clauses would normally be quite common in Western business contracts in America and Europe. However, the Chinese negotiators would normally prefer an agreement to be written in the form of general agreed principles rather than including many specific detailed clauses. If the international negotiator insists on including a lot of boiler plate legal clauses in the final contracts, then these could lead to very long and difficult negotiations.

In addition, the Chinese negotiators normally insist that all the finalized agreements and contracts plus their different terms and clauses should also comply with the general, standard Chinese contract forms and requirements. This is a very important requirement to meet in order for the Chinese and international negotiators to gain the required Chinese government approvals for the major Sino-foreign joint venture agreements, supplementary contracts and local contracts that they have negotiated.

In China, all the finalized joint venture agreements and contracts that have been negotiated between the Chinese and international negotiators need to be submitted to relevant Chinese government authorities, such as the Ministry of Commerce (MOFCOM), for review and final approval. If these agreements and contracts do not meet the basic Chinese legal requirements, then this would result in lengthy and difficult reviews with various Chinese legal and contract experts from different ministries. This would then lead to a long delay in the final approval by the PRC Government ministries for the various proposed contracts.

Negotiations building-up and building-down approaches

There are significant cultural differences between Chinese and international negotiators in their preferred approaches to negotiating the different key contract terms and the details of their final agreement. Analysis of different business negotiation cases in China shows that there are generally two key different negotiation approaches, i.e. a 'building-up approach' or a 'building-down approach'.

In the 'building-up' negotiation approach', the negotiators on both sides normally focus on negotiating the key business principles from both sides first. After agreeing the relevant key business principles, the negotiators could then gradually build-up the detailed terms and conditions of the final agreement as they progress with the negotiations.

In the 'building-down' negotiation approach, the negotiators on one side normally start with tabling a long draft agreement containing all the details that the negotiators from one side would want to see in the final agreement. Then the negotiators on both sides would have to go through the draft agreement clause by clause with the opposing negotiators. This would often lead to lengthy and difficult negotiations on the details of each of the draft clauses.

A good case example is that many negotiators from major Western, multinational companies, especially America and Europe, usually adopt the building-down approach in the early days of business negotiations in China. These negotiators, often American or European lawyers, would typically spend a lot of time in their overseas head-office to develop a long draft, legal agreement with all the detailed terms and clauses based on their various international agreements before they start their negotiations in China. When they actually start their negotiations in China, these Western negotiators would then present their massive, long draft proposed agreements to the Chinese negotiators. These would often come as a shock to the Chinese negotiators who would either adjourn the negotiations so they could study the draft first or they would ask the international negotiators to carefully explain each and all the key clauses in their draft agreement. Both would then normally lead to long and difficult negotiations by both sides.

On the other extreme, the international negotiators should also be aware that some Chinese negotiators could also choose to start their negotiations in China with some Western negotiators by presenting the standard Chinese contract, to which they might have made some minor adjustments for their proposed deal. Then the negotiators from both sides would have to spend a lot of time in typical building-down negotiation mode, on reviewing and negotiating the detailed wording of each of the proposed clauses in the Chinese standard contracts. These negotiations can often be long and hard with a lot of details being negotiated from each clause from the start. This would result in a long period of difficult negotiation before the negotiators might be able to agree on a joint agreement with the right terms.

Taking the aforementioned negotiation scenarios into consideration, it would generally be recommended that in modern business negotiations in China, the Chinese and international negotiators should work together and adopt the building-up negotiation approach in their contract negotiations. The negotiators on both sides should, at the start of negotiation, agree to first concentrate on negotiating the key business principles and conditions that would be important for both sides to finalize the proposed deal. After agreeing all the key business principles, then the negotiators can start to negotiate the other relevant key terms and conditions for the business contracts. After agreeing all the key business principles and relevant conditions, then the Chinese and international negotiators can work with their lawyers on drafting the right terms and clauses with detailed wording for the final agreements and contracts. During drafting, there might be requirements for more negotiations and clarifications on some key business principles, but these should be done within the framework of the key business principles agreed by both sides. This building-up negotiation approach would generally be more business-focused and more in line with the negotiation culture and requirements in China. In addition, the negotiation process should run more smoothly resulting in faster deals.

Negotiation and deal-making cultural differences

An important cultural driver of business negotiations in China is the different negotiators' basic attitude towards negotiation and deal making. Analysis and literature surveys of different business negotiations have shown that most negotiators would generally approach deal making and business negotiations with one of two basic attitudes. They would either be negotiating with a win–win compromise attitude or a win-lose confrontational negotiation attitude.

Typically, the negotiators with the win–win attitude see negotiations and deal making as a collaborative, problem-solving process with the negotiators on the opposite side. They would generally be negotiating with the opposing negotiators over the various key issues over which they would be willing to make the necessary compromises to get to a win–win agreement for both sides. Different business negotiations in China have shown that this collaborative negotiation approach is more in line with Chinese negotiation customs and cultural requirements.

The famous US oil tycoon and billionaire J. Paul Getty gave very good advice on win–win collaborative negotiations many years ago. "My father said that you must never try to make all the money that's in a deal. Let the other fellow make some money too, because if you have a reputation for always making all the money, you won't have many deals." What he said many years ago is still very relevant today on the importance of win–win collaborative negotiations.

On the other hand, the negotiators with the win-lose negotiation attitude would often approach negotiations with strong, confrontational attitudes. They would often take very strong confrontational positions during negotiations with little possibility for compromise with the negotiators on the other side. These negotiations would be more in line with the older, more conservative negotiations in both the Eastern and Western business cultures. Analysis of business negotiation results shows that most of the agreements reached by these win-lose negotiations would be unsustainable in the longer term. The party who felt they lost out in the win-lose negotiations would normally be trying their best to get out of these agreements as quickly as possible.

Hence it would generally be recommended that before an international negotiator enter new negotiations in China they have the right negotiation training so they can develop skills to recognize the type of negotiators they might be dealing with. Then the negotiators can adapt their negotiation approach and process accordingly to get the best possible negotiation outcome.

Many surveys and analyses of negotiation cases have shown that cultural differences in negotiation attitude exist and that the Asian negotiators, especially Chinese and Japanese, often approach negotiations with the win–win, collaborative, negotiation attitude. In fact, it would be quite normal during business negotiations in China that the Chinese negotiators would be stressing to the foreign negotiators that all the negotiations in China should follow the key negotiation principle of 'mutual equity and win–win' for all the parties involved in the negotiations. The international negotiators should understand these important Chinese negotiation requirements and have the appropriate collaborative negotiation skills to undertake win–win negotiations with the Chinese negotiators.

Negotiation communication approaches and styles

Analyses of different business negotiations cases in China have shown that the correct management by the international and Chinese negotiators of different communication approaches and styles during negotiations in China can have a strong influence on the outcome of the negotiations in China.

The personal styles of different negotiators during negotiations could also have a big influence on the negotiation process and outcome. This could include the different ways that negotiators from various cultures engage with the other negotiators. One important aspect is the different ways that negotiators use their titles during normal communication and social engagements. Another aspect would be how they might dress during the negotiations, i.e. formally or informally.

Various negotiation studies have shown that cultural differences strongly influence the personal style of negotiators. A negotiator from countries with more formal styles, such as the German negotiators, would often insist on addressing the opposing negotiators by their formal titles and ranks, such as Herr Doctor or Herr Ing, etc. These negotiators with formal attitudes also often try to avoid discussions of their private or family life during negotiations. They often prefer to stick just to the business negotiations with little social exchanges.

On the other hand, a negotiator with cultural preferences for a more informal style, such as American or Canadian negotiators, often try to start the negotiations on an informal, first-name basis. They would often try to quickly develop a friendly and social relationship with the negotiators on the other team. These informal negotiators would also often like to take off their jackets and roll up their sleeves during negotiations.

During negotiations in China, it would be important for the Chinese and international negotiators to recognize that negotiators from different cultures have their own styles, customs and formalities. However, these different negotiation styles should all fit in with the overall Chinese negotiation customs and requirements in order to achieve a successful negotiation in China.

A good negotiation example would be that many Western negotiators, especially those from America or United Kingdom, would often try to call the Chinese negotiators by their first name as an act of friendship right from the start of negotiations. In contrast, for Japanese negotiators, the use of the first names at the first negotiation meeting would often be considered an act of disrespect. German negotiators would also often behave more formally than other European negotiators, and they would often address the other negotiators by their full titles.

As a general rule, it is recommended that it might be safer for the international negotiator to first adopt a formal but relaxed approach at the start of their initial business negotiations in China. They could then observe the behaviour and reactions from the opposing Chinese negotiators before they would decide to move on to a less formal negotiation style or continue with a formal negotiation approach. This stepwise, cultural negotiation approach is generally less risky when compared to the approach of a negotiator trying to assume an informal style too quickly and early in the negotiations. The careful traditional stepwise approach would also minimize misunderstanding and reduce the possibility of wrong signals being sent to the Chinese negotiators.

The communication methods that negotiators use during negotiations can also vary greatly between negotiators from different cultures. Some negotiators would prefer the direct and simple methods of verbal communication. Other negotiators would prefer the indirect and more complex methods of communication. They might also choose to use figurative forms of speech, facial expressions, gestures and different forms of non-verbal body language depending on their cultural backgrounds.

For negotiators from cultures that values directness, such as the American or the Dutch, their negotiators would normally give clear and direct verbal responses to negotiation proposals and questions from the Chinese negotiators. However, for negotiators from cultures that would rely more on indirect communication, such as the Asian and Japanese cultures, their replies to negotiation proposals might be less direct and could involve different vague comments and non-verbal gestures.

In China, it would also be very unlikely that the international negotiators would receive any definite 'yes' or 'no', or any clear commitment or rejection of their negotiation proposals from the Chinese negotiators. It can be quite common during negotiations in China that the Chinese negotiators would often say that they need to study the new proposal first before they give any response to the international negotiators. This would allow time for the Chinese negotiators to review the proposals from the international negotiators and then discuss these with their senior executives involved in directing the negotiation to decide on a suitable negotiation response.

It would be important for international negotiators undertaking negotiations in China to be trained in different communication skills, such as active listening skills and non-verbal communication skills. Then they could use these different communication skills during negotiations in China to improve their understanding of the real messages from the Chinese negotiators and to minimize misunderstandings and avoid friction.

Many negotiation studies have shown that negotiators from Far East, especially the Chinese and Japanese negotiators, often prefer an indirect communication style whilst Western negotiators would prefer a more direct communication style. During negotiations in China, the Chinese negotiators would rarely directly reject or disapprove of proposals made by the international negotiators during initial negotiation rounds. If a Chinese negotiator indeed rejects any negotiation proposal directly, then it would clearly indicate to the international negotiator that this is a very important and essential issue for the Chinese negotiators.

Another good example of negotiation communication in China is when an international negotiator tabled a new negotiation proposal during negotiations in China, then the Chinese negotiator would often tell the foreign negotiator that they would take their new negotiation proposal away to 'Yan Jiu', which literally means to study and research further. The Chinese negotiators might indeed want to study the new negotiation proposal internally before they negotiate the proposal with the foreign negotiators. On the other hand, the Chinese negotiator might be trying to infer to the international negotiators that the new proposal did not look attractive and needed improvement before they could negotiate it. Hence the international negotiators should listen actively and carefully to the replies from the Chinese negotiators including their non-verbal communications to effectively deduce the true messages being sent by the Chinese negotiators.

During negotiations in China, many inexperienced international negotiators have misinterpreted the messages from Chinese negotiators as they have not been trained in relevant communication skills and non-verbal communication skills. As Chinese negotiators do not normally not give a direct 'yes' or 'no' reply to international negotiators, they need to have the appropriate training to understand that some indirect, non-verbal communication from the Chinese negotiators can be a polite way to indicate to the foreign negotiator that their negotiation proposal did not look appropriate and would have little chance of being accepted by the senior Chinese management. If the international negotiator misunderstands, thinking that the Chinese negotiators are still considering their proposal whilst they are really rejecting it, then this could lead to serious misunderstandings and very difficult negotiations.

China negotiations time concepts

Another key cultural influence on the negotiation process and progress in China would be the different attitudes that negotiators from various cultures have towards time and time keeping. For negotiations in China, it would be important for international negotiators to recognize two important time concepts, i.e. punctuality and the concept of time for negotiations.

On negotiation time punctuality, it is important for foreign negotiators to understand that they should always try to be punctual and on time for their planned negotiations in China. If they are not punctual and have no good reasons for being late, then the Chinese negotiators might get the wrong impression that the foreign negotiators are trying to show that they are superior to the Chinese negotiators or applying time delaying tactics. This could often result in reciprocal actions by the Chinese negotiators, i.e. also arriving late for future negotiations meetings.

These 'negotiation time-keeping gaming tactics' by negotiators on both sides can often lead to serious negotiation time delays, which can seriously slow down negotiation progress. In addition, these could also lead to loss of face issues which could create poor guanxi between the negotiators on the two sides.

On the concept of time required for negotiation in China, it is important for the international negotiators to realize that the Chinese negotiators normally like to take time with their negotiations before reaching a mutually acceptable deal. They normally like to take time in the initial negotiating stages for the Chinese and international negotiators to get to know each other well and build up good guanxi. The Chinese negotiators also like to first decide if they can trust the foreign negotiators or not, before embarking on the negotiations for the proposed long-term business joint ventures with the foreign party.

Some inexperienced Western negotiators have often tried to accelerate negotiations in China and to shorten the negotiation time periods. The Chinese negotiators often consider these aggressive attempts by the foreign, Western negotiators to shorten the negotiating time possibly as cheap, negotiation tactics to hide important issues or to take advantage of the Chinese party.

A good negotiation example is that Western negotiators, especially some American and European negotiators, often want to negotiate faster and make deals quickly. They often try to reduce the initial negotiation formalities to a minimum and try to get down to business negotiations quickly. They would often say that time is money and they would want to try to negotiate fast so they can get on to another deal. However, these aggressive time-pushing negotiation tactics may back-fire as the Chinese negotiators might get the wrong impression that they are trying to cover up things or take advantage of them in the negotiations. Then the negotiations between the Chinese and international negotiators could get more difficult and take more time.

Negotiation risk approaches and tactics

The cultural backgrounds of negotiators have also been found to have a big influence on the willingness of negotiators to take risks during negotiations. Negotiation research and case analysis results have shown that negotiators from some cultures are more conservative and risk averse than others. These negotiators would be less willing to take any risks during negotiations. They would also be less willing to share information and try new approaches during negotiations. They would also be very reluctant to tolerate uncertainties during negotiations.

A good negotiation example is that some Asian negotiators, especially Chinese and Japanese negotiators, have often been found to be more risk averse than Western negotiators. They would normally ask for large amounts of information from the opposing negotiators on the different business issues being negotiated so they could consider all the possible risks. In addition, they would also have complex and intricate group decision-making processes which would tend to minimize their risk exposure, but more time would be required for their group decision making.

On the other hand, some international negotiators, especially Americans, French and English, would be higher risk takers. They would often be more willing to take some risks during negotiations. They would be more willing to share various pieces of company and project information with the negotiators on the other side. They would also be more willing to try new negotiation approaches and accept some uncertainties during negotiations.

It is also important for international negotiators to understand that the Chinese negotiators' attitude towards risk might also be influenced by their company cultures and backgrounds. Normally the negotiators from the large Chinese SOEs have a more conservative approach towards negotiation risks. The Chinese SOEs often have their own specific internal system for risk evaluation and control which their Chinese negotiators can study and evaluate after the negotiations with risk control specialists in their company.

On the other hand, some modern Chinese negotiators, especially those with entrepreneurial backgrounds or from the more progressive Chinese private companies, would have a more relaxed attitude towards risk. These modern entrepreneurial Chinese negotiators might be more open to accept uncertainties and risks during their negotiations with international negotiators. They might also have been educated overseas, i.e. the United States or the United Kingdom, and would behave in similar ways to some Western negotiators.

In most large joint venture negotiations in China, the foreign negotiators would often have to negotiate with Chinese negotiators from large SOEs or leading local government companies who would be more conservative and quite risk averse. If the foreign negotiators have to negotiate with a risk-averse negotiator in China, then it would generally be recommended that the foreign negotiator should not try to rush the negotiating process too hard. If they try to push the negotiations too fast for the risk-averse Chinese negotiators, then it might heighten their perception of risks in the proposed deal. In the worst case, the Chinese negotiators might suspect that the international negotiators are trying to cover up some key issues or trying to take advantage of the Chinese negotiators.

Taking the aforementioned Chinese negotiation characteristics into consideration, it is generally important for international negotiators during initial negotiations in China, to reply openly and factually to requests from Chinese negotiators for relevant information on the international company. They should ensure that the Chinese negotiators are given sufficient information about the foreign company and the proposed deal details so they can explain these to their senior management and government leaders. These would then help the true Chinese decision makers to decide if they can trust the foreign company and to authorize their negotiators to enter into formal negotiations with the international negotiators. Hence the foreign negotiator should change their normal, aggressive, Western negotiation approach to allow plenty of time for the negotiations in China.

Chinese negotiations customs, management and tactics

To undertake successful business negotiations in China, the negotiators must have the appropriate skills and experience to understand and appreciate the different negotiation customs and cultural differences. They need to manage these well during actual business negotiations in China to aid a smooth negotiation process and to achieve successful negotiation outcomes.

To start successful negotiations in China, it would be normal custom for both the negotiation teams to first discuss and agree the negotiation venue and logistics before negotiations begin. This would normally include where the first negotiation meeting should be held in China and who should attend. The negotiation agenda and programme should also be agreed beforehand. All these discussions could possibly become the start of the first phase of business negotiations by the negotiators on both sides if not managed well. It is very important that all these detailed negotiation arrangements should be pre-discussed and agreed by the international negotiators with the Chinese negotiators. This would ensure that there would be no surprises or mishaps at the start of negotiations. This would also help to ensure that the business negotiations would start on a friendly basis and minimize the risk of any "loss of face" and poor guanxi, which could be caused by a wrong choice of venue or poor logistical arrangements.

The initial opening phase of business negotiations in China would normally involve introductions and getting to know each other. These might occur over an informal welcome dinner or lunch held by the Chinese negotiators. During the welcome meal, there might be long informal, social discussions over family, career, home countries, education and interests, etc. These might cause some inexperienced foreign negotiators, who were unfamiliar with Chinese culture and customs, to become quite impatient and wonder what these discussions have to do with the formal business negotiations.

It is important for the international negotiators to realize that these informal exchanges are very valuable for two very good reasons regarding business negotiation. First, the Chinese negotiators use these informal gatherings to get more detailed, first-hand information on the foreign negotiators. Different Chinese negotiators try to collect detailed, personal, background information on each of the foreign negotiators. This might include important information on their background, taste, style, family and interests. This information could become very useful and relevant in the later stages of intensive negotiations.

Second, these initial engagements also help to build trust and guanxi between the Chinese and foreign negotiation teams. Building good guanxi between the negotiators could be very useful in the later stages of tough, intense business negotiations. Negotiations in China would normally involve very intense, high-level interpersonal activities and exchanges between the Chinese and international negotiators. Therefore, both the negotiation teams would have to be well-informed about their counterparts and their backgrounds, in addition to the key business topics in the negotiations.

In addition, the negotiators in both parties should try to find out more about the culture, codes of ethics and values of the opposing negotiators' organization. This could be gained via detailed competitor analysis during negotiation preparations or via verbal discussions during the negotiation opening. This competitor information can be very helpful in developing the appropriate negotiation strategies and to avoid costly misunderstandings during the intensive negotiation stages later.

One of the biggest dangers during business negotiations in China for all negotiators is being too eager or focused on reaching agreement quickly. This could often be caused by tight deadlines and time pressures imposed on the international negotiation team by senior management in their overseas corporate head office. The senior international management would often be keen to reach a deal quickly and to announce it globally. This would be good for their public image and would also be helpful for their share prices. However, the time expectations of the overseas management should be managed and balanced against the reality that negotiations in China can often take longer. Imposing tight deadlines on a negotiation team to achieve a deal quickly in the West might be normal business practice; however, for an international negotiation team in China, these artificial internal deadlines can become very disadvantageous during negotiations. In the worst case, the Chinese negotiators might exploit these to pressurize the international negotiators to give some early concessions in exchange for reaching an agreement quickly. Hence it would be important that the international chief negotiator should have a good, honest, open discussion internally with their senior international management to agree realistic negotiation milestones and timelines, prior to starting negotiations in China.

In addition to realistic negotiation timelines, it would also be important for both the Chinese and international negotiators to discuss and agree realistic negotiation mandates and 'bottom lines' with their top management in advance of the initial negotiations in China. These bottom lines must be the absolute 'must haves' that the negotiation team would need to achieve during negotiations in China. Having clearly agreed bottom lines is very important as this would help to establish clear 'negotiation objectives' for the whole negotiation team.

It is very important for negotiators on both sides to discuss and agree realistic negotiation mandates and bottom lines with their senior management and corporate sponsors. This will help manage management expectations and avoid unrealistically high expectations of negotiation outcomes in China. These discussions with top management by the negotiators can be tough and should be carefully planned by the negotiators. They should impress upon their top management the tough negotiation environments in China. In particular, they should update their management that negotiations in China can take much longer periods with many possible compromises being required during negotiations.

Business negotiations normally take longer in China. The Chinese negotiators normally like to first assess and build trust with their opposite foreign negotiators before they begin serious negotiations. The actual business negotiations in China can also take longer than in the West as the Chinese negotiators like to have all the relevant detail and information on each business issue prior to making up their mind on specific issues. They can then analyze each issue with the relevant information and update their management accordingly to decide the appropriate negotiation strategy and mandate. During negotiations, the Chinese negotiators would also stress the importance of negotiating each key business issue based on the key negotiation principle of equity and win–win negotiation.

During business negotiations in China, it would be customary for the negotiators on both sides to negotiate and trade different alternatives and compromises on different business issues in order to achieve a final win–win agreement which would be acceptable to both sides. Hence the negotiators on both sides should always make sure that they have flexible negotiation mandates involving suitable negotiation alternatives plus possible options to fall back on during their business negotiations in China.

Alternative negotiation positions and options during intense negotiations in China would normally help to improve the negotiating positions of the negotiators and increase the level of confidence of the negotiation team. It is very important during negotiation preparations to try to evaluate and forecast the other negotiation party's alternative positions before starting the negotiations. If one could determine that the opposite party does not have any good alternative positions, then this could improve one's negotiating power to drive a much more favourable deal during business negotiations in China.

To help establish realistic negotiation alternatives, one important negotiation analysis for the negotiators to do before starting negotiations in China would be to analyse and determine the 'relative bargaining or negotiating power' of the Chinese negotiators. This would normally include detailed negotiation scenario analysis on what would happen to the Chinese Partner if no agreements were to be reached in the negotiations. This would normally involve detailed analysis of how far the Chinese party would be prepared to move before deciding to stop the negotiations or taking the non-settlement alternatives. Developing these potential negotiation scenarios for each critical negotiation business issue would often help the international negotiators to better understand whether the Chinese Partners have stronger non-settlement options and greater relative bargaining power. These would in turn help the international negotiators to develop the appropriate negotiation strategy and counter-arguments to be used during business negotiations in China.

During business negotiations in China, it is customary for both negotiations teams to trade negotiation positions to make the required compromises to develop win–win agreements for both sides. Hence the negotiation teams should also try to identify potential areas for possible concessions or compromises during their negotiation preparations, prior to starting negotiations. They should be aware of what possible 'win–win alternatives' are available for them to table during negotiations in China. The negotiation team should also decide how best to table these during the negotiations. The negotiators also need to decide what negotiation techniques to employ and how to use them effectively to achieve successful negotiations in China.

In addition, making concessions and compromises at the right times during negotiations in China could help to promote better guanxi and relationships with the Chinese negotiators. Hence it would be important for the international negotiators to carefully study and plan the right moment to table their proposed concessions to the opposing negotiators. This would then help to maximise the value of these compromises plus contribute to building better guanxi and trust with the Chinese negotiators.

During long, difficult business negotiations in China, it is important that members of the foreign partner negotiating team should not have any open disagreements amongst themselves in the company of and observation by the Chinese negotiation team. The whole team should always try to present itself as a unified front to the Chinese negotiation team. In reality, this might be difficult to manage as negotiations in China can be long and difficult. There can be a lot of pressure on the international negotiators which might lead to friction and difference in views. Negotiations in China can also be highly unpredictable and unexpected developments can occur which might add to the pressure. In some cases, various negotiation tactics or time-delaying tactics could be applied to delay the negotiations or to throw the negotiators off guard. The negotiation team should be well trained and be ready to deal with these tough negotiation tactics from the opposing negotiators. The negotiators should also always try to keep calm and maintain patience during these periods of tough, difficult negotiations in China.

Part II
Negotiation team selection and preparation

4 Team selection for business negotiations in China

英雄所见略同
Yīng xióng suǒ jiàn lüè tóng
The views of different heroes are generally similar.
Great minds think alike.

Executive overview

Selecting the right negotiation team would be one of the critical requirements for achieving successful business negotiations in China. The chief negotiator should be experienced and empowered to lead the negotiation team in China. The negotiators should have the key negotiation competencies and skills required for business negotiations in China. The chief negotiator should assign different strategic primary and secondary negotiation roles to the various negotiators during business negotiations. The negotiation team should optimize and synergize teamwork so that the team can negotiate effectively as a unified, integrated negotiation team against the opposing negotiation team.

Negotiation team selection tactics

For high-level business negotiations in China, it is very important that a fully competent and capable negotiation team is carefully selected by senior management. It is critical to have the right combination of negotiation skills available within the negotiation team for the planned negotiations. It is also important to ensure that there is good chemistry and teamwork between the various negotiators in the team. The whole negotiation team need to work effectively together as an integrated, unified team for an extended period of time in China during the business negotiations which could last up to several years.

It is important that the chief negotiator and negotiation team members are selected by senior management for possessing the appropriate knowledge and negotiation skills relevant to the business negotiations to be undertaken in China. The negotiators should not be chosen on the merit of their corporate position or seniority if these do not add value to the planned negotiations in China.

The Chinese negotiators are normally experts in their specific areas of responsibilities. They would quickly find out if the international negotiators were inexperienced or lacking in relevant knowledge. This would then reduce the credibility of the chosen international negotiators and undermine their ability to represent the foreign company competently during negotiations in China. In addition, this would undermine the credibility of the whole international negotiation team in the eyes of the Chinese negotiation team. These could lead to more difficult negotiations and uncertain negotiation outcomes.

Business negotiations in China also involve a high degree of cross-cultural negotiations. These would often create intense pressure and strong challenges on different negotiators. So, the chosen negotiators would have to be strong physically and mentally to handle all the pressures and to navigate the various cultural nuances. Choosing negotiation team members who are able to work with the different negotiation cultures in China would give the negotiation team a stronger, competitive advantage. If the selected negotiators have little respect for the Chinese negotiation culture and customs, then this could lead to poor guanxi and some very difficult negotiations in China. This could adversely affect the negotiation process and outcomes during negotiations in China.

Senior management should also choose negotiators whose natural cross-cultural communication and negotiation styles and skills would work well within the local cultural requirements of China. This would help the negotiators to quickly build guanxi and good relations with the Chinese negotiators. These could then help them to quickly build trust with the Chinese negotiators at the initial stages of their negotiations in China. These good relationships should help to support smoother negotiation progress in China.

Another noteworthy consideration is that the Chinese negotiators normally prefer to deal with international negotiators who would be considered 'keqi' in China. According to Chinese customs, an international negotiator would be considered keqi if he or she is behaving well and humbly. The Chinese negotiators would normally find some of the more aggressive, confrontational Western negotiators difficult to work with. This could lead to poor guanxi and lower trust between the Chinese and international negotiators. It would also be important to note that a negotiator could be both keqi and assertive at the same time in China. Different assertiveness negotiations techniques will be discussed later in this book in subsequent chapters.

Different global negotiation experiences have also shown that it would generally be very hard to turn a Western negotiator who was aggressive and confrontational into a 'keqi', i.e. a humble and courteous negotiator in China. Senior international management should bear in mind this important negotiation behavioral quality when they are selecting negotiators for their negotiation team for China. It should also be noted that a negotiator can be considered both keqi (i.e. humble and courteous) and assertive during negotiations in China. In fact, many actual business negotiation experiences in China have shown that having these qualities will help win the respect of the Chinese negotiators and lead to better guanxi. There is a good old Chinese negotiation saying that

"Good negotiators should negotiate hard across the table but could be friends under the table".

In some high-level business negotiation cases, senior management have sometimes employed the negotiation tactic of deliberately injecting some new aggressive and confrontational negotiators into the negotiation team. Some senior management use this negotiation tactic to push some key issues or to try to accelerate the negotiation progress. This can be a dangerous and complicated negotiation tactic to play in China and would need very good negotiation management to succeed. These negotiation tactics sometimes work as a new aggressive negotiator might help to secure some short-term gains from the opposing negotiators. However, they can also have backfire if the opposing negotiators decide that they want to stand firm and confront the aggressive new negotiator. These confrontations could then quickly lead to poor guanxi and reduced trust between the two negotiation teams, which might be difficult to rebuild.

Senior management should also consider the important cross-cultural negotiation behaviour and skill requirements in selecting the appropriate negotiators for their negotiation team in China. Cultural knowledge can be a significant advantage especially if they select competent negotiators who can speak the Chinese language and understand Chinese culture. These negotiators could then provide deeper insights on the negotiations for the whole international negotiation team. They could also advise on what would and would not work during negotiations in China. In addition, they could also provide direct observations and feedback about how new negotiation proposals would be received by the Chinese negotiators. During long business negotiations in China, the chief negotiator could also assign one of these negotiators to play the important informal role of the 'negotiation intermediary' with the Chinese negotiation team.

Many leading, multinational companies have adopted a new approach for choosing their China negotiation team selection. The international top management of many leading multinational companies now select their negotiators from both their overseas head office together with suitable senior local staff from their Chinese subsidiary. This helps to provide the international negotiation team with the relevant functional expertise and business knowledge plus the relevant Chinese cultural and local input.

Some international companies which do not have subsidiaries in China, have sometimes chosen to hire local, Chinese, cultural advisors and translators to advise their business negotiation team in China. They should carefully vet and check out these potential advisors. In particular, they should undertake careful and diligent checks of their backgrounds and experiences. They should check out the types of business negotiations that the advisers have been involved in previously to ensure that they have the relevant experience. A very important and sensitive check in China would be to ensure that these advisors do not have any hidden problems or reputational issues with the Chinese negotiators. In addition, the international negotiation team must also ask these local negotiation advisers and translators to sign the necessary confidentiality agreements to help minimize any confidentiality concerns and reduce the possibility of leakages during negotiations.

Senior management should also select negotiators who are good, strong team players who could contribute to the overall cohesiveness of the team and promote teamwork during their long business negotiations in China. This would be very important as business negotiations in China can often take long periods from over a few months to a few years depending on the complexity of the deal. During these negotiations, there would be intense pressure on each of the negotiators and the whole negotiation team. So, the negotiators must be able to work well together to promote teamwork and the effectiveness of the whole negotiation team. If a negotiator is too independent then they could become a maverick team member who could then damage the overall teamwork plus cause more harm to the team than benefit.

Complex corporate politics and requirements can also push the senior management of both the international and Chinese companies into selecting negotiators from different powerful internal stakeholders' representative groups. This would often be required in large, complex organizations so as to satisfy the different stakeholder requirements and interests. If this is the case, the senior management should appoint a very strong senior chief negotiator to lead the whole negotiation team and empower him appropriately to lead the team. This would then help the chief negotiator to organize and integrate the negotiators from different stakeholder groups into the negotiation team so they can function effectively as a whole negotiation team.

A chief negotiator must be suitably empowered by senior management to lead the negotiation team and be accepted by all the different stakeholder groups plus factions of the host company. In addition, the chief negotiator should be a strong leader but not a dictator. He or she must be able to lead and manage the whole negotiation team well to ensure that there would be good team work between all the different negotiators. This would be essential to maximize their negotiation effectiveness and team efficiency.

Very good advice on effective leadership was given many years ago by the famous US President and chief negotiator General Dwight D. Eisenhower: "You do not lead by hitting people over the head – that's assault, not leadership." What he had said over 50 years ago is still very true today about how a good chief negotiator should lead his negotiation team effectively, in both China and worldwide.

Prior to the start of negotiation in China, the top management of the international company must appoint their chief negotiator formally and provide him with a signed and chopped formal letter of appointment. This would be required as the Chinese chief negotiator would normally require the international chief negotiator to show them their appointment letter at their first negotiation opening meeting in China, in line with formal Chinese negotiation requirements. A lot of Western companies have overlooked this important negotiation requirement which can possibly lead to delays in the initial stages of negotiations in China.

In addition, the selected international negotiation team should also be suitably empowered to represent the different factions of the international company. The top management of the international company should ensure that there are general buy-ins and support for the negotiation team in China from the different stakeholders and factions in the company. These would be essential to support the negotiation team in their long and difficult business negotiations in China.

Senior management should also select and nominate their negotiation team members at the earliest possible time so the selected negotiation team would have time to work together to prepare adequately for their forthcoming negotiations in China. The negotiators should work together to develop their negotiation plan, choose their negotiation process and develop their various negotiation strategies. They should also undertake appropriate in-depth research on the Chinese company to help understand their organization, structures, business and culture, as these would be important information for the business negotiations.

For some new international negotiators China would be a distant, unfamiliar environment. So, it would be important that they would be provided with the necessary relevant training on negotiations in China. These should include appropriate training in negotiation tactics, cultural awareness, negotiation culture plus Chinese relationship and guanxi management, etc.

It would also be very important for senior management to carefully consider what should be the right size of their negotiation team for China. Analysis of high-level business negotiation experiences in China has shown that having too many negotiators in the international negotiation team could send the wrong messages to the Chinese negotiators. They might misconceive that the foreign company have a large amount of resources and money to spend on the negotiations. A large negotiation team could also intimidate the Chinese negotiator and might over-complicate the formal and informal communication processes during negotiations. On the other hand, too few negotiators in the international negotiation team could also create the wrong impression that the foreign party might not be very keen on the negotiations or might not be prepared to commit to the potential deal.

Taking the aforementioned negotiation factors into consideration, analysis of different successful negotiation teams in China has shown that negotiation teams comprising five to six core negotiators have normally functioned well in China. Senior management should ensure that the selected negotiators will bring sufficient skill sets and knowledge bases to the negotiation team to support their intensive negotiations over long periods in China. The negotiation team could also then bring in specific additional experts and lawyers, as and when required.

Valuable advice on the quality and quantity of a negotiation team was given over 50 years ago by the famous British philosopher Sir Julain Sorrell Huxley (1887–1975), who said, "the quality of people and not merely the quantity, that is what should be aimed for". Although the saying might be over 50 years old, it is still very relevant regarding negotiation team selection and size.

Negotiation team primary management roles

For successful business negotiations in China, it is a very important task for management to assign clear roles and responsibilities to each member of the negotiation team. During team selection, they should evaluate and ensure the best fit of each selected negotiator to the team so that they have the competence and skills to hold specific roles required during the business negotiations in China. The chief negotiator can then assign each negotiator clearly defined primary and secondary negotiations roles to enable the team to negotiate effectively in China.

Different international companies have different approaches for selecting their negotiation team members plus assigning them with different roles in the negotiation team. Analysis of various negotiation team compositions in China have identified the different key primary and secondary negotiation roles required for successful business negotiations in China. The primary negotiation roles would normally be based on the negotiators' different functional expertise, such as finance, technology and manufacturing. The secondary negotiation roles would include the important China negotiation roles such as note taker, observer, facilitator and intermediary, which are required to support successful business negotiations in China.

The chief negotiator should normally be a senior business leader with appropriate authority in the international company to negotiate the required new agreements and contracts with the Chinese parties. Management should empower the chief negotiator to make decisions on behalf of the company and negotiation team during their long business negotiations in China. The chief negotiator would also be responsible for leading the negotiation team plus assigning clear roles and responsibilities to each of the negotiation team members. He should have good depth and breadth of experience together with a successful record of accomplishment on negotiating major contracts. He should be able to demonstrate effective negotiation skills particularly for cross-cultural negotiations and relationship management which would be essential for successful negotiations in China.

Analysis of different high-level business negotiation teams in China has also shown that some international companies have sometimes nominated their senior legal counsel to be the chief negotiator and to lead their negotiation team in China. In these cases, it would then be very important for the top management to also nominate other negotiators with strong business expertise and wide commercial experience to support the chief negotiator and legal counsel during the business negotiations in China.

The chief negotiator should be supported in the business negotiations in China by suitable negotiation team members with different functional expertise, such as legal, finance, technology and manufacturing. Analysis of different leading China negotiation teams highlighted that the following negotiation team primary support roles would normally be important for successful negotiations in China.

An experienced, senior finance negotiator with strong business understanding and financial analysis skills should normally be included in the negotiation team. He or she should have the necessary financial skills to undertake quick, high-level assessments during intense negotiations in China. This is essential if new valuations or finance proposals are to be tabled by the Chinese negotiators during negotiations in China. After each round of negotiation, he or she should undertake the required detailed, financial analysis prior to the next round of negotiations. In addition, he/she would have to liaise and undertake the required follow-up action with the financial function in head office and get their support and input on any new financial proposals and evaluations.

An experienced, senior, technical, or manufacturing negotiator should normally be included in the team. He should have good knowledge and experience in the specific advanced technology processes and manufacturing operations that the international company would be planning to establish and invest in. The technical negotiator should have the special ability and skills to explain the technicalities of the special processes to the Chinese negotiators in simple, layman language during negotiations. Many technical experts have tended to overcomplicate their technical explanations with too much detail. This could then create the wrong impression on the Chinese negotiators and lead to unnecessarily difficult negotiations.

An experienced lawyer with good understanding of the Chinese law and legal systems and requirements should be included in the negotiation team. He could then provide expert legal advice plus explain complicated legal terms to the Chinese parties. After the teams have negotiated all the required key business principles, the lawyer could then work with other legal experts to prepare and write the final new agreements and contract for signing by top management.

If the new joint venture or project being considered also involves new marketing operations, then an experienced marketing negotiator should be included in the negotiation team. He should have good knowledge of the Chinese market, supply chains, logistics, agency, system houses, etc. He could then support the relevant negotiations on joint venture marketing and the marketing service contracts.

One or two good, experienced translators should be included in the negotiation team in China to ensure proper translation during the negotiations. A good translator could also help with various informal communications with the Chinese negotiators during the negotiations and over dinners or lunches. Many leading international companies would use their own inhouse translators for these sensitive business negotiations in China. Companies without suitable inhouse translators could hire a local translator from a reputable agency. However, it would be essential that they check that the agency translator would have sufficient language skills to undertake the required translations during negotiations. They must also ask the translator to sign the necessary confidential agreement to avoid unnecessary leakages during negotiations.

To control the size of an international negotiation team in China, other functional experts from the international company could be brought in to support the negotiations in China as and when required. They could then provide specific expert input or assessment in key areas that might come up during negotiations in China. These could include international company experts on specific technology, processes, site configuration, utilities, buildings, human resources, accounting, customer database, etc. Typically, these experts should not be involved in any direct negotiating with the Chinese negotiators. Their primary role would be to provide the expert information data requested by the other party and to answer questions from the Chinese negotiators. However, the international negotiators would have to pre-brief each of these experts well before they enter the negotiating room so that they could give their expert comments in line with the stated negotiation positions of the international negotiation team.

Negotiation team secondary management roles

In addition to the various formal primary negotiator roles covering business, finance and technical areas, analysis of actual negotiation roles and practices in China has also suggested that there are some essential secondary informal negotiator roles. These secondary negotiation roles would normally include facilitator, observer, note taker and intermediary. These have been found to be essential to support the long, complex business negotiations in China. During negotiations in China, the chief negotiator should also assign these informal secondary roles to each of the negotiators in addition to their primary, professional negotiation roles.

For negotiations in China, the chief negotiator should appoint one of the international negotiators to be a 'facilitator' and 'intermediary' to help develop informal relationships with the Chinese negotiators and to maintain a good, informal channel of communication during intensive negotiations. He or she should normally be an international negotiator who could speak Chinese and have a good understanding of Chinese culture and negotiation customs. During long business negotiations in China, there are often formal negotiations during the negotiation meetings as well as informal communication over coffee or lunch breaks. The international negotiator with the facilitator and intermediary roles could help with the informal communications with the appropriate Chinese negotiators. These can often provide very useful pieces of additional information for the negotiation teams to support the ongoing negotiations.

During difficult, intense negotiations in the later stages of negotiations in China, they could also act as the 'negotiation intermediary' between the two negotiation teams providing an informal bridge for communication and messages between the negotiation teams. These could help to maintain good guanzi and effective communication with the Chinese negotiators. In addition, the 'negotiation intermediaries' on both the negotiation teams could help to informally explore potential compromises and alternative negotiation options without formal commitments from both the chief negotiators. However, these informal explorations could be very sensitive and should only be undertaken after careful discussion with the whole negotiation team plus with direct approval of the chief negotiator.

The chief negotiator could also consider appointing one of the negotiators to be a 'summarizer' and 'challenger'. They could help the chief negotiator greatly by carefully following the various arguments and new proposals from the Chinese negotiators plus to ask for appropriate clarification at the right moment. Clarification could help the international negotiation team to get more relevant information from the opposing negotiators, particularly during intensive negotiations. These should also give the chief negotiator more time to think and consider suitable responses. However, the appointed challenger should also be very tactful in their interventions in the ongoing negotiations so as not to over-interrupt the negotiation progress and process. In addition, they must act tactfully so as not to undermine the authority of the international chief negotiator and upset the Chinese negotiators. These interventions could typically involve asking politely for clarification on the different points made in the negotiations plus summarizing the ongoing negotiations. As this could be a very sensitive, informal role, the chosen negotiator must have excellent communication skills plus have good judgement on when to ask for clarification and when to be silent.

For negotiation in China, the chief negotiator should always appoint one of the negotiators to be a 'note taker' or 'recorder' for the team. He or she should be responsible for making detailed notes about what had been said by both teams during the negotiations. In particular, they should carefully note down what the Chinese negotiators might be requesting and what new negotiation offers might they be tabling. After each negotiation round, they should also prepare the draft negotiation minutes for the team. For negotiations in China, it might be necessary and useful to prepare two sets of minutes. One set of minutes should be the joint negotiation minutes which would need to be discussed and agreed with the Chinese negotiators. It should be clear and concise plus on the important areas discussed, key areas agreed plus outstanding areas still to be negotiated. The other set of negotiation minutes should be for internal use and should contain detailed notes of the negotiation, especially counter arguments and new offers from the Chinese negotiators.

For long, intensive negotiations in China, it has also been found to be useful to appoint one of the negotiators to be an 'observer' for the team. Their key role would be to observe the behavioural subtleties plus non-verbal communication and body language of the Chinese negotiators. These are normally very important during negotiations and could often help to provide additional information about how well the negotiations are going in China. In particular they should closely observe if there are any signs of tension or disagreement between the opposing negotiators. During negotiations in Chinese, open signs of disagreement and emotion would be rarely shown by the Chinese negotiators. However, their body language could often help to provide additional indications if there was any tension or friction between the Chinese negotiators. The observer should alert the chief negotiator on their critical observations so that the chief negotiator can then decide if they need to adjust their negotiation arguments or approach.

Negotiation team management and tactics

Good management of a negotiation team in China is critical to achieve successful business negotiations. Analysis of various negotiation team management has highlighted that it is key to consider the right team size, assigning the right roles for each negotiator, good negotiation team preparation and planning, plus good team communications.

During team selection, it would be important to consider what would be the right size team for the planned business negotiations in China. Having too many negotiators might send the wrong messages to the Chinese negotiators of a foreign company with a large amount of resources and money to spend on the negotiations. On the other hand, too few negotiators in the international negotiation team could also create the wrong impression that the foreign party might not be keen or committed to the deal. Analysis of different business negotiation teams in China has shown that negotiation teams comprising five to six core negotiators have normally functioned quite well. As the famous philosopher Julian Huxley said, "it is quality of man and not merely the quantity that we should aim for".

Clear roles and responsibilities should be assigned to each member of the negotiation team by the chief negotiator so that they all know what they need to do during the intense negotiations. This should include the formal and informal negotiation roles. The formal roles should be based on the professional skills and expertise of the negotiators. These would normally include legal, finance, technology, marketing, etc. In addition, the chief negotiator should assign additional secondary informal roles to each of the negotiators on the team. These would normally include facilitator, challenger, note taker and observer, etc.

The chief negotiator should also decide together with the team who should be the spokesman and who would represent the team on different issues. For negotiations in China, it might be useful to appoint different team members to be the spokesperson for different key negotiation issues based on their functional expertise. This would then allow the chief negotiator more room for negotiation in the later negotiation stages.

Business negotiations in China can be very stressful for the negotiators and some negotiation situations can become quite volatile. These could also lead to some inexperienced negotiators becoming volatile and inject their own agendas into the negotiation. These situations can seriously undermine the effective functioning of the whole negotiation team and impede their negotiation efficiency. Hence the chief negotiator should caution the whole negotiation team from falling into these undesirable situations and to undertake immediate remedial action if these unfortunate situations occur.

Good advice for chief negotiators was given over 2,500 years ago by the famous Chinese philosopher Confucius (551–479BC) in his *First Ten Books*. The Master said, "guide them by edicts, keep them in line with punishments and the common people will stay out of trouble but will have no sense of shame. Guide them by virtue, keep them in line with the rites and they will, besides having a sense of shame, reform themselves". Whilst these sayings were made over two thousand years ago, they are still very relevant to how a chief negotiator should be leading the negotiation team during long negotiations in China.

The chief negotiator should also be aware of and understand the different personality profiles of the various negotiators in their negotiation team. It is very important for the chief negotiator to ensure that all the different personalities in the negotiation team are aligned with one another so that all the negotiators would work together effectively as an integrated, unified negotiation team. During negotiations, it is important for the whole negotiation team to project the image of a unified negotiation team to the opposing negotiators. If the opposing negotiators observe that there are disagreements amongst the negotiators, then they might exploit these with various negotiation tactics.

The chief negotiator and the international team would also have to consider how they wish to position themselves and how they would like to be perceived during the negotiation in China. Analysis of business negotiations in China shows that they normally choose to appear strong but amenable. However, they should review these continuously so they can adjust these in line with negotiation progress and developments.

It is very important for the negotiation team to plan ahead and decide the manner by which the negotiators will communicate with each other during negotiations in China. It will normally be difficult for each team member to communicate verbally with each other during negotiations in China at the negotiation table. There is also a risk of sensitive information being overheard by the opposing negotiators. Hence it would be important for the team to establish appropriate signals and non-verbal communication protocols which the negotiators could then use during negotiations.

The international negotiators should also be careful that the opposing negotiation team might have negotiators who have been trained in understanding different foreign languages plus observing non-verbal communication between different cultures. Some inexperienced international negotiators have assumed that the Chinese negotiators were not able to understand their native foreign languages only to discover that some Chinese negotiators have been specially trained with different language skills to cater for these negotiation situations.

An interesting example of a business negotiation case in China was a team of European negotiators who agreed that they would try to communicate using the slang language of their native European language during their business negotiations in China. They thought it would be very unlikely that the Chinese negotiators would be able to understand any European slang language. At the end of the negotiations, it came as a great shock to the international negotiators to discover that one of the Chinese negotiators had actually been specially trained with the required language skills to understand their European slang. They found out afterwards that during initial negotiation planning, the Chinese negotiators correctly predicted that the European negotiators might be trying to communicate with each other using their native slang. So, the Chinese chief negotiator specially included a Chinese negotiator who had the appropriate language training to enable him to understand the slang used by the international negotiators. This turned out to be a very good negotiation choice by the Chinese chief negotiator, as they were then able to understand the confidential verbal communication between the European negotiators during the business negotiations without their awareness. After the negotiations were successfully completed and the agreements signed, the international negotiators discovered the special language skills of the opposing Chinese negotiation team.

Corporate head office support to China negotiation team

During negotiations in China, it would be important for the international chief negotiator to carefully manage the communication channels and relationships with their overseas international head office and senior management. Before negotiations commence in China, the chief negotiator and his team should agree their negotiation strategies and mandates with all the relevant senior management and stakeholders in the international company. During negotiations in China, the chief negotiator and his team should update the head office after each negotiation round on their negotiation progress plus any new negotiation offers being made by the Chinese negotiators. Then the international negotiators should discuss and agree with their corporate sponsors any revisions in negotiation strategies plus get their support for relevant new mandates, prior to starting the next round of negotiation in China.

The international negotiation team in China will also need good backup and support from the different business units and corporate functions in the corporate head office during the negotiations and between each negotiation round. This would normally include competitor analysis, financial analysis, market updates, preparation of legal documents and draft agreements for the negotiations. It would also be important for the negotiators to get buy-ins and support from these important functions and businesses on their new negotiation strategies and mandates.

Many leading multinational companies have also established formal negotiation organizational structures in their head office to support their international negotiating teams in China. Many leading international companies have appointed a senior corporate sponsor, who would normally be a C-level senior executive in the international company, to champion the negotiations and have overall responsibility for their business negotiations in China. In many cases, the senior corporate sponsor would also ask other senior executives from the different divisions that would have strategic interests in the negotiations in China to join him in a head office-based, high-level, corporate China negotiation steering committee. This would be a good cross-functional business practice as negotiations in China often require strategic decisions affecting different businesses and functions across the international corporation.

The international chief negotiation and negotiation team should regularly update their corporate, high-level, negotiation steering committee on their negotiation outcomes and key progress after each major round of negotiations in China. The steering committee can then review these and provide guidance on appropriate changes in negotiation strategies together with new management mandates for the negotiation team.

Negotiation decision makers and high-level steering committee

During negotiations in China, it is also very important for the international negotiators to find out who from the Chinese negotiation team would have the real authority to make decisions during the negotiations. It is often not easy to find out who the real decision makers are and it might require tactful, in-depth investigations. In business negotiations in China, the negotiation teams would quite often not be able to negotiate directly with the real high-level decision makers from both the Chinese and international negotiation teams. Hence the negotiators should carefully evaluate and clearly determine the authority of the opposing negotiators that they are negotiating with so that they could adjust their negotiation plans and strategies accordingly. In addition, they should structure their key negotiation messages and proposals very clearly and keep them simple. This will help ensure that the negotiators report these correctly to the real decision makers after the negotiations. In this case, the joint negotiation minutes would be even more important as each of the chief negotiators and their negotiation team would be using these to brief their real decision makers and top management after each of the major rounds of negotiation.

For negotiations in China, when it is not apparent who the senior decision makers are in the Chinese negotiation team, it might be advantageous for the international negotiation team to consider the negotiation tactic of not revealing the identity of their real decision maker to the Chinese negotiators. Some leading international companies and their negotiation team in China have adopted this negotiation tactic so that their senior representatives or real decision makers are not readily identifiable to the Chinese negotiation team and they might also not be present at the negotiations in China. In adopting this negotiation team tactic, the international company and their negotiators could make it more difficult for the Chinese negotiators to identify the center of power in the international negotiation team. However, this could be a dangerous, complex negotiation tactic which could backfire if not managed well.

Analysis of successful business negotiations in China shows that there could be an effective negotiation tactic and high-level negotiation approach that the chief negotiators on both sides could use to flush out the real, top decision makers on both the Chinese and international sides. Some leading Chinese and international companies have empowered their chief negotiators to discuss the establishment of a high-level joint Chinese and international negotiation steering committee which would meet regularly during the long business negotiations in China. This would require top-level management commitment from both the Chinese and international companies that their most senior corporate sponsor for the negotiations in China would agree to join the proposed high-level committee. If both sides agree to establish the high-level negotiation committee, then the chief negotiators and their negotiation teams should try to negotiate all the key business issues and try to develop win–win compromises on most of these. A few key outstanding high-level negotiation issues would need to be referred to the high-level committee for their review and guidance. Both the chief negotiators should ensure that each of their decision makers is well briefed prior to their high-level meeting. During the planned, joint, high-level negotiation meeting, the two senior decision makers can then discuss possible negotiation compromises to the key outstanding negotiation issues and then give appropriate instructions to their chief negotiators for the subsequent negotiations.

This high-level negotiation steering committee approach has been shown to be effective in the negotiation of different major Sino-foreign joint venture agreements and contracts. It could help to promote more effective negotiations in China, but it would require clear commitments from both the top Chinese and international decision makers. The Chinese and international chief negotiators would also need to carefully manage the negotiations of the various key business issues to ensure that only a few of the top issues would require negotiation by both the top Chinese and international decision makers at the high-level committee.

Negotiation skills and tactics training

For successful negotiations in China, it is very important that the negotiators be properly trained so that they have the required negotiation skills and tools for undertaking effective negotiations.

Many international companies train their negotiators with input from leading international negotiation consultancies or agencies. Some companies use negotiation courses or programmes from leading universities and business schools in the United States and Europe.

Analysis of the best international negotiation practices by leading multinational companies has shown that some leading companies, which have undertaken a lot of negotiations in China, find it very beneficial to organize a confidential inhouse negotiation academy which would organize special inhouse training courses for their chief negotiators and international negotiators. The experienced negotiators from the company can then share their global negotiation experiences with the other negotiators in the company. This will often provide new international negotiators with invaluable, firsthand, confidential, negotiation advice which is generally not available from consultants or universities.

Analysis of international negotiator training needs for Chinese business negotiations have shown that many negotiators have found it useful to receive training on interpersonal skills, negotiation tactics, Chinese negotiation culture and customs, etc. In addition, many international companies have also found it useful to organize negotiation workshops for their negotiations team prior to actual negotiations in China.

Good interpersonal skills are very important for effective negotiations in China. This could help the international negotiators to build up good guanxi and a trusting relationship with the Chinese negotiators. This would then contribute to smoother negotiations and the ability to negotiate a win–win agreement in China. Hence training to improve interpersonal skills of negotiators would usually be considered essential for international negotiators. This training should cover the important Chinese negotiation customs of how to 'give face' and build 'guangxi' with the Chinese negotiators. These are complicated forms of Chinese interpersonal skills and negotiation tactics which could contribute significantly to building respect and trust between the negotiators. If applied successfully, this could help to make the negotiations go smoother and improve the chances of achieving successful and mutually beneficial negotiation results. However, if these interpersonal skills are not applied correctly, this could lead to poor relations and bad guanxi which could seriously affect the negotiation process and adversely influence the negotiation outcomes.

Analysis of multiple international company negotiation experiences in China has highlighted that the international negotiators should receive specific negotiation training in four key aspects of the Chinese negotiation interpersonal skills and culture which are critical for effective business negotiations in China.

First, they should receive training in the important interpersonal skill to build 'guanxi' which means 'relationships'. This is the central concept of Chinese interpersonal skills and relationship management. It is important for the international negotiators to build good guanxi and trust with the Chinese negotiators during negotiations in China.

Second, the international negotiators should be trained in the important interpersonal skill of mastering 'mianzi' which literally means 'face' in Chinese. It is very important for a negotiator to master this interpersonal skill, especially the art of 'giving face' and 'losing face' during negotiations. These would help the negotiators to win and counter arguments effectively during complex negotiations whilst maintaining good guanxi with the Chinese negotiators.

Third, the international negotiators should be trained in the important interpersonal skill of mastering 'Gei ni mian zi' which literally means 'giving face' in Chinese. This is one of the most useful and positive interpersonal engagement skills for international negotiators in China. However, it can also be a complex interpersonal skill to learn and master for most international negotiators. It would be very worthwhile for international negotiators to learn skills in 'giving face' in China as these could, if properly applied, help the international negotiator to build trust and good guanxi quickly with the Chinese negotiators.

Finally, they should be trained in the complex art of 'Diu-lian' or 'Diu mian zi' which means 'losing face' in China. These can be a very powerful interpersonal skill and strong tactic to apply during negotiations in China. However, it must be used very carefully and by very experienced, trained international negotiators. If it is applied well, then it can help to deliver some powerful messages and counter arguments to the Chinese negotiators directly during complex negotiations in China. However, if it is applied wrongly, then it can cause bad guanxi and adversely affect the negotiation process and its outcomes. In addition, there might be a strong reaction from the opposing negotiators, who should be handled well.

Analysis of various business negotiations in China shows that effective communication skills, in both verbal and written forms, is essential for effective negotiations in China. It is very important for negotiators to be able to present their arguments clearly and concisely during negotiations in China, especially taking into account the language differences. Many companies have given their negotiators communication training to equip them with the necessary verbal and communication skills for effective negotiation in China.

For negotiation in China, one important communication skill for international negotiators, especially technical and process experts, would be in the art of 'storytelling'. In view of the cultural and language differences, it would be essential for an international negotiator to tell his negotiation case simply and clearly to the Chinese negotiators. Many negotiators have found that the art of storytelling has helped them in delivering their verbal responses during negotiation clearly and smoothly. This often helps the Chinese negotiators to understand them better especially if it involves translations.

Good active listening skills have also been shown to be very important during negotiations in China. Analysis of different business negotiation cases shows that good active listening can help the international negotiators to get a fuller understanding of the different complex arguments from the Chinese negotiators.

In particular, the international negotiators should have the necessary communication skills to carefully read between the lines of what the Chinese negotiators say during negotiations to get the real meaning of the messages being given during negotiations. This would help to reduce misunderstandings and help the international negotiation teams to develop more effective counter arguments and proposals to use in their negotiations in China.

Analysis of different negotiation situations in China have also shown that it would be important for the negotiators to have the necessary communication skills to be aware of both the important verbal and non-verbal communication cues from the Chinese negotiators. These can be quite complex, especially when taking into account the cultural and behaviour differences between East and West. Many international companies have included special training for their negotiators so they are trained in observing body language and other non-verbal signals from the Chinese negotiators. This can then help the international negotiators to better analyze the messages and counter arguments from the negotiators in China.

Many companies have also found that good business decision-making and problem-solving skills are important for their negotiators to have in China. A lot of the modern business negotiations in China would involve complex business situations. Most international negotiation teams in China would be operating far from their corporate head office. The large time zone differences between China, Europe and the USA means that most international chief negotiators and their negotiation teams would be undertaking negotiations in China whilst their head office support staff are sleeping. China is six to eight hours ahead of Europe and 12 to 15 hours ahead of the USA. Hence most international negotiators would often have to negotiate in China and make quick decisions on the ground during their negotiations without being able to refer these to their Western head office. With the large time differences, the international negotiators would often not be able to communicate and discuss their negotiation issues with their head office first before replying to the Chinese negotiators.

Analysis of China business negotiation cases also shows that the international negotiators should have good assertiveness skills so they can demonstrate to the Chinese negotiators that they have confidence and conviction in their negotiating positions. This could be very important as the international negotiators would normally be probed during from various angles by the Chinese negotiators to see if there are any weaknesses or gaps in their negotiation position.

Business negotiations in China can be long and intensive. Hence the negotiators should have the skills to be patient and remain calm during long periods of complex negotiations. Many companies have found it useful to hold training for their negotiators on how to remain calm and focused during negotiations. The negotiators should also have the skills to act calmly and deal rationally with complex negotiations during long, intensive negotiation situations in China. They should also be trained with suitable skills to control their temper to avoid losing their temper in front of the Chinese negotiators if the negotiations became heated in China. If tensions rise during negotiations in China, then the chief negotiator and the negotiation team should try to look for ways to control or diffuse this.

Analysis of various business negotiation cases in China shows that it is very important for the negotiation team to prepare well ahead of their negotiations in China. Many negotiation teams have found it useful to rehearse and practise their negotiations prior to the actual negotiations in China. A good business practice that many negotiation teams have found useful, is to hold 'negotiation workshops' with simulated negotiation scenarios. During these workshops, the negotiators can role play different parts appropriate for their forthcoming negotiations in China. These simulated negotiation role play exercises help the negotiation team develop a sense of what might happen during the actual business negotiations. This could also help the international negotiators to learn from their potential negotiation mistakes and improve their negotiation approaches or arguments accordingly. During the different role-playing scenarios, the negotiators should consider how the opposing Chinese negotiation team are likely to react during the negotiations in China. In particular, the negotiator should consider how the Chinese negotiators might react to different possible negotiation offers and what counter offers or arguments they are likely to respond with.

5 Preparation for business negotiations in China

有其父必有其子
Yǒu qí fù bì ǒu qí zǐ
The son always takes after his father.
Like Father like Son.

Executive overview

Business negotiations in China have become very complex and good preparation prior to starting negotiations in China are important to achieve effective and successful negotiation outcomes. Analysis of various high-level business negotiations has highlighted the different key business negotiation preparations that should be undertaken by the negotiation team prior to starting business negotiations in China. It would also be critical for the negotiation team to develop suitable business negotiation strategies with different options for their negotiations in China. In addition, they should apply different advanced negotiation tools, including negotiation scenario analysis, strategic negotiation and counter argument planning. The chief negotiator and the team should also obtain the appropriate negotiation mandates and bottom lines from senior management prior to business negotiations in China.

China business negotiations preparation

Analysis of various high-level business negotiation cases in China has shown that it is very important for a negotiation team to undertake various key business negotiation preparations and plan their negotiations well prior to starting negotiations in China. These preparations would support the chief negotiator and the negotiation team to have smoother negotiations and achieve more successful outcomes with the Chinese negotiators.

International negotiators need thorough negotiation preparation and planning as their opposing Chinese negotiators normally undertake extensive negotiation preparation and research before they begin any negotiations. The Chinese chief negotiator and the negotiation team are usually experienced and well trained in their different specialist functional areas. They would also have had extensive negotiation training within their own Chinese company. In addition, they might also have attended advanced negotiation training with the relevant government authorities, such as the Chinese Ministry of Commerce.

The Chinese negotiators have normally been trained to undertake extensive negotiation preparation, such as competitor research and analysis, before starting negotiations with international negotiators. They would also have been trained to develop detailed negotiation strategies and plans to prepare for the different negotiation situations that might arise during long business negotiations in China.

Hence during business negotiations in China, the international negotiators often find that the Chinese negotiators would be very knowledgeable about the foreign company and its negotiators. This is a direct result of the extensive research and preparation that the Chinese negotiators undertake as part of their negotiation preparations. These would normally include undertaking detailed competitor analysis on the foreign companies and in-depth background research on each of the international negotiators, especially the international chief negotiator. These preparations help the Chinese negotiators to better understand the latest strategies and developments of the international company. This will also help them to identify potential areas of conflict and possible compromises during negotiations. It can also help them to create more options for win–win compromises between the two sides during negotiations.

As part of their competitor analysis, it is very useful for the international negotiators to undertake research to find out more about the culture, the code of ethics and values of the Chinese company. This should include research into the Chinese company's key business principles, code of ethics, governance code, anti-corruption standards, compliance standards and systems. This information helps the international negotiators to develop the appropriate negotiation approaches in compliance with the high ethical standards required by both the Chinese and Foreign companies. In addition, this helps prevent any costly misunderstandings or serious non-compliance incidents during the intensive business negotiations in China.

As part of their negotiation preparations, the Chinese negotiators normally try to research the backgrounds of the foreign chief negotiator and each of the negotiators. This enables them to build detailed negotiation profiles of the international chief negotiator and all the foreign negotiators. These profiles help the Chinese negotiators to better predict the possible behaviour and reactions of the international negotiators during the long intensive business negotiations in China.

As part of the Chinese negotiation team's preparation, the Chinese chief negotiator and his team normally prepare a confidential Chinese negotiation report covering their key negotiation objectives, negotiation plans, plus different potential negotiation strategies and options. The Chinese chief negotiator will usually present and discuss these with their corporate sponsors and top management so as to get their input and mandates. In some sensitive negotiations, such as those involving international trade or strategic investment areas, the Chinese chief negotiator will present their negotiation report to the relevant government authorities, such as the China Ministry of Commerce, and get their support and input. The Chinese chief negotiators normally only begin their negotiations with international negotiators once they have obtained all the relevant negotiation support and mandates from their corporate sponsors and relevant government authorities.

During negotiations in China, the Chinese negotiators stress the importance of negotiating in line with the vital principle of 'mutual equity' and 'win–win' in China. They often emphasize this to the international negotiators during negotiations so they can work together towards win–win agreements which are mutually acceptable to both sides. It is important for all the negotiators to understand that a mutually beneficial, win–win agreement in China can only be reached after negotiating and meeting all the key strategic needs and 'must haves' of both the Chinese and international negotiators.

Negotiations in China can often be long and difficult. Hence it is very important for both negotiating teams to develop, during their negotiation preparations, good negotiation plans and strategies for the different rounds involved in the long negotiations. They should also develop suitable strategies for the different possible negotiation scenarios which might occur during negotiations in China, together with possible negotiation options which they can employ during lengthy negotiations.

Taking the detailed preparation by the Chinese negotiation team into consideration, it is important that the international negotiation team should also allocate and spend sufficient time on their negotiation preparations and planning. They should thoroughly prepare the various key negotiation aspects and ensure that they develop an appropriate negotiation plan supported by relevant negotiation strategies. In addition, the chief negotiator and the team should pre-agree their negotiation strategies with their corporate sponsor plus obtain the appropriate negotiation mandates from their management prior to starting negotiations in China.

The international chief negotiator and the negotiation team should realize that business negotiations in China can involve very intensive, high-level interpersonal activities and tough exchanges between the Chinese and international negotiation teams. Therefore, the international negotiation team should also do careful background checks on their opposing Chinese chief negotiator and negotiation team. They should be well informed about their counterparts and their backgrounds, in addition to the various business negotiation issues. They should try to find out the background and profiles of the Chinese chief negotiator and each of the Chinese negotiators. This should include information on the negotiator's background, education, career history, interests and family. In addition, they should research the personality types, spoken languages and body language of the opposing Chinese chief negotiator and negotiators. These detailed profiles of the Chinese negotiators could be very useful during intensive negotiations as the international negotiators could use these to better predict the opposing Chinese negotiators' potential negotiation stances and reactions during difficult intensive negotiations in China.

It is also very important for the international negotiation team to prepare well and agree realistic negotiation schedules and mandates with their management in advance of their negotiations in China. In particular, the international negotiators should agree realistic negotiation bottom lines and mandates with their corporate sponsors and senior management, to avoid unrealistically high expectations from them on the negotiation outcomes from China.

Negotiations in China could take a long time with unforeseeable outcomes. So, the international negotiators should try to identify potential areas for compromises on the less important negotiation issues so as to create some 'win–win alternatives'. Then the international negotiators could decide when best to table these concessions during their negotiations in China so as to create good guanxi and improve the negotiation outcomes.

It is also very important for the negotiation team to find time to rehearse and practise their negotiations prior to actual negotiations in China. The chief negotiator should assign clear roles and responsibilities to each member of the negotiation team so that they know what they need to do during the intensive negotiations in China.

An international negotiation team in China also requires good backup and support from the different business units and corporate functions in their head office. The negotiators need input during their long negotiations in China and also between each negotiation round. This input should include competitor analysis, financial analysis, market updates, preparation of legal documents, draft agreements for the negotiations, etc. The international negotiators should also regularly update their corporate sponsors on their negotiation progress. They also need to get the buy-in and support from their corporate sponsors and relevant corporate stakeholders on their revised negotiation strategies and new mandates prior to starting the next round of negotiations in China.

Very good advice on negotiation preparation was given many hundreds of years ago by the famous Chinese military philosopher Sun Tze in his famous book, *The Art of War*: "If you know the enemy and know yourself, you need not fear the result of a hundred battles." This ancient saying from hundreds of year ago is still be very much applicable today to the detailed and thorough negotiation preparations that all negotiators should undertake prior to starting any negotiations.

Pre-negotiation mapping of contract clauses

It is very important for international negotiators to understand that the Chinese chief negotiator and negotiation team will most likely review in detail all the other contracts that the foreign company have already negotiated and signed in China as part of their negotiation preparation. In China, all Sino-foreign joint venture agreements and contracts have to be submitted to the relevant Chinese government ministries, such as Ministry of Commerce, for review and final approval after negotiations and agreement between the parties. All these contracts would be included in the extensive confidential China Sino Foreign contract database in the relevant ministry. During their negotiation preparations, the Chinese negotiators can access these with appropriate approval. This would then allow the Chinese negotiators a unique first-hand insight into all the key confidential terms and clauses that the foreign company have already negotiated and conceded with other Chinese companies in China.

During tough negotiations in China it will be usual for the Chinese chief negotiator to strongly challenge the international chief negotiators on all their proposed new contract terms and clauses. The Chinese chief negotiator will normally question the international chief negotiator directly on why the international company are proposing tougher terms than they had already conceded in other contracts which they have negotiated and agreed in China.

These serious challenges can create some very embarrassing moments for the international chief negotiator if he is unprepared. In the worst case, the international negotiators might be unaware of these concessions because they were done by other negotiators in another division of the international company. This could then cause severe loss of face to the international negotiators who would most probably have to adjourn the negotiations in China so they can thoroughly check the earlier concessions made previously by other international negotiators from their company in China.

The key lesson from the aforementioned business negotiation is that it is very important for the international chief negotiator and his team to review all the previous contracts that different divisions of the international company have already negotiated and signed in China as part of their negotiation preparation. It is also highly recommended that the international negotiators undertake the required 'negotiation mapping and comparison' of all the previously agreed contract terms and clauses with their proposed new contract terms and clauses that they would be planning to table for the new negotiations in China. This would then help to highlight if they need to revise some of their proposed new clauses after mapping them with earlier contract clauses which have been already been negotiated and agreed.

Negotiation preparation analysis tools

During negotiation planning, the Chinese and international negotiation teams should use various advanced negotiation analysis tools to improve their negotiation analysis and planning. These various advanced negotiation tools and tactics, such as competitor analysis, SWOT analysis, negotiation scenario analysis, contract terms and clause mapping, plus 'Best Alternatives to a Negotiated Agreement' (BATNA), etc., will help them to undertake better negotiation preparations for their forthcoming business negotiations in China. The details of each of the key negotiation analysis tools and techniques will be described in more detail below.

An important part of the negotiation preparation is for the negotiators to undertake detailed competitor analysis of the opposing company and negotiators. These will help the negotiators to gain a good understanding of the strategic intents, interests, motivations and concerns of the opposing company and negotiators before starting the negotiations. International negotiators have often found that the Chinese negotiators are very well informed about the foreign company, its competitiveness, results, strengths and weaknesses. This is because the Chinese negotiators normally undertake detailed competitor research and analysis of the foreign companies prior to starting negotiations.

Hence it would be important for the international negotiators to undertake similarly detailed competitor analysis of the Chinese company and negotiators. They could apply the systematic 'Strength Weakness Opportunity Threat' (SWOT) competitor analysis technique to better analyze the opposing company. The negotiators should start by undertaking detailed searches on the opposing company to find out their plans, strategies and developments globally and in China. They should then apply SWOT analysis to help them better understand the strengths and weaknesses of the opposing company. Then they should investigate the potential opportunities for cooperation with the opposing company. In addition, they should carefully consider the possible threats from the opposing company in China and globally.

The negotiators should also undertake systematic investigation of the different key strategic areas of the proposed joint project. This could help to build up a better picture of the opposing party's motivation, ambitions, priorities, concerns and strategic intents. This would then help the negotiators to better understand the strategic aspirations of the opposing negotiators plus to identify potential areas of conflict and compromise during negotiations. This could also assist the negotiators to develop more options for possible win–win compromises between the two sides during negotiations.

Another important negotiation analysis tool that the negotiators should use during negotiation preparation would be 'Negotiation Scenario Analysis' (NSA). The negotiators can use the NSA technique to generate various possible negotiation scenarios for their forthcoming negotiations in China with the opposing negotiators. These different scenarios then help the negotiators to develop better negotiation strategies to handle each of these potential negotiation scenarios. The negotiators should first identify the key negotiation issues after undertaking appropriate competitor analysis and deal analysis. They can then apply NSA to develop the various possible negotiation scenarios and possible outcomes. This would help the negotiators anticipate how the negotiations might proceed in China. This should also include the possible negotiation offers and arguments from the opposing negotiators. This information would then help the negotiators to develop suitable negotiation strategies plus counter arguments and offers for each of these negotiation scenarios. Subsequently, this will assist the negotiators in achieving their desired negotiation outcomes during actual negotiations in China.

A very important negotiation analysis for negotiators to undertake is to analyze and determine the 'Relative Negotiating Power' (RNP) of the opposing negotiators. This would normally include detailed 'worse case negotiation scenario analysis' on what would happen if no agreement could be reachable during the negotiations in China. The analysis should include a careful evaluation and assessment on how far the opposing negotiators would be prepared to move before deciding to end negotiations or take the non-settlement alternatives.

In normal negotiations, the Chinese and international negotiators negotiate hard with each other and make suitable compromises on different business issues to try to find mutually acceptable solutions. However, in some special cases the opposing negotiators might not be prepared or have not been empowered to give any further concessions. So, some negotiators might rather risk taking the 'non-settlement outcome' as part of their zero-sum negotiation strategy, to force some internal realignments amongst their powerful internal stakeholders.

Developing the various potential 'worse case non-settlement negotiation scenarios' can help the negotiators to better understand whether the opposing negotiators have any stronger non-settlement options which would then give them greater relative bargaining power. This in turn would help the negotiators to develop appropriate negotiation strategy with suitable counter-arguments to use during their business negotiations in China.

A very important negotiation contract analysis for the negotiators to undertake during negotiation preparation and prior to starting negotiations in China is an in-depth 'Contract Terms and Clauses Mapping' (CTCM). The international negotiators should be aware that the Chinese negotiators have good access to the confidential business contracts and agreements that the international company have already negotiated and signed in China. In China, all the major business agreements negotiated by Chinese and international partners must be submitted to relevant government ministries, such as the China Ministry of Commerce, for review and final approval. As part of their negotiation preparations, the Chinese negotiators would normally access the confidential contracts database so they can see all the key terms and concessions already made by the international company in China.

Hence the international negotiators must also carefully undertake detailed pre-negotiation CTCM of all the contracts that different divisions of their international company have signed in China. Then the negotiators should carefully pre-study all the key terms and clauses in all these contracts that the international company have already negotiated and agreed in China. The negotiators should then map these agreed contract clauses and terms against the proposed new key terms and clauses which they would be planning to table in their planned negotiations in China. Based on these, they can more easily see any overlapping areas so they can then develop appropriate new terms and clauses for their negotiations with the Chinese negotiators. This would also help the international negotiators to avoid the potential serious challenges from the Chinese negotiators during negotiations in China.

Analysis of business negotiation cases in China shows that if international negotiators have tried to negotiate new key terms and clauses without understanding or making references to previous agreements, then they make themselves vulnerable to severe challenges from the Chinese negotiators. The Chinese negotiators would normally strongly challenge the international negotiators on why they are changing their negotiation positions from past agreements that they have already signed in China. In many cases, they would even show evidence of past agreements already signed in China by the international company.

These strong and normal challenges on contract clauses and terms by the Chinese negotiators could be very embarrassing for the international negotiators, especially if the Chinese negotiator were able to expose that the international negotiator did not know what their company have previously agreed and signed in China. In some cases, the Chinese negotiators might even refer to other terms and clauses that other international competitors have already negotiated and conceded with other Chinese companies in China. The Chinese negotiators would use these to seriously challenge the international negotiators on why they would be reluctant to agree to these new terms when their competitors have already done so in China.

In the worst case, the Chinese chief negotiator could also choose to put more pressure on the international chief negotiator by saying that if they do not agree to their proposed new terms and clauses, then it would be very difficult for their final negotiated joint agreements to be approved by the relevant Chinese government authorities. These tough negotiation tactics can put the international negotiators in a very difficult, face losing situation during intensive negotiations in China. Hence it would be very important that the international negotiators undertake the CTCM analysis during their negotiation preparations so they develop suitable counter negotiation arguments to use in their future negotiations in China.

Chinese business negotiation strategies and plans

It is important for international negotiators to realize that the Chinese negotiators devote a lot of time to developing their negotiation strategy and plans prior to the start of negotiations with the foreign negotiators. The Chinese chief negotiator and the negotiation team would normally have to prepare, as part of their negotiation preparations, a detailed, internal, confidential negotiation report which would summarize their proposed negotiation objectives, plans and strategies. Within the Chinese system, the Chinese chief negotiator would then have to present and agree their proposed negotiation strategy and plans with their corporate sponsors and senior company management. In some special cases, they would also have to discuss and agree these with relevant Chinese government authorities, especially if the negotiations involve international trade or involve sensitive strategic business sectors in China.

Analysis of Chinese negotiation strategies and plans shows that the Chinese negotiation team normally develop their negotiation strategies and plans in line with the Chinese business negotiation norms and customs. In China, the Chinese word for negotiation is 'tan pan' which literally means a combination of discussions and judgements. In Chinese business negotiations, it would normally be a high priority for both parties to first build trust and good relationships with each other. Only after both parties feel that they can trust each other would the two negotiation teams start their negotiations. Then the negotiations would have to be undertaken in line with the key Chinese negotiation principle of 'mutual equality' and 'win–win'. This would promote both negotiation teams to negotiate all the key business principles and develop win–win agreements which would be mutually acceptable by both parties.

It would usually take some time to build trust and good initial guanxi between the two negotiation teams at the beginning stages of negotiations. This would normally involve extensive exploratory dialogue and engagement between the two negotiation teams. Each of the negotiation teams would also try to evaluate the other negotiation team's capabilities and strengths as well as their trustworthiness. In some cases, the Chinese negotiators might have to report these to their corporate sponsors so they can then decide internally if the international negotiators are trustworthy for them to continue with the formal negotiations.

During early negotiations, the Chinese negotiators, in line with the Chinese negotiation process, try to negotiate and reach some mutual early agreements on some less important business issues to help build trust and good guanxi between the two sides. These early compromises would help the negotiators on both sides to better negotiate other parts of the deal to make a 'mutually beneficial' and 'win–win' deal in the end with mutually acceptable agreements and contracts.

Taking the above into consideration, the primary objective of the Chinese negotiation team's strategy and plan for the initial negotiation phase would normally be more focused on creating a good, comprehensive framework for long-term, sustainable cooperation rather than rushing into agreeing and drafting a written agreement quickly. The Chinese negotiators would normally prefer the dynamic, ongoing negotiation approach which would take into account the actual changing business situations. Their initial negotiation strategies and plans normally would be more focused on building trust between the two negotiation teams and would consider the dynamic overall situation. The Chinese negotiators normally prefer to negotiate and agree all the key business principles first. Only after this has been done would the Chinese negotiators be prepared to start to negotiate and prepare the detailed written contracts and agreements. Many traditional Chinese negotiators also consider business negotiations that solely focus on developing written contracts and agreement quickly to be more aligned with the Western-style negotiation process. They might suspect that the international negotiators are trying to take advantage of them and 'pull the wool over their eyes' on some important negotiation issues.

International Western negotiators undertaking business negotiations in China should understand and master these significant differences in negotiation style and approach when developing their specific negotiation strategy and plans. The international negotiators, who might be more task-based and time-conscious, must balance their wish for quick negotiation outcomes and habit of developing written contracts as soon as possible against the slower pace of business negotiations in China.

In addition, the international negotiator should try to make all efforts to support the important requirements to first build trust, promote guanxi and establish good interpersonal relationships with the Chinese negotiators in China. If the international negotiators work within the Chinese negotiation process, this should help develop suitable negotiation strategies and plans which should work better during their negotiations in China. On the other hand, if they choose to ignore these important negotiation requirements, then their negotiations in China will generally be difficult with uncertain outcomes.

During negotiations in China, the Chinese negotiators would often stress the key Chinese business negotiation principle of negotiating on an 'equal and mutually beneficial' basis. Their negotiation strategy would usually be focused on negotiating and achieving a mutually beneficial win–win agreement for both sides in the end. This would normally involve having to negotiate and agree all the key strategic business principles and 'must haves' of both the Chinese and international negotiators. These negotiations would normally be long, complex and difficult covering all the different key negotiation issues.

However, in some cases, some Chinese negotiators might push hard to promote their company's negotiation agenda and aspirations. The international negotiators should be very vigilant of these strong negotiation pressures during negotiation in China and should negotiate hard with the opposing negotiators to try to find mutually beneficial negotiation solutions. In China, it would be possible for international negotiators to be considered both 'keqi' and assertive during negotiations. Different negotiation assertive techniques will be discussed later in this book.

Taking the above into consideration, it is important for both negotiating teams to develop good negotiation plans and strategies for the different possible negotiation scenarios which might occur during the long negotiations in China. It is also very important that the negotiators on both sides keep their negotiation strategies and plans dynamic based on the actual negotiation progress. Both negotiation teams should update their senior management regularly after each negotiation round on their negotiation progress. They should also gain support for their revised negotiation strategies and new mandates prior to starting the next round of negotiations in China.

Analysis of different Chinese negotiation plans shows that Chinese negotiators are normally required to develop a detailed negotiation report covering their negotiation plan, together with relevant negotiation strategies plus their key negotiation objectives and negotiation options. The Chinese chief negotiator will usually first present this to their corporate sponsors and senior management to seek their support. In many cases, the Chinese chief negotiator would also have to present these to relevant government authorities to seek their endorsements, especially if the negotiations cover sensitive strategic areas or have an impact on international trade. Based on this, the Chinese chief negotiator and negotiation team are given appropriate negotiation directives and mandates from their corporate sponsors and relevant government authorities before negotiations with international partners commence.

Taking the above into consideration, it would also be useful for the international negotiation teams to prepare and develop an appropriate negotiation report containing their proposed negotiation plans and strategies prior to starting their negotiations in China. They should carefully evaluate and determine their strategic negotiation goals plus what they think they can realistically achieve in their negotiations in China. They should also include their different negotiation options and various possible negotiation approaches in their negotiation report.

Then the international chief negotiation and negotiators should discuss their 'negotiation strategy and planning report' with their corporate sponsors and senior international management. The report should highlight their key negotiation objectives and plans, plus appropriate negotiation strategies together with different negotiation options and approaches. The negotiation team should also consider different potential 'negotiation scenarios', including the possible arguments from the other party and their potential counter arguments. The international chief negotiator should discuss and agree their proposed negotiation plans and mandates with their senior management and corporate sponsors. This will help the international negotiators to gain the required management support for their proposed negotiation approaches plus for senior management to grant the appropriate negotiation mandates to the international negotiation team.

Analysis of different negotiation strategies for China shows that when the international negotiators develop their detailed negotiation strategies for China, they should adapt their negotiation strategies and tactics to the specific Chinese style of negotiations. In particular, the international negotiators, who may be more task-based and time-conscious, should balance their aspirations for quick settlement on specific negotiation issues and key contract terms with the slower-paced and the sometimes seemingly abstract focus on first building guanxi and interpersonal relationships by the Chinese negotiators. For the international negotiators to negotiate effectively within the Chinese negotiation framework, they should understand and accommodate the Chinese-style negotiation approaches. This would enable them to develop appropriate negotiation strategies and strategic plans that would work on a local level in China.

One of the biggest dangers during negotiations in China for all negotiation teams is being too eager to reach agreement quickly plus without having suitable alternatives and options to fall back on. Having alternative options during a negotiation normally helps teams to increase their negotiating position and level of confidence. It would also be important to estimate and evaluate the other party's alternative positions before starting the negotiations. If a chief negotiator can determine that the opposite negotiators do not have any good alternative positions, then this could help to greatly improve their negotiating power to drive a much more favourable deal against the opposing negotiators.

Reviews of negotiation cases in China show that it is very important for the negotiators to agree realistic negotiation timing and 'bottom lines' with their top management in advance of the start of negotiations. These agreed negotiation bottom lines must be the absolute 'must haves' that the negotiators would need to achieve from the negotiations in China. Having clearly agreed bottom lines would then establish clear 'negotiation objectives' for the negotiators. During their negotiations in China, the negotiators should not accept any deals or counter offers below these agreed bottom lines. All the key corporate stakeholders and negotiators should agree to these and these should be communicated to all the negotiators in the team so that they all clearly understand these bottom lines. Having agreed bottom lines can often protect the chief negotiator and the negotiation team from being pushed into accepting bad deals during the heat of intensive negotiations in China.

Analysis of negotiation cases in China shows that in addition to having good negotiation bottom lines, the negotiators should also consider the worst possible negotiation scenarios during their preparations. Best negotiation practices show it is important for negotiators to consider their potential 'BATNA'. This negotiation analysis and tactic can help negotiators to strengthen their position during negotiations in China. The BATNA can involve potential counter offers, another potential new project or the status quo which the negotiators have developed and agreed with their corporate sponsors during their negotiation preparations. Once the negotiators have discussed and agreed these BATNA with their corporate sponsors, then these become their new bottom lines. The BATNA can change and improve over time as different negotiation options and counter offers are tabled during negotiations in China.

Realistic negotiation timelines and schedules should be agreed by the chief negotiator with their management to avoid unrealistically high expectations on short negotiation timings. The negotiators and their corporate sponsors should realize that business negotiations in China normally take much longer periods to negotiate the different issues. The corporate sponsors should set a realistic timeline for their negotiators to avoid putting undue pressures on their negotiators. Unrealistic tight negotiation timelines can sometimes pressurize negotiators to agreeing too quickly to negotiation concessions without adequate time to negotiate.

The negotiation teams should also try to identify areas where concessions and compromises might be made on less important business negotiation issues as part of their negotiation preparation. They should be aware what different potential 'win–win alternatives' are available and how to negotiate these to reach a suitable compromise with the Chinese negotiators. The negotiators can determine how and when is best to offer these concessions during their negotiations to achieve the desired negotiation outcomes. This would normally include which negotiation techniques to employ and how best to apply them during negotiations in China to achieve successful win–win outcomes and build guanxi.

In addition, there should be formal communication systems in place in the international company to keep their negotiators informed of the different statements made by senior international management on China and globally. This would be important as the Chinese negotiators would also be monitoring these news developments. During negotiations, the Chinese negotiator might often quote the latest news statements by the international company to test the responses from the international negotiators. It would be very embarrassing and cause serious loss of face if the international negotiators were unaware of this news relating to their own company.

An interesting tough business negotiation tactic used by some Chinese chief negotiators would be to say to the international chief negotiator something along the line that "During the recent visit by your CEO to China, he assured our CEO during dinner that your company would provide these products and service free as part of the agreement that we are negotiating". Then it would be very important for the international chief negotiator to show that he was aware of the details of these important statements by his senior management. Otherwise, the international chief negotiator might lose face if he was unaware of these statements and could not respond adequately to the Chinese negotiators. By the way, the international negotiators can use the same negotiation tactic on the Chinese negotiators on key messages that their Chinese company management might have given overseas or in China.

Negotiation roles and team building

Analysis of successful business negotiation teams shows that a negotiation team should be well organized and operationally ready for their forthcoming negotiations in China. One of the key objectives for a negotiation team is to become 'operationally ready' for their intensive business negotiations, in China. The chief negotiator should organize and align the different negotiators, who have been drawn from different company divisions and internal corporate functions, to work most effectively as an integrated negotiation team in their negotiations in China.

The chief negotiator should assign clear roles and responsibilities to each of the negotiators. In addition, the negotiators should be trained to work together as a highly disciplined, cohesive negotiation team which follows agreed, unified negotiation plans and strategies. The integrated unified negotiation team approach should help the international negotiation team to negotiate more effectively in China. This integrated, disciplined negotiation team approach for China is different from the typically more open, unscripted Western style of negotiations, where each negotiation team member might give their input when they like during business negotiations between Western parties.

In the unified, integrated negotiation team approach, analysis of best negotiation team practices shows that there should be one designated speaker for the negotiation team on each key issue during negotiations in China. The designated speaker should normally be the chief negotiator at the start of negotiation. However, many negotiation teams have also found it useful to appoint different designated speakers for different negotiation topics as negotiations proceed in China.

Analysis of business negotiations in China shows that each negotiator should be appointed to be the team speaker on their specific functional speciality or area of expertise. This practice of rotating the designated speaker allows the chief negotiator to reserve his negotiating position so he can be more flexible in his negotiations in the later stages. However, the designated speaker and other team members speaking during the negotiations should all speak in line with the team's negotiation plan and script to demonstrate their corporate consensus and teamwork. If the negotiator deviates from the agreed negotiator script, then they risk the opposing negotiators observing and exploiting the contrasting views amongst the team.

During business negotiations in China, it would be normal practice for the Chinese negotiators to engage the international negotiators in some small talk during tea breaks, lunch or dinners. It would be important that the negotiators should never openly disagree with each other or try to air unresolved internal issues with each other in front of the opposing negotiators during these breaks in negotiations. Experienced negotiators would be trained to observe and pick up on these disagreements and disputes amongst the opposing negotiation team. They would then try to attack these weaknesses and exploit the differences during formal negotiations.

Analysis of successful, integrated and unified international negotiation teams shows that the chief negotiator should also assign different primary duties and secondary negotiation roles to each negotiation team member. The primary duty is normally based on the negotiator's primary area of expertise and functions within the company, such as technology, finance, manufacturing, etc. The secondary role includes being the notetaker, translator, observer, facilitator and intermediary for example. These different functions are normally required for successful negotiations in China, and they might overlap with each other in some areas of responsibilities.

The designated note taker normally serves a very important role in each negotiation team in China. During negotiations, the Chinese or international negotiators might often refer to different statements, offers, counter offers or concessions made during earlier negotiations. Hence it would be important to have detailed minutes of negotiations and accurate documentation of the different rounds of negotiations. This would help the negotiators to contest various claims from the opposing negotiators.

After each negotiation round, the designated note taker on the Chinese and international negotiation teams should work together to prepare the joint negotiation minutes for both teams. These should be signed off by the chief negotiators of both teams. Then the chief negotiators and their teams can use these joint negotiation minutes to update their senior management on the negotiation progress plus discuss new negotiation strategies and mandates.

The choice of the right translator during negotiation is key to efficient negotiations in China. Analysis of successful China negotiation experiences has shown that many leading international companies have found it useful to use their own Chinese translator during business negotiations in China. This would be to avoid any sensitive and subtle negotiation points being lost or wrongly translated during negotiations in China. In addition, the translator could also help to provide more insights to the international negotiators on various observations of the Chinese negotiators' behaviour or discussions in their native Chinese during negotiations. It would also be useful to involve the translator in negotiation preparations and workshops so they get an insight into the context of the negotiations. This will help them to improve their translations and express the points better during sensitive negotiations.

Many successful international negotiation teams have found it useful to appoint an observer during their negotiations in China. During business negotiations in China, non-verbal communication amongst the Chinese negotiators is usually as important as the spoken, verbal communication. The designated observer or facilitator should be a negotiator who is familiar with Chinese culture and trained in interpretation of Chinese, non-verbal communication and expression.

A specific instance which shows how this training is useful is that Chinese and Asian negotiators are normally unlikely to answer "no" directly during negotiations. A direct "no" could sometimes be seen as a failure and lead to 'loss of face' for the Chinese negotiators. Hence Chinese negotiators normally tend to express their rejections or refusal in many different, indirect ways, both verbally and non-verbally. The designated international observer should then help to interpret these non-verbal signals and pass their observation results to the chief negotiator.

This will help the international negotiator to more accurately judge if the Chinese negotiators are really rejecting their proposals or indeed considering the negotiation proposal from the international negotiators further.

For successful negotiations in China, the role of a designated 'negotiation intermediary' within both the Chinese and international negotiation teams is very important. This is in line with the important Chinese negotiation cultural characteristic of wanting to avoid direct confrontation during negotiations which could create personal embarrassment and losing face to the Chinese negotiators. Hence it is desirable for the Chinese and international chief negotiators to each appoint one of their negotiators to be the designated intermediary. Then the intermediary on both sides can speak informally to each other during breaks in negotiations to ask for clarification on different points made during negotiations. In some special cases, the intermediary could be used by the chief negotiator to informally test new ideas or negotiation proposals with the opposing negotiators. Usually the exchanges of pivotal information between negotiation intermediaries is conveyed informally during tea breaks and over dinner or lunch. Very often these are in the form of informal 'small talks' which do not cause embarrassment or loss of face to either of the negotiation teams. It normally takes time for a negotiation intermediary to build trust with their designated counterpart on the other negotiation team. In addition, the intermediary must be empowered and trusted by their chief negotiator. The intermediary must also act fully in line with the chief negotiator's instruction and follow the team's negotiation mandate and plans.

Negotiation workshops and war gaming

Analysis of successful business negotiation cases shows that it is important for negotiators to find time to practise and rehearse their negotiation roles prior to starting actual negotiations in China. As part of a negotiation team's preparations for negotiations in China, the chief negotiator should assign clear roles and responsibilities to each member of the negotiation team so that they know what they need to do during the intense negotiations in China.

Many negotiation teams have found that formal negotiation workshops with role plays on the most likely negotiation scenarios to be very useful in their negotiation preparations. These workshops help the negotiation team to get a better foretaste of different potential negotiation situations in China and practise for these. Hence many leading international and Chinese companies have held formal 'negotiation workshops' for their negotiation teams with different role plays for various likely negotiation scenarios prior to starting actual negotiations in China.

Analysis of good business negotiation workshops shows that it would be useful for the 'negotiation workshops' to include different role plays together with realistic, simulated negotiations scenarios. During these workshops, the negotiators normally undertake different role plays appropriate for their designated roles in the forthcoming negotiations in China. These simulated negotiation role play exercises help the negotiators to get a good foretaste of what could happen during their actual forthcoming negotiations in China. It also allows the negotiators to learn from their different mistakes and to improve prior to starting actual negotiations in China.

During the different role-playing scenarios, the negotiators should also consider how the opposing negotiators might potentially react during the negotiations in China. In particular, the negotiator should consider how the opposing negotiator might react to different possible negotiation offers including what counter offers or arguments they would be likely to respond with. This will help the negotiators to prepare themselves better prior to starting actual business negotiations in China.

Analysis of different negotiation preparations cases has shown that it is useful to include 'war gaming' techniques in the planned negotiation workshops. In particular negotiators should consider applying war gaming techniques to analyze and prepare for potential stressful negotiation situations. Negotiation experiences have shown that these could help the negotiators to better prepare for the worst possible negotiation cases. This would also help negotiators to effectively handle potential conflict and stressful situations which can easily occur during tough negotiations in China and globally. The negotiators, through a combination of war gaming and role play, can learn how to handle these potential tough situations whilst maintaining good guanxi with the opposing negotiators.

Preparation for the beginning of negotiations in China

To ensure a successful start of negotiations in China, it is important to make good plans on the details of the logistics and venue arrangements for the first negotiation team meeting. The Chinese and international negotiation teams should discuss and agree the planning of their negotiation opening meeting together prior to the start of negotiation. These preparations are essential for a smooth start to the negotiations in China, in addition to having good negotiation strategies and plans.

Good opening of negotiation arrangements can also help to build trust and guanxi quickly with the Chinese negotiators. Alternatively, failure to plan the negotiation opening meeting well could lead to early disagreements between the negotiation teams. In the worst case, serious arrangement mishaps could result in serious loss of face and poor guanxi with the Chinese negotiators which could undermine the negotiation process in China.

The negotiation teams should carefully consider and discuss when and where the first negotiation meetings should be held in China. In particular, they should carefully choose the proposed dates of their negotiation meetings in China. They must avoid proposing to hold their negotiation meetings in conflict with the dates of the main Chinese holidays. They should avoid holding negotiations during the October Chinese national holidays and the Chinese New Year holidays when most Chinese are away for a week or more. If the international negotiators choose to neglect these important Chinese dates, then this could lead to rejection of the proposed dates by the Chinese negotiators. In the worst case, this might lead to the Chinese negotiators being unhappy and reverting with some embarrassing counter offers on negotiation dates that could cause difficulties for the international negotiators.

An interesting example of an instance when this occurred was when an inexperienced international negotiation team once asked their opposing Chinese negotiators if they could hold some quick negotiations meetings close to one of the main Chinese national holidays when most of the Chinese negotiators would be away. This resulted in the Chinese negotiators being upset and counter requesting the international negotiators to travel to China to attend important negotiation meetings near to Christmas and the New Year. The international negotiation team then realized their mistake. They rescheduled the proposed negotiation dates so that these would not conflict with any of the Chinese national holidays. When they resubmitted their proposed negotiation dates to the Chinese negotiators, they also apologized for their mistake and oversight. The Chinese negotiating team accepted their apologies and confirmed that the new negotiation dates were acceptable. They also agreed to cancel their request for the international negotiators having to travel to China near to Christmas and New Year to attend negotiation meetings.

The first negotiation meeting agenda and programme should also be discussed and agreed beforehand by the two negotiation teams. However, in some cases this could easily become part of the opening negotiations. It would be good to prepare and propose the meeting agenda well in advance so that the negotiators on the other side have time to consider these. This will help to avoid surprises and allow time for the Chinese negotiators to come back with suitable revisions and amendments. In China, it is normally good to start a negotiation meeting with a joint negotiation agenda which has been agreed by negotiators on both sides. This will help to give a smooth start to the negotiation and improve the effectiveness of the negotiation meeting.

It is important for the international negotiators to ensure that all the detailed arrangements for the negotiation meeting are pre-discussed and agreed with the Chinese negotiation team through designated intermediary or through assigned logistics staff on both sides. All the details should be covered and agreed so as to ensure that the negotiations start on a friendly basis with no undue pressures or advantages being placed upon either negotiation team through the wrong choice of venue or a poor logistical arrangement.

Chinese business negotiation etiquette and tactics

Prior to start of business negotiations in China, it is helpful for the international negotiators to familiarize themselves with some basic Chinese business etiquette and customs. The Chinese negotiators normally appreciate and respect the international negotiators who have taken the time and effort to learn basic Chinese business etiquette. This will often help to build guanxi and trust in the initial negotiation meetings in China.

On the other hand, the Chinese negotiators are likely to look down upon foreign negotiators who attend negotiation meetings in China without making the necessary preparations and show a lack of interest and respect for the local Chinese culture and customs. This could often lead to poor guanxi and low trust levels which might negatively affect the subsequent negotiations.

The international negotiator should recognize that in their first business meeting with the Chinese negotiators, it is customary to begin with the introduction of the negotiators and teams on both sides. It is common to shake hands briefly and polite to nod slightly when greeting the Chinese negotiators for the first time. When the international negotiators are being introduced to the Chinese negotiators, it is important to have some eye contact but it would be generally recommended to avoid 'eye fixing' or staring. In China, it is generally considered impolite to look straight or stare directly into the eyes of another Chinese person for long periods, as this is considered to be a lack of respect. At the same time, it would also be considered impolite for the eyes of the international negotiators to be wandering all over the place during introductions and conversations with Chinese negotiators. During introductions and normal conversation, it would also be good manners in China to not interrupt a Chinese person whilst he is speaking or in mid-sentence. It is normally recommended that the international negotiator should listen politely and reserve his comments until after the Chinese negotiator has finished speaking.

During introductions, it is customary for both sides to exchange business cards when meeting for the first time. During business card exchanges in China, it is important to present the business cards with both hands to the Chinese negotiators as a sign of respect. If an international negotiator presents their business card with just one hand to a Chinese negotiator, this is considered to be a sign of disrespect. In addition, the international negotiator should treat with respect each of the business cards they receive from the Chinese negotiators. It is customary to spend some time reading each business card and its contents. It is also considered good manners for the international negotiators to memorize the correct names and titles of each of the Chinese negotiators for subsequent meetings.

The Chinese negotiators normally also appreciate having a Chinese translation on the back of the business card of the international Western negotiators. Hence as part of their negotiation team preparations, bilingual business cards should be prepared and printed for each of the international negotiators by the international company, ahead of their first negotiation meeting in China. The international negotiators should bring lots of their bilingual business cards to China as these could run out quickly.

The international negotiators should also try to learn some basic Chinese in preparation for their negotiations in China. It is generally appreciated by the Chinese negotiators if the foreign negotiators make the effort to learn some basic Chinese, but they normally do not expect the international negotiators to learn a lot of Chinese.

Two good useful Chinese phrases would be 'nihao', which literally means 'hello' in Chinese, and 'xiexie', which literally means 'thank you' in Chinese. These two simple but popular Chinese phrases could come in very handy during the initial negotiation meetings as ice breakers for the international negotiator when they first meet with the Chinese negotiators.

In preparation for their first meetings in China, it would also useful for the international negotiators to read up on some recent, positive news on China and the Chinese company, such as sports, awards, achievements, etc. These news stories could come in very handy as ice breakers for the international negotiators during their general social discussions or small talks with the Chinese negotiators during the initial meetings, dinners and lunches. The Chinese negotiators would appreciate the international negotiators showing some interest in China and its culture. It would also help to give the Chinese negotiators a sense of respect and a demonstration of their interests in China. It would also be generally recommended that the international negotiator avoid bringing up controversial topics, such as politics, religion and sensitive international relationships issues.

When attending the planned negotiation meetings in China, the international negotiators should ensure that they arrive punctually for the planned negotiation meetings. It would normally be considered bad manners and a sign disrespect if an international negotiator arrived late for planned business meetings in China without any good reasons. If there really were difficult circumstances which prevented one from being on time, such as traffic jams in Beijing, then it would be good manners for the international negotiators to inform the Chinese negotiators as soon as possible.

In the negotiation meeting room, the international negotiators should sit at their assigned places during the formal negotiation meetings. If there are no assigned seats, then the international negotiators, as foreign visitors, should normally sit in the meeting room facing the main entrance door of the meeting room. This is an old Chinese custom based on the historical tradition of an assassin normally entering a meeting room through the main doors if they would want to kill important visitors during special meetings. So, the foreign guest would historically be seated facing the door so they could see the assassin coming in first and then could take appropriate protective actions. In modern-day China, these assassination incidents are very unlikely to take place, but these ancient traditions and customs are still followed as a general rule.

In China, the host or chief negotiator would also normally sit at the middle of the table rather than either end of the table. The other negotiators would then be seated in line with their seniorities on either side of their chief negotiator. If a translator is used for the negotiations, then the translator is normally seated next to the chief negotiator or designated speaker so it would be easier for them to make translations.

During negotiations in China, it would be normal for the international negotiation team to have lunches, dinners and some drinks together with the Chinese negotiation team. It would generally be considered good manners to accept the lunch or dinner invitations from the Chinese negotiators and hosts. There are famous sayings in both China and Western businesses along the line that "business is better done over dinners and drinks". If an international negotiator refuses to accept these invitations from the Chinese negotiators, then this could lead to misunderstandings and doubts by the Chinese negotiators on the commitment and sincerity of the international negotiators.

These dinner and lunch occasions are often a good opportunity for the international negotiators to have social interaction and establish better guanxi with their Chinese negotiating counterparts. In some cases, important messages or offers might be passed informally from the Chinese negotiators to the international negotiation team during dinner. These informal messages should be quickly passed onto the chief negotiator and the rest of the team after the dinner so the negotiators can analyze the messages and develop suitable responses.

At the start of meals, the Chinese negotiators might ask the international negotiators what they do not like to eat when they meet for the first time. It would be acceptable for international negotiator to specify these politely, otherwise they might regret not saying so later during the meal. It would often be acceptable for international Western negotiators to say that they could not take some very spicy food, fish heads, pigs heads, snakes, chicken feet, etc. These are usually the most common Chinese food that most Westerners have trouble eating in China. During the meals, the international negotiators should always accept the food offered to them and not leave what they can't eat on their plates. It is often appreciated if the foreigners use chopsticks during meals, though it would also be acceptable to ask for a knife, fork and spoon in a large restaurant in China. However, it would be considered very bad manners to stick the chopsticks into rice, food or fruits during meals, as this would be considered equivalent to a symbol of stabbing in China.

During dinner, it is a common custom in China to 'ganbei', which literally means giving toasts to each other in Chinese. In the past, the strong, white Chinese liquor with high alcohol content, such as 50 to 70 per cent proof, was often poured into small glasses for the toasts. However, nowadays these strong white liquors have often been replaced by red wine or beer. It would be considered good manners and polite to accept these toasts. There is a famous old Chinese saying that "friendship is built by drinking together".

Normally the Chinese negotiators find many reasons to ganbei or toast the international negotiators over meals. These could include toasts to good cooperation, friendship, partnership, plus health, etc. Some inexperienced international negotiators would find these a bit overwhelming but they should understand that the main purpose of all these ganbei and toasts are to build good guanxi and to emphasize the positive aspects of the business relationship in China.

During meals, it would be customary in China for the Chinese negotiators to engage the international negotiators on social small talk. The international negotiators should not be surprised by the Chinese negotiators asking them about their company salary and benefits. In China, this would be a popular question and it would be acceptable to discuss money and salary, without revealing the confidential details during meals. So, it is recommended and polite for the international negotiators to give some general factual answers on their salary and benefits, but without revealing the confidential details. The international negotiators can also engage the Chinese negotiators to discuss sports, food, health, music or weather, as these are also popular subjects to discuss over a meal in China.

Generally, it is recommended that the international negotiator refrains from raising or discussing formal businesses or negotiation issues over the dinners unless their Chinese host or the Chinese negotiators have first brought these issues up during dinner. In China, meals are generally considered to be a good time to build guanxi and good relationships and to become more relaxed with each other. The Chinese negotiators rarely bring up formal negotiation issues unless they have pre-planned these as part of their negotiation tactics.

Sometimes the designated Chinese negotiation intermediary would pass some negotiation messages informally to the designated international negotiation intermediary. Then it would be very important for the negotiation intermediary to immediately share these important messages, after the meals, with their chief negotiator and the rest of the negotiation team. Then they could review and analyze these messages plus prepare suitable responses to give during the next negotiation meeting.

After the negotiation teams have gotten to know each other well, then in some special cases, the Chinese negotiators might choose to converse informally over meals and relay some important negotiation proposals to the international negotiation team. This would often be planned well beforehand by the Chinese negotiators after discussions with their chief negotiator and senior management. The international negotiators, especially the designated intermediary, must ensure that they pick up these important messages accurately. Then after the meals, they should immediately discuss these important informal negotiation proposals with the chief negotiator and the rest of the negotiation team so they can develop appropriate responses for the next negotiation round.

Part III

The negotiation cycle and stages

6 Chinese business negotiation

The opening stage

种瓜得瓜

Zhòng guā dé guā

If you plant a melon seed, then you should get a melon when it is grown.

You reap what you sow.

Executive overview

The opening stage of business negotiations in China is very important as it shapes the stage for rest of the long business negotiations. It also sets the tone for relationships between the negotiation teams. There are important negotiation formalities and official requirements that the negotiation teams need to comply with in China. The international negotiators should understand and follow these Chinese negotiation processes and protocols to ensure good guanxi and smooth negotiations. It is critical that the international negotiators start to build trust and guanxi with the opposing Chinese negotiators. At the start of negotiations, the Chinese negotiators normally stress that the key China negotiation principle of mutual equity and equal benefits is followed to achieve win–win negotiation outcomes in China.

Preparations for opening of negotiations in China

High-level business negotiations cases in China have been analysed to identify the key requirements for successful opening negotiation meetings in China. It was found that to start successful negotiations in China, is very important that both the Chinese and international negotiators are well prepared and have developed good negotiation strategies and plans. In addition, the negotiators should have undertaken good planning of the negotiation venue and coordination before negotiations actually begin. This would include where the negotiation meetings should be held in China and who should attend.

The negotiation agenda and programme, plus all the logistics for the opening meeting should be discussed and agreed beforehand by both the Chinese and international negotiation teams. The international negotiators should also realize that these discussions for the arrangements for the opening of negotiations can be sensitive. In some cases, these might even lead to the onset of some difficult negotiations, even before the formal opening of negotiations between the two negotiation teams.

Successful negotiation cases in China also show that it is very important that all these detailed arrangements for the opening negotiation meeting should all be pre-discussed and agreed with the Chinese negotiators. This will ensure that the negotiations start on a friendly basis between the two negotiation teams with no 'loss of face' and impact to good guanxi. Alternatively, a wrong choice of venue or poor logistical arrangements could lead to severe loss of face and poor guanxi between the two negotiation teams. These could then seriously undermine the future negotiation process and negotiation outcomes.

An important element of the opening negotiation meeting and initial first phase of business negotiations in China involves introductions between the international and Chinese negotiators. This helps the negotiators on both sides to get to know each other and start to build trust between the two sides. These normally take place first during the formal negotiation opening meeting followed by an informal welcome dinner or lunch for both the negotiation teams.

Business negotiations in China can often be complex and long. In addition, negotiations normally involve very intensive high-level interpersonal activities and exchanges between the Chinese and international negotiators. An important part of the preparations for negotiations in China is for both the Chinese and international negotiator to find out as much as possible about each other plus to get to know each other well. If the negotiation teams are well-informed about their counterparts and their backgrounds, then this can help them to develop the appropriate negotiation strategies and approaches for the various key negotiation issues. In addition, it is very important for negotiators to start building trust and good relationships between the two sides right from the start of negotiations.

For the international Western negotiators who are normally more time conscious, they might want to get these initial negotiation preliminaries over and done with as quickly as possible. Some inexperienced negotiators might believe that these preliminaries are wasting time and they prefer to get into the formal business negotiations as soon as possible. However, this could be counter-productive as these preliminaries are important elements of the Chinese negotiation customs and process. The Chinese negotiators use this opportunity to find out more about the international negotiators plus to try to build good guanxi and trust with the international negotiators. This will help to build a good foundation for smooth negotiations in the future and good relationships between the negotiation teams. Hence the international negotiator should also play an active part in these introductions and informal exchanges at the opening stages of negotiations. If not, then this could lead to lost opportunities, poor guanxi and low levels of trust.

The chief negotiator should allocate clear roles and responsibilities to different members of the negotiation team prior to the start of negotiations. During business negotiations in China, the negotiation team should act as a unified team and should have an appointed spokesman for the team. Analysis of actual business negotiations in China shows that the chief negotiator should be the spokesman on key negotiation issues and then different team members should be assigned to be the speaker on their respective specialities in the negotiation team. It would be desirable not to have the chief negotiator as the spokesman for the team all the time. This would then allow the chief negotiator more room and flexibility in the later stages of negotiations.

The chief negotiator should assign one of the negotiation team members to be the official notetaker. After each negotiation round in China, the notetakers for both negotiation teams should work together to prepare a set of short, joint minutes of the negotiation with key agreed items, open items and action points. Both the chief negotiators should then sign the joint negotiation minutes. The chief negotiator and the negotiation team can then use the agreed joint minutes to update their management after each negotiation round. They can also discuss any changes to their negotiation strategies and obtain the necessary new mandates from their management, prior to the next round of negotiation.

For effective business negotiation in China, it is essential to include one or two good, competent translators in the negotiation team. During negotiations, they have to make clear and accurate translations of the proposals. It would also be advisable to include the translators in the negotiation team preparation sessions. These would help them to build up their basic understanding of the technicality of the business and negotiation processes so that they can then make better translations during the negotiations.

In China, a lot of foreign companies might employ external or agency translators for their negotiations and business meetings when they do not have suitable internal staff. If the international team decide to hire an external translator from an agency for important business negotiations, then it would be important to require the translators to sign the necessary secrecy or confidentiality agreements, prior to start of the confidential business negotiations.

Opening meeting tactics for Chinese business negotiations

The first opening negotiation meeting in China is important for both the Chinese and international negotiation teams. It shapes the stage for the long business negotiations in China between the two teams. It also sets the tone for the relations and guanxi between the two negotiation teams. There are important Chinese negotiation formalities and official requirements that both the negotiation teams need to comply with in China.

It is important for all the negotiators to be punctual and arrive on time at the planned negotiation opening meeting. If there are unavoidable delays, e.g. traffic jams in Beijing, then the international negotiators should inform the Chinese negotiators as soon as possible. All the physical arrangements and logistics for the negotiation meetings should be pre-discussed and arranged well in advance of the meeting with the Chinese negotiators. It is important to do this beforehand to avoid any disagreements which could cause loss of face to either side at the opening meeting.

Reviews of different high-level Chinese negotiation cases show that at the start of formal business negotiations, both the Chinese and international negotiation teams should be led by their appointed chief negotiators. Each of the chief negotiators should have been formally appointed by their respective top management before the opening meeting. The companies should have provided their chief negotiator with the appropriate formal appointment letter. In China, it is normal practice at the first formal negotiation meeting that the chief negotiators from both sides show each other their respective 'Letter of Appointment' from their head office. The letters of appointment should have been both signed by the CEO and also stamped with their official company chop. This is a common legal practice and requirement in China.

At the start of negotiations in China, the Chinese chief negotiator would normally ask their lawyer to check and verify the Letter of Appointment from the international company. They would also ask the international chief negotiator to supply a copy of the appointment letter for the Chinese company's files. The international chief negotiator should also ask to see the Chinese chief negotiator's appointment letter and ask him to supply an official copy. This formal exchange and confirmation of appointment letters should also be minuted in the first joint negotiation minutes to be prepared by both teams, to show that both negotiation teams have been properly empowered by their top management.

It is also customary at the first negotiation meeting in China that each of the chief negotiators introduce each of their negotiation team members to the other side. The chief negotiator has several options for the introduction of their negotiators. He or she could choose to keep their introductions of the team short and concise. However, as a minimum he should mention their name, position and responsibilities. An alternative approach which some chief negotiators prefer is after giving a short introduction of the negotiation team member, he would then invite each of the negotiators to briefly introduce themselves. This has become quite a popular practice as it provides an opportunity for each of the negotiators to add some important messages about themselves. However, these personal introductions by each of the negotiators should also be kept brief and concise.

The exchange of business cards between the negotiators is an important part of the introductions during the first negotiation meeting. The international negotiators should observe the Chinese custom of holding their name card with both hands when presenting one's name card and receiving the Chinese negotiators' name cards. On receiving each name card, they should also take a short time to read the contents whilst holding it with both hands, so as to show respect to the Chinese negotiator.

The international negotiator should understand that titles and ranks are still considered to be of high importance in China. It is important for the international negotiators to use the right titles when addressing the Chinese negotiators. During negotiations, the highest ranked Chinese host, would normally sit in the middle of the long negotiation table with the rest of the Chinese negotiators seated in order of seniority on his left and right.

After negotiator team introductions, it is normal practice for the chief negotiators from each side to give a short speech on the negotiations. This is a good opportunity for the chief negotiators to put forward their key negotiation messages and desired negotiation process to the other side. They can also give some key messages about their key negotiation objectives and aspirations. Some chief negotiators might choose to include some key messages on their key 'bottom lines' and 'must haves' in their speech. However, they should be very careful about disclosing too much of their negotiation bottom-lines and positions right at the start of their negotiations. Each of the chief negotiators should spend time in preparing their opening speech to make them concise and punchy.

Very good advice for chief negotiators in preparing their key opening speeches was given over 1,700 years ago by the famous philosopher Plotinus (204–270) in *Enneads I 6, 9*, when he said that man should "remove all that is superfluous and straighten what is crooked". Although this saying is from over 1,700 years ago, it is still very relevant today.

The Chinese negotiators normally stress at the opening of negotiation and during negotiations, that the key negotiation principle of 'mutual equity and equal benefits' should be applied in all their negotiations and agreements. To ensure that all the agreements reached would be equitable, fair and reasonable for both parties, the negotiation teams might also discuss adopting suitable independent or international criteria. However, these might also lead to lengthy negotiations as both sides would be keen to ensure that these independent, international criterion would not give any unfair advantages to the other side.

Active listening and speaking tactics in Chinese negotiations

For business negotiations in China, it is customary that each negotiation team should have designated spokesman during each of the detailed negotiation rounds. At the opening of negotiations, the chief negotiators should normally be the spokesmen so they can outline their key negotiation messages and approaches.

During subsequent detailed negotiations, different negotiation team members may be assigned by the spokesman for their different specialized areas. Analysis of different Chinese business negotiation experience has shown that it would be desirable not to have the chief negotiator as the spokesman all the time. This would then allow the chief negotiator more room and flexibility to negotiate key issues in the later stages of intensive negotiations.

The nominated spokesperson should carefully prepare their planned speech and remarks before the start of each negotiation rounds. It is important for the international negotiators to realize that whilst it might be common for them to give PowerPoint presentations in Western business meetings, it is not very usual for negotiators to give PowerPoint presentations during negotiations in China. Normally most of the negotiations in China would be done verbally and face-to-face. If they really need to give a presentation, then the international negotiator should discuss with the Chinese negotiators whether they can give a PowerPoint presentation during negotiations. If this is agreed by both sides, then they should ensure that they bring the necessary computer, projector and screen for the presentation as these might not always be available, especially if these negotiations are held away from the main Chinese cities. During their presentation, they should expect that the opposing negotiators might take photos of their slides with their smartphones or cameras. At the end of their presentation, they should be prepared to share their whole presentation file with the opposing negotiators.

Taking the above into consideration, it is normally recommended that the international negotiator who is also the designated spokesman for their negotiation team should prepare their speech in the form of well-planned clear remarks which they then deliver verbally to the Chinese negotiators. It is also be important for the international negotiators to be trained in the appropriate 'storytelling' techniques so that they can then deliver their verbal remarks in a clear and simple storytelling way during negotiations in China. This is particularly important taking into account the language and cultural difference between Chinese and Western negotiators and the need for translation.

During negotiations in China, the international negotiators should actively listen to the Chinese negotiators. They should not interrupt the Chinese negotiators during their delivery and speech until after they have stopped talking. Normally it would be considered impolite and bad mannered to interrupt a Chinese negotiator in the middle of their speech. The international negotiators should make notes of their questions and save all their questions and counter arguments until the end.

During active listening in China, the negotiators should also learn to tolerate periods of silence during the negotiations. One of the most common mistakes of inexperienced negotiators is to rush in to fill periods of silence with some rushed and unprepared remarks. This would not be a good negotiation tactic as experienced negotiators quite often make use of silence as one of their negotiation tactics to apply some pressure on the opposing negotiators. Most inexperienced negotiators are therefore tricked into making some rushed, unprepared comments which they would regret afterwards. Hence it is recommended that negotiators should resist being tempted into making some rushed remarks during periods of silence in their negotiations in China. A simple but effective negotiation tactic would be just to keep silent and not be tempted to make any unprepared comments during periods of silence in the negotiations.

In addition, the international negotiators should, during active listening, also closely observe the Chinese negotiators' non-verbal behaviour, as well as listening actively to their verbal remarks and speeches. Analysis of negotiation behaviour has shown that sometimes well over half of the messages given by a Chinese negotiator are delivered via non-verbal channels. The most common non-verbal communication channels in China would include changes in tones in the negotiator's voice, facial expressions, body language and eye contact.

After the negotiators have actively listening to the opposing negotiator's speech, they would be expected to reply and ask questions to clarify what has been said. It is acceptable during negotiations in China for negotiators to say that they did not understand the points made by the opposing negotiator and to ask for further clarification. In fact, many experienced negotiators use this simple negotiation tactic to try to get more valuable information during negotiations. In addition, applying this simple negotiation tactic also helps to buy more time so the experienced negotiators can think through their response before replying to the opposing negotiators. Another useful negotiation tactic is to try to keep one's questions open-ended and try to use paraphrasing so that the opposing negotiators would then be required to confirm or clarify their meanings and provide more details. Both of these simple negotiation techniques can help the negotiators to get much more valuable information on the negotiation issue from the opposing negotiators which can help them to better develop their counter response.

Chief negotiator's opening speech tactics

At the start of formal high-level business negotiations in China, it is customary for both the Chinese and international chief negotiators to each give a short speech on their key negotiation messages. This would normally take place after the introductions of the negotiation teams to each other. It is an important and valuable opportunity for both the Chinese and international chief negotiators to outline their key negotiation objectives, aspirations, proposed negotiation approach, key negotiation issues, etc.

Each of the chief negotiators should prepare their speech carefully so it covers all their key points in a clear and unambiguous way. The chief negotiator should also have pre-agreed their speech with their top management and corporate sponsors so that they can give the speech on behalf of the team and their companies. The chief negotiator should also share their speech with the rest of the negotiation team prior to start of negotiations.

It is important for each of the chief negotiators, in their keynote speeches, to outline their key negotiation objectives and aspirations for the forthcoming business negotiations in China. They should also share their desired timelines for the negotiations and any required target dates for the agreements. However, they should be aware that giving target dates at the start of negotiation might expose them to the risk of the opposing negotiators applying negotiation time pressure tactics during the later stages of negotiations.

In many negotiations in China and globally, negotiators on both sides often agree to set target dates for their signing ceremonies at the start of negotiations. These would normally be based on reasonable and realistic estimations of how long the negotiations would likely take. Then, later on in the negotiation, experienced negotiators could start to apply time delay negotiation tactics to apply pressure to the opposing negotiators causing them give concessions in order to meet the pre-set target dates.

The chief negotiators should also in their speeches, highlight their views on the key business and ethics principles that the future joint venture should adopt and adhere to. These could include board governance, governance standards, global accountancy standards, codes of ethics, etc. However, the international negotiators should be aware that if they propose to adopt international standards then these will most likely result in the Chinese negotiators counter arguing for

Chinese standards and requirements. Hence the international negotiators should plan for this most likely negotiation scenario in their negotiation preparations. They should formulate suitable responses and counter arguments which they can give during their negotiations in China.

The chief negotiators can also mention in their keynote speeches, some of the more sensitive, commercial and business principles such as shareholding, number of board directors and the nomination of key staff. Analysis of many business negotiations in China has shown that these issues normally require a lot of complex and long negotiation in China between the Chinese and international negotiators.

The chief negotiator should also highlight in their keynote speech, their desired negotiation process and approaches. During business negotiations in China, the Chinese negotiators normally prefer to discuss and agree all the key business principles first. Only after agreeing all the key business principles will they agree for the lawyers from both sides to start drafting the final agreements.

Negotiation opening tactics and lessons

One of the most critical negotiation strategy decisions to make during the opening of negotiations in China is which side should make the first negotiation opening offer. At the start of negotiations there are a lot of uncertainties and a lack of reliable information about the opposing negotiators' true bargaining positions. Hence there is often not enough data to determine what first offers the opposing negotiators would be likely to find acceptable. Furthermore, the negotiators also have to guard against the possible negotiation situation where some experienced negotiation opponents might offer misleading information and responses in an attempt to derail the negotiations right from the start to gain a bargaining advantage.

Considering the inherent ambiguity and uncertainty of most business negotiations in China, many negotiators prefer to open their negotiations in a conservative manner. They often prefer to wait for the opposing negotiators to make the opening offers apart from some key bottom lines which they would want to highlight at the start of negotiations. This negotiation strategy of waiting to receive the opening offer from the other side has both pros and cons. On one hand, it could help get some valuable information about your opponent's bargaining position. However, there might be some significant disadvantages as it might allow the opposing negotiators to seize the first negotiation initiatives plus enjoy the anchoring effects of their first negotiation offers.

Negotiators should balance a conservative negotiation opening strategy against the powerful effects that making the first offers during negotiations might generate significant anchoring effects. Making the first offers can normally help the negotiators to gain control of the negotiation process from the start. There has been a large amount of psychological research on Western and Chinese negotiation which suggests that negotiators who have made the first offers during negotiations are generally be more likely to come out ahead during the subsequent negotiations. However, with the higher complexity and longer periods of negotiations in China, it would be difficult to say with a high degree of certainty whether a negotiator who had made the first offer during negotiations in China will always come out ahead on all the negotiation issues during the subsequent long and complex negotiations.

However, it is important to recognize that in situations of great ambiguity and uncertainty during negotiations in China, making a first negotiation offer can generally have a strong anchoring effect on the negotiations. This would then allow the negotiators to exert a stronger pull throughout the rest of the negotiations in China.

Hence the negotiators on both sides should carefully consider which negotiation opening tactic they would like to use at the start of negotiations in China. They should carefully evaluate the various advantages and disadvantages before deciding on their preferred negotiation opening approach. If the negotiation team are able to find sufficient information during their negotiation preparations to allow them to clearly predict the opposing negotiator's likely negotiation positions then it could be advantageous to consider making the first negotiation offers. This could then help to establish some strong, powerful negotiation anchors right from the start of negotiations.

In addition, if there are some special key business principles and inflexible bottom lines in the negotiations which have been mandated to the negotiators by their top management. then it would be important to highlight these at the start of negotiation to the opposing negotiators. A good international negotiation example would be that many international companies have international codes of ethics and business principles which their board has agreed and published globally. These international company codes would generally be fixed and not open to negotiation by most international Western companies in their negotiations in China.

An interesting example of an actual business negotiation case in China was when the negotiators from a leading international European company insisted from the start of negotiation that their international code of ethics and business principles must be accepted by the Chinese negotiators for their future joint venture in China. The international negotiators told to the Chinese negotiators that the board of the international company had instructed them that they could not even discuss any minor wording changes during their negotiations in China as their codes of practice have in fact been published globally plus accepted by their shareholders and key stakeholders globally. After long and complex negotiations, the negotiators on both sides finally agreed that the future joint venture should adopt the international company's codes of ethics and business principles without changes but the joint venture should also adopt the entire Chinese book on Chairman Mao's quotations without changes. When the top management from both the international and Chinese companies signed their final Joint Venture Agreement, it included in the appendix both the international company codes of ethics as well as Chairman Mao's quotations.

Analysis of different business negotiation cases in China has also shown that the Chinese negotiators normally want to negotiate all the key business principles first before developing the written contracts. However, some international companies and their negotiators would want to first develop a preliminary draft agreement, including all the key terms and clauses, based on international standards and contract forms. Then the international negotiators would table these drafts to the Chinese negotiators at their opening negotiations in China. This Western approach would then result in the Chinese negotiators seeking a lot of explanations and clarifications from the international negotiators. In the worst case, the Chinese negotiators might adjourn the negotiations. They usually say that they would want to first study in detail the draft agreements and prepare their responses before resuming the negotiations. This could then lead to a long delay in negotiation which would often be unacceptable to many international companies and negotiators.

Great advice on having the right opening negotiation strategy was given some two thousand years ago by the famous Chinese scholar, Confucius who said in his *The First Ten Books*, "To attack a task from the wrong end can do nothing but harm." Although he said this nearly two thousand years ago, it is still very relevant for negotiation teams to have the right opening negotiation strategy and plans.

Initial negotiations tactics and risks

During the opening of negotiation and subsequent business negotiations in China, one of the most important negotiation strategies and requirements is for the entire international negotiation team to project the image of a unified, integrated negotiation team to the Chinese negotiation team. In particular, the members of the international negotiation team should not have any open disagreements amongst themselves as would be common back in their international office or during Western negotiations. The Chinese negotiators have been trained to observe these differences and they would be looking out for any disagreements between the international negotiators. Experienced Chinese negotiators would then use and exploit these weaknesses in their negotiations later. Hence it is very important that the international negotiators always try to present themselves as a unified team to the Chinese negotiation team.

During opening negotiations in China, it is important for the international negotiators to use various negotiation tactics to find out who on the Chinese negotiation has the real authority to make decisions during the negotiations. In many Chinese and international negotiation teams, the chief negotiator might be empowered to lead the team but the real decision makers are much more senior. In many negotiation situations, it is not be easy for the negotiators to find out who the real decision makers are during their business negotiations as this is an integral part of both the negotiation team's tactics.

Hence it would be important for the negotiators to realize that in many business negotiations in China, the negotiation team might not be able to negotiate directly with the real, high-level decision makers at the negotiation table. Then the negotiators should try to assess and evaluate the authority of the opposing chief negotiators and negotiators with whom they have to negotiate across the table, so that they can adapt their negotiation tactics accordingly.

In these negotiation situations, one useful and proven negotiation tactic is for the negotiators to structure their key negotiation messages clearly and simply to ensure that the opposing chief negotiator and negotiators report these accurately after the negotiation round to their real decision makers not present at the negotiation table. In these cases, the joint negotiation minutes are even more important as both the chief negotiators and their negotiation teams would be using these to brief their real decision makers and top management, after each of the negotiation rounds.

Analysis of successful high-level business negotiations in China has shown that there could be one powerful and effective negotiation tactic that the Chinese and international chief negotiators use to really find out who would be the real decision maker for the Chinese and international companies respectively. However, the chief negotiators would have to manage this very well and must first get full support and endorsement from their top management.

Both the international and Chinese chief negotiator must first check and confirm beyond any doubt that the real Chinese and international decision maker is not present at the negotiation table and not be part of the negotiation team. Then the chief negotiators can propose to each other that they establish a joint, top-level, executive negotiation steering committee. This top-level, bilateral, negotiation committee would involve the most senior corporate executive from both sides who would have the real decision-making power for the negotiations in China.

The international and Chinese chief negotiators and their negotiation teams would then continue to negotiate and discuss all the various key issues during the negotiation rounds in China. However, they should identify a few key negotiation issues which require the top-level decision makers to review and provide guidance. Both the chief negotiators should discuss and agree what these key issues are and then include these key issues in the joint agenda for the top-level committee. Both the chief negotiators and their teams should then each brief their top executive well before the top-level committee meeting. At the top-level committee meeting, the two top decision makers can discuss the key issues and make the necessary compromises. Then they can give their appropriate new negotiation directions and mandates to their chief negotiators to help the negotiations move towards developing a win–win outcome for both sides.

An example of a successful, high-level business negotiation committee case in China was when a top-level executive negotiation committee was established and worked successfully on the joint venture agreement negotiations for a mega petrochemical joint venture between a leading China SOE and a leading international company. After the chief negotiators from both sides established sufficient good guanxi and trust between them during initial negotiations, they shared with each other that both their real top-level decision makers would not be present at the negotiation table in China. They then discussed various options and agreed to establish a top-level, executive, negotiation steering committee. This top-level, bilateral, negotiation committee involved the most senior corporate executive from the Chinese and international companies who were the corporate sponsors responsible for the negotiations in China and had the real decision-making power on the various negotiations issues. The international and Chinese chief negotiators and their negotiation teams then continued to negotiate and discuss all the various key negotiation issues during many negotiation rounds in China over a negotiation period of over three years.

However, the Chinese and international chief negotiators would regularly identify a few top negotiation issues which would require top-level decisions and input. Both the chief negotiators then discussed these issues and agreed to include these key issues in the joint agenda for the top-level, executive committee meeting. Both the chief negotiators and their teams would brief their respective top executive well before each of the regular the top-level committee meetings. Then at the top-level negotiation committee meeting, the two top decision makers would discuss the various key issues and make suitable compromises on each of the key issues. They would then provide the required negotiation directives with new mandates to their respective chief negotiators. Both the chief negotiators and their team would then try their best to negotiate these key issues in line with their new mandates to find suitable win–win solutions which would be mutually acceptable to both the Chinese and international companies.

One of the biggest dangers and tactical errors during opening negotiations in China is when negotiators are too eager to reach agreement quickly. Many inexperienced negotiators are keen to reach some early agreements but without having suitable alternatives and options to fall back on. Hence it would be important for both the negotiation teams to pre-agree suitable alternative options and bottom lines with their management before a negotiation round in China as this will help to clarify their negotiating positions. It is also important to estimate and evaluate the other party's alternative negotiation positions, strengths and weakness. If a negotiator can determine that the opposite party do not have any good alternative negotiation positions, then this could improve one's negotiating power to achieve a more favourable negotiation outcome in the end.

Negotiations in China can be highly unpredictable and unexpected developments can always occur. In many cases, various negotiation tactics, such as time delaying, might be used by experienced negotiators to delay the negotiations or to throw the opposing negotiators off-guard. The negotiation teams should always be on the lookout for these tough negotiation tactics from the opposing negotiators so they can deal with them appropriately. The negotiators should also try to keep calm and maintain patience during these periods of difficult negotiation in China.

Joint negotiation minutes preparation

After the opening of negotiation and then after each negotiation round in China, it is highly recommended that the Chinese and international negotiation teams prepare a set of joint negotiation minutes. Each chief negotiator should appoint a designated note taker in their negotiation teams. The designated note takers should then work together to prepare, discuss and agree joint draft minutes of the negotiations which should comprise the key agreed items, open items and action points. Sometimes this can involve some more debate and discussions, especially if there are sensitive negotiation issues involved.

After the note takers have prepared and agreed the draft minutes, then the chief negotiators of both teams should formally review and agree these draft minutes. Sometimes this can become another mini-negotiation especially if there are sensitive negotiation issues which the chief negotiators on both sides need to establish clear negotiation positions prior to briefing their top management after the negotiation round.

After agreeing the joint minutes, then both the chief negotiation should sign the joint negotiation minutes, after each major negotiation round. These signed minutes can then help both the chief negotiators and their negotiation teams to brief their respective senior management and corporate sponsors on the negotiation progress and key issues negotiated.

Hence it would be very good negotiation practice that after each major negotiation round in China, the Chinese and international chief negotiators and their negotiation team prepare joint negotiation minutes which summarize their negotiation progress and new findings. Then the chief negotiators could use the joint minutes as part of their updates to their respective corporate sponsors and senior management. They could also discuss and agree any revisions in their negotiation strategies with their corporate sponsors. The chief negotiators should also get the required new negotiation mandates from their management, prior to going into the next round of negotiations.

Chinese negotiation engagements and dinner tactics

After the start of formal high-level business negotiations in China, it is normal practice for both the Chinese and international negotiation teams to have a dinner or meal together. During the meal, it is normal for the negotiators on both sides to undertake informal, social discussions over their family, career, home countries, education and interests. This might cause some of the inexperienced foreign negotiators, less familiar with Chinese culture and customs, to become quite impatient and to wonder what do all these discussions have to do with the formal business negotiations. However, it is very important for the negotiator to appreciate that these informal exchanges are important and valuable for two very good business reasons.

First, the Chinese negotiators use these informal gatherings as an opportunity to get more detailed first-hand information on the international negotiation team. Different Chinese negotiators normally try to collect detailed personal information about each of the foreign negotiators, especially on the international chief negotiator. These might include key information on their background, taste, style, family, interests and ways of thinking. This would help them build a profile of each of the opposing negotiators and these might become very useful in the later stages of intensive negotiations.

During these social engagements, the Chinese negotiators might also ask the international negotiators about their salary and company benefits. This might come as a shock to many Western negotiators as these are not common topics to discuss during Western business meetings. However, they should understand that these topics are common discussion topics in China.

Second, these initial social engagements also help to build good relations and trust between the two negotiation teams. These in turn would help to build good guanxi between the Chinese and international negotiators. This would be very useful, especially in the later stages of business negotiations which would often be tough and complex.

During the Chinese dinner or banquet, it is important for international negotiators to understand that there are very strict Chinese protocols for seating round the table. Normally the Chinese host sits at the top of the table with the most important and second most important international negotiators sitting on either side of him. If the international chief negotiator needs a translator, then the translator normally sits next to him to facilitate translations. However, in some cases, the translator might need to sit behind the international chief negotiator, if there is not enough space at the table. The other negotiators are then seated in order of their seniority around the table.

During dinner, it is important for the international negotiators to actively participate in informal social discussions with the Chinese negotiators seated on either side of them. It is normal to have informal discussions over dinner about family, career, home countries, education and interests, etc. International negotiators should realize that the Chinese negotiators would be keen to find out as much background information on them as possible. In addition, the Chinese negotiators would be trying to build good relationships and guanxi with the international negotiation team. Hence it is similarly a good opportunity for the international negotiators to find out as much background information about the Chinese negotiators as possible and to start to build good relations with the Chinese negotiators.

During a dinner banquet in China, it would be considered good manners for the international negotiators to use chopsticks and to accept the food offered. It would also be fine for the international negotiators to ask for a knife and fork in most leading hotels in big cities in China, plus to leave what they could not eat on their plates. During the meal, it would also be considered good manners for the international negotiators to engage the Chinese negotiators in social conversations. During the Chinese banquet, it is normal to have a lot of toasts of drinks or 'ganbei' between the chief negotiators and negotiators on both sides. Ganbei is somewhat equivalent to the Western 'cheers'. In the past, Chinese negotiators used the strong Chinese white liquor for ganbei or toasts. However, this has now been mostly replaced by red wine or beer.

It is customary for the Chinese chief negotiator, if he is hosting dinner, to first welcome the international chief negotiator and the international negotiation team to the dinner together with a toast. The international chief negotiator should then provide a short response and thank the Chinese chief negotiator and the Chinese negotiation team for their welcome together with a toast.

During dinner, it is also an acceptable custom for individual negotiators to toast the opposing negotiators around the table. The main purpose for ganbei or toasts during dinners in China is to emphasize the positive aspects of the business negotiations and to help to build good relations or guanxi.

There is a famous, old Chinese saying which said that "Good negotiators should fight across the negotiation table but they should also drink across the dining table". This saying is quite old, but it is still very relevant for the negotiations in China to date.

During dinner, the international negotiators should appreciate that it is not customary to discuss official business over food and drinks after a long day of negotiations. Chinese banquets are normally a time to relax, to enjoy each other's company and to build good relations or guanxi. An exception might be if the Chinese negotiators first choose to bring these negotiation issues up during dinner. They might then be trying to pass some important negotiation messages or proposals informally to the opposing negotiation team. Then it would very important for the international negotiation team to review these messages carefully after the dinner and to prepare the appropriate response to give in the forthcoming negotiations.

At a Chinese banquet, after a long day of opening negotiations, there is usually no requirement for either side to make formal speeches unless the Chinese chief negotiator chose to do so. The Chinese chief negotiator usually makes a very short opening remark welcoming the international negotiators and wishing that they would enjoy the food and drinks. This is then followed by the first round of ganbei or toasts. It is also customary for the international chief negotiator to make a short response and thank the Chinese hosts for their good arrangements and propose a second round of ganbei and toasts.

At the end of dinner, it is customary for the international chief negotiator to thank the Chinese host for their good food and arrangements. It is generally a good idea to thank the Chinese negotiators for the positive atmosphere of the opening negotiations and that the negotiation teams look forward to continuing their negotiations.

It is also desirable for the international chief negotiator to learn some basic Chinese phrases and include some of these in his speech. A useful Chinese phrase is "xiexie" which is pronounced as "she-yeh", and means "thank you very much". The international chief negotiator should at the end of his speech propose a final ganbei or toast of thanks to the Chinese negotiation team and he could also say "xiexie" or "thank you very much".

Before the end of dinner, the arrangements for the next day of negotiations are normally discussed and agreed between the Chinese and international negotiation teams. This should be done by suitable members of the international and Chinese negotiation team who have been assigned by their chief negotiators to be responsible for making the detailed negotiation arrangements for both sides. This will ensure that the next round of negotiations will go smoothly.

7 Chinese business negotiation stages and tactics

国以民为本
Guó yǐ mín wéi běn
The foundation of a country is made up by its people.
People are a country's roots.

Executive overview

Chinese business negotiations have become very complex and can take a long time with many negotiation rounds. The chief negotiators and the negotiation teams need to manage the negotiation process well and in line with the required Chinese protocols. They also need to maintain good guanxi and relations with the Chinese negotiators during the long negotiations in China. It is important for the negotiators to assess their negotiation progress in China realistically. The negotiators should also regularly update their senior management overseas on their China business negotiation progress and get their support for revised negotiation strategies and new mandates. The negotiators should also use the appropriate negotiation tactics on making their negotiation offers and counter offers to try to drive the deal negotiations to the stage of final closure.

China business negotiation stages

Business negotiations in China are normally long and complex, involving many negotiation rounds and stages. It is very important for the negotiation teams to be mentally and physically ready to handle the long period of negotiations which can be very stressful and difficult.

The Chinese word for negotiation is 'tan pan' which literally combines the two Chinese characters, 'discussion' and 'judgement'. At the initial stages of negotiation after the opening stage, it is quite normal for the Chinese negotiators to first spend quite some time on evaluating and probing the different aspects of the international negotiators and trying to find out more background information on the international negotiators. The reason for this is that Chinese negotiators need to evaluate quickly and decide internally if they trust the international negotiators and the foreign partner so the two parties can consider working together on their proposed joint investments on a long-term basis. The Chinese negotiators normally only agree to begin serious negotiations with the international negotiators after they have reached a positive internal decision on their trustworthiness during the initial engagements.

The international negotiator should understand this very important Chinese negotiation milestone requirement. They should focus their initial negotiation strategy and efforts on building trust and creating good guanxi with the Chinese negotiators. Their key initial negotiation objective should be to convince the Chinese negotiators that they are trustworthy and that the two parties can work together for the benefit of both the Chinese and international companies on a long-term, sustainable basis.

During the initial negotiation stages the Chinese negotiators normally have many specific questions about the international company and the proposed deal for the international negotiators. These questions normally cover the key gaps in knowledge that the Chinese negotiators have found during their negotiation preparation and competitor analysis. The Chinese negotiators normally want the international negotiators to give them the required answers factually so that they can build a more complete picture of the international company and the proposed deal. The Chinese negotiators usually have already found a lot of information about the international company during their negotiation preparation and competitor analysis. Hence it would be important for the international negotiators to answer the various questions from the Chinese negotiators in the initial negotiation rounds, with accurate factual information, and to provide face-to-face confirmation on the various key areas that the Chinese negotiators want the international negotiators to provide.

Analysis of different Chinese negotiation cases shows that an effective and well-proven negotiation tactic for the international negotiators to quickly build trust with the Chinese negotiators at the early stages of negotiation is for the international negotiators to agree to participate in positive, open dialogue with the Chinese negotiators on their requests for specific information on themselves and their company. Supplying this required information promptly and openly will help the Chinese negotiators to build a more complete picture of the foreign company. This will help the Chinese negotiators to better evaluate the foreign partner's potential capabilities and commitments. This in turn will then support the Chinese negotiators in their sensitive discussion with their corporate sponsors and top Chinese management on whether the foreign company is a trustworthy partner for the longer-term.

Some inexperienced international negotiators might not understand the importance of these special early negotiation requirements. They might instead try to push their own negotiation agenda aggressively right from the start of negotiations in China. This will most likely lead to serious negative feedback and resistance from the Chinese negotiators. In addition, this could lead to poor guanxi and low trust levels creating difficult negotiations in the future.

One interesting example of a high-level business negotiation case in China involved an international negotiation team dominated by international, Western lawyers representing a leading multinational company. They were involved in negotiating a major joint venture agreement with a leading Chinese SOE. The international lawyers spent months during their negotiation preparation preparing a very long and complex draft joint venture contract, based on some of their standard international joint venture agreements. From the start of their negotiations in China, these international lawyers were only interested in pushing their proposed joint venture agreement in English upon the Chinese negotiators. They tried their best to pressure the Chinese negotiators to adopt their proposed draft agreement as the basis for their Chinese joint venture agreement negotiations. They also ignored all requests from the Chinese negotiators to translate the draft joint venture agreement from English into Chinese, plus their requests for additional information about the international company. After some difficult initial negotiation rounds, the Chinese negotiators eventually had enough and told the international lawyer negotiators to postpone negotiations for one to two years so the Chinese negotiation team's translators could translate the draft joint venture agreement, which was several hundred pages, into Chinese. Then the Chinese lawyers would need to review each of the proposed clauses in the draft joint venture contract to see if they were acceptable. In addition, the Chinese lawyers said they would also need to redraft the whole joint venture agreement to the Chinese contract standards so that the joint venture agreement would be acceptable to the Chinese authorities. The Chinese negotiators insisted to the international negotiators that they could only resume negotiations after the completion of all these actions, which could take one to two years. This came as a big shock and surprise to the international lawyers and negotiators. They discussed this with their top international management who did not accept the negotiations being stalled for a few years and the proposed Sino-foreign joint venture being delayed for a longer time. In addition, the top international management were also very concerned about the potentially negative international media exposure if news leaked of the breakdown in negotiations in China. The international negotiation team was then forced to completely change their negotiation strategy. They apologized to the Chinese negotiators on their wrong negotiation approach and made a large concession at the start of negotiations in agreeing to put aside their proposed draft joint venture contract. Instead, the international negotiators agreed to follow the normal Chinese negotiation process in future negotiations. This created a loss of face to the international chief negotiator and their lawyer negotiators. Their international corporate sponsor and top management also replaced some of the senior lawyer negotiators with senior business negotiators. After these initial upsets and concessions, the international negotiation team resumed negotiations with the Chinese negotiation team on a more collaborative, integrative basis. Then after over three years of difficult, integrative negotiations, the international and Chinese negotiators finally managed to negotiate a new joint venture agreement including many associated contracts, which were mutually acceptable to the international and Chinese partners.

Chinese business negotiations mid-stage management

Business negotiations in China are generally viewed as an ongoing, dynamic process which can take time and effort by the negotiators on both sides. After the initial negotiation rounds, the negotiations in China normally move onto the extended, middle stage of negotiations which could involve many negotiation rounds on different key negotiation issues. There are normally long negotiation sessions for each of these key negotiation issues. The Chinese and international negotiators also make appropriate compromises on different business negotiation issues to develop final, win–win contracts, which are acceptable to both the international and Chinese negotiators.

Many Chinese negotiators prefer the long Chinese negotiation process with multiple, long mid-negotiation stages. They normally consider the alternative approach of quickly creating some new written contracts proposed by inexperienced Western negotiators to be more in line with the Western-style negotiation process. The Chinese negotiators normally prefer to discuss and negotiate all the key business principles first with the international negotiators. This might involve many different rounds of negotiations so they can cover all the key business negotiation issues. The Chinese negotiators normally only agree to start developing the detailed written contracts after all the key business principles have been negotiated and agreed by the negotiators on both sides.

There have been some interesting examples of business negotiations in China when Chinese chief negotiators have insisted to the international chief negotiator that the lawyers from both sides should not be allowed to become involved in the initial negotiations of the key business principles, and that instead, the lawyers should be seated in a separate room to be consulted on specific legal issues when required. Then, after all the key business principles have been negotiated and agreed, the lawyers could be asked to develop the draft written contracts in line with the framework on the agreed business principles.

These significant differences in Chinese and international negotiation styles and cultures can sometimes lead to some misunderstandings and unfavourable perceptions between the Chinese and international negotiators. Some inexperienced international negotiators might perceive the Chinese negotiators to be slow, inefficient and taking too long with their negotiations. On the other hand, some Chinese negotiators might perceive the international negotiators as being too pushy, rushing too much, untrustworthy, impersonal and too focused on getting results and immediate gains.

To achieve successful negotiation outcomes in China, it is very important for the international negotiators to balance their needs to achieve quick results and settlement on specific contract issues with the slower and longer negotiation process in China. To negotiate effectively within a Chinese negotiation framework, they need to have patience and work with the Chinese negotiation process. Although the negotiation process in China might take longer, this will eventually help both sides to achieve mutually acceptable, win–win negotiation outcomes on the key business principles. This will allow the negotiators and lawyers from both sides to develop the new written agreements and contracts quicker and within the frameworks of the agreed business principles. The written contracts should then be more easily accepted by both sides and will work better on the local level in the future.

Taking the above into consideration, the international chief negotiator and negotiation team should try to manage the expectations and aspirations of their corporate sponsors and different stakeholders in their negotiations in China. The top international management are often keen to have quick negotiation results so they can sign the contracts in China as quickly as possible. The international negotiators need to help them understand that negotiations in China take longer, involving long, complicated negotiation rounds. It is very important that the international chief negotiator agrees with their international sponsors a realistic negotiation timeline with achievable negotiation objectives and target dates for their negotiations in China.

During the long rounds of negotiations in China, it is very important that the international negotiators continuously update their negotiation strategies and plans with their latest insights into the Chinese negotiator's negotiation agenda and positions. This normally takes the whole negotiation team a lot of time and effort. The chief negotiator should lead the whole negotiation team to undertake thorough post negotiation reviews after each major negotiation round. In particular, they should evaluate objectively which of their negotiation strategy and tactics worked well and which performed poorly. Then the negotiators can revise their negotiation tactics accordingly in preparation for the next round of negotiations. In addition, the negotiators should seek support from their corporate sponsors for any required changes in negotiation strategies and new negotiation mandates prior to starting the next negotiation round in China.

Negotiation team operational readiness management

During the long negotiations in China, the operational readiness of the negotiation team is critical for successful negotiations. It is also very important for the negotiation team to be highly disciplined and cohesive and function as a unique, integrated negotiation team. The whole team should follow a unified negotiation plan with appropriate negotiation strategies and tactics, during their long negotiations in China. This is often quite difficult for some inexperienced, Western international negotiators to accept. They should understand that negotiating in China is different to their typical Western-style negotiations during which the negotiators are often free to voice their own opinions and ideas when they wish during the negotiations.

If the negotiators openly disagree with each other during their negotiations in China, then this is often perceived as a sign of weakness and lack of control by the opposing negotiators. The whole negotiation team should always try to present itself as a unified, integrated team to the opposing negotiation team. The international negotiators should try to discuss and work out all their differences before coming to the negotiation table in China.

The chief negotiator should assign specific roles and responsibilities to each of the negotiators for their negotiations in China. For the long negotiation process in China, this will involve different primary and secondary negotiation roles for each member of the international negotiation team.

The chief negotiator should assign each negotiator as the team spokesman on specific issues during negotiation relating to their specific areas of expertise, such as technical, finance, marketing, etc. Analysis of different China negotiation cases has shown that it is generally a good idea that the chief negotiator is not the spokesman all the time. This will then allow the chief negotiator more room for negotiations and flexibility in the later stages of negotiations.

The chief negotiator should also assign secondary negotiation roles for each negotiator to cover during their long negotiations in China. These normally includes important roles including note taker, observer and intermediary.

The chief negotiator should assign one negotiator to be the official note-taker for the team. After each negotiation round, the appointed note-takers from the Chinese and international negotiation team should prepare and agree joint minutes of the negotiation with key agreed items. The chief negotiators should then discuss and agree the joint negotiation minutes after each negotiation round. They should also both sign the agreed joint negotiation minutes. These signed minutes can then be used by each negotiation team to update their corporate sponsors and senior management. The negotiators should also discuss any required changes in their negotiation strategies with their management, and seek their endorsement of appropriate new negotiation mandates, prior to starting the next round of negotiations.

The designated negotiation observer should closely monitor the behaviour of the opposing negotiators during negotiations, especially their non-verbal communications and body language. They should alert the chief negotiator and the rest of the team to any special or unusual behaviours they observe so they can analyze together and then take the necessary or appropriate action during the subsequent negotiation.

The designated negotiation intermediary plays an important role during negotiations in China, particularly in the later, intensive stages of negotiations. They normally exchange informal messages with the designated intermediary on the opposite negotiation team during breaks in negotiations. They must then share these messages with the chief negotiator and the rest of the team as these can be very relevant and important for the ongoing negotiations.

Business negotiations experiences have shown that negotiations in China often take a long time and can become very difficult. It is normal for both the Chinese and international negotiators to negotiate hard on each of their different negotiation issues. Both the Chinese and international negotiators normally employ various tough negotiation tactics and strategies during their negotiations. Hence it would be important to train and prepare the negotiators well to deal with the difficult negotiations in China.

Chinese negotiation decision makers

During long negotiations in China, it is very important for the Chinese and international negotiators to find out who the real decision makers are in the opposing negotiation team. This is often not easy and it will often require tactful, in-depth investigations.

In many negotiations in China, the real high-level Chinese and international decision makers often choose not to join the actual negotiations in China. Instead, the chief negotiators require that their negotiation teams update them on their negotiation progress after each negotiation round. Then they decide if there should be any changes in the negotiation strategies and tactics. Then the Chinese and international chief negotiators and their negotiation team implement these in their next round of negotiations with the international negotiators.

Hence the chief negotiator and their negotiation team should be prepared that they might not be able to negotiate directly with the real, high-level Chinese and international decision makers at the negotiation table in China. It is important for both the Chinese and international chief negotiators to structure their key messages and negotiation proposals very clearly. This will then ensure that the opposing negotiators can report these important messages correctly to their real decision makers after the negotiation round. The joint negotiation minutes prepared by the teams after each negotiation round are very important as both the chief negotiators and their negotiation teams will use these to brief their real decision makers and top management, after each of the negotiation rounds.

Analysis of actual high-level business negotiation cases has shown that an effective negotiation approach in China is for the international and Chinese chief negotiator to discuss the establishment of a high-level, negotiation steering committee to be attended by the top decision makers from both sides. Some leading international companies and Chinese SOEs have established these bilateral, high-level negotiation steering committees which have helped them to successfully negotiate their major joint venture agreements and contracts. However, it requires top-level management commitment and careful management by the chief negotiators to ensure that the bilateral, high-level negotiation steering committee will work effectively in China. Details on the establishment of the high-level committee and the appropriate negotiation approaches have been described in more detail in another chapter in this book.

Western companies and international negotiation teams often underestimate the degree of linkage between business and government in China. If the business negotiations in China touch on sensitive issues and international trade issues then the Chinese negotiators would normally have to seek support and agreement from relevant Chinese government agencies in addition to support from their own company management. Various government stakeholders at the national, provincial and local levels normally have major input into the business negotiations by Chinese SOEs with international companies.

It is very important for the international negotiators to ensure that their negotiation proposals do not cause any conflict with the national and local government directives and regulations in China. If there is any potential conflict, then this will be spotted and raised by the various Chinese experts from the different China government ministries who review the joint venture agreement and contracts submitted by the international and Chinese companies after negotiation. It is very unlikely that negotiated business agreements will be approved by the relevant Chinese government authorities if there are any areas of conflict with Chinese law and regulation.

The international negotiators should allow the Chinese negotiators sufficient additional time to engage with relevant Chinese government authorities to seek their support after each negotiation round plus on their review of the final agreements after their negotiations. They should also be prepared for long periods of slow negotiation progress in China until the Chinese chief negotiator has received clear support from both the relevant government departments and their senior company management on the different key issues in the negotiations.

Chinese negotiation intermediary role and tactics

Analysis of multiple business negotiations in China has shown that many Chinese and international chief negotiators have appointed one of their senior negotiators to be the informal negotiation intermediary to liaise with the opposing negotiation team. This special negotiation role has been shown to improve negotiation progress and maintain guanxi during tough negotiations in China.

Hence it is highly recommended that both the Chinese and international chief negotiator appoint one of their senior negotiators as the designated negotiation intermediary to work with the other negotiation team. This is a special and sensitive negotiation role in China, but it is in line with the Chinese negotiation customs and practices. The international chief negotiator should select an international negotiator on the team who is familiar with Chinese culture and can preferably also speak Chinese to take the role of the negotiation intermediary during the long negotiations. Similarly, the Chinese chief negotiator should select a Chinese negotiator who is familiar with international culture and can preferably speak the foreign language of the international negotiators. Building the roles of the trusted intermediary on both the Chinese and international negotiation team will take time on both sides. However, this will help to provide an unofficial but useful conduit for informal discussions between the two sides during the long negotiations. It will also allow the informal passing of sensitive information between the two sides via the intermediary channel. This will be an important part of the negotiation team operational readiness in China.

The role of negotiation intermediaries is in line with the Chinese negotiation culture and customs. In the Chinese negotiation culture, there is normally a preference to avoid direct confrontation. Confrontation can often cause personal embarrassment plus loss of face during formal negotiations between the Chinese and international negotiators. The negotiation intermediaries on both sides should speak informally to each other during breaks in the negotiations, e.g. tea, lunches, or dinners. The intermediaries can ask each other for important clarification plus explore different negotiation ideas informally with each other without formal involvement and commitment from the chief negotiators.

Analysis of actual negotiations in China shows that some of the most sensitive negotiation information and proposals are often conveyed informally over dinners or during 'small talk' during breaks in the negotiations. Both the Chinese and international negotiation intermediaries can then become important messengers for their Chief negotiators during tough negotiations in China.

It is very important that both the Chinese and international designated negotiation intermediaries act fully in line with the instructions of their chief negotiators. They should never deviate away from the negotiation team's agreed negotiation strategies and positions as this would risk opening a second parallel negotiation. They should also share the messages and informal proposals urgently with their chief negotiator and negotiation team so that these can be reviewed immediately.

Some inexperienced international negotiators find the negotiation intermediary role in China very difficult to accept as it is not a normal role in Western negotiations. In some cases, some inexperienced Western negotiators might even distrust the appointed negotiation intermediary on their negotiation team. They might even become jealous of their close contact with the Chinese negotiators.

A good negotiation intermediary should always be aware of all the requirements and sensitivities of their role. They should always be available and ready for possible approaches from the opposing negotiators. They must also ensure that they report all the informal messages they have received from the Chinese negotiators, promptly and accurately to their chief negotiator and their negotiation team. The chief negotiator should then evaluate the implications of these informal messages promptly with the whole negotiation team so they can jointly develop suitable counter messages or proposals to be used in the next round of negotiation.

Chinese negotiation relationship management tactics

During long negotiations in China, both the Chinese and international negotiators normally do their best to negotiate hard with each other to promote their companies' business aspirations and priorities. In these long intensive negotiations, it is important for the negotiators on both sides to maintain a good negotiation relationship and guanxi with each other despite the tough negotiations.

An important negotiation guideline in China is for both the Chinese and international negotiators to ensure that the ongoing negotiations never be made personal. Negative, personal criticism of a negotiator on the opposite side should be avoided as much as possible by both the Chinese and international negotiators. Analysis of different business negotiation cases in China has shown that bringing a negotiation problem to the personal level rarely improves the business negotiations in China and can even backfire and create greater problems.

Some aggressive, inexperienced negotiators might have the tendency to want to attack and destroy the negotiator on the other side. These aggressive tactics might be common in some Western negotiations but rarely work in China. It might even result in the Chinese chief negotiator requesting that the international chief negotiator control the aggressive international negotiator. In the worst case, the Chinese chief negotiator might request the international chief negotiator to remove the aggressive international negotiator from the international team as the Chinese negotiators may not want to negotiate with him.

A simple but proven negotiation relationship building technique in China is for the negotiators to 'give face' to the negotiators on the other side during negotiations. An experienced negotiator chooses the appropriate face-giving tactic to use tactfully during negotiations to help promote good relationships and guanxi.

A good example of a simple but effective face-giving negotiation technique would be for the international negotiators to praise the achievements of the Chinese company to the Chinese negotiators during formal negotiations, such as a public award or good financial results. This would often help to build and maintain good guanxi during the long, tough negotiation rounds in China.

During negotiations, it is also important for the international negotiators to show respect to Chinese negotiation customs and practices. One simple but very important negotiation tactic in China is for the international negotiator not to interrupt the Chinese negotiators during their speeches and remarks. Some inexperienced Western negotiators might be impatient and interrupt the Chinese negotiators with remarks or questions, like they often do during Western negotiations. They then discover that these negotiating behaviours are not appreciated much in China. Frequent interruptions can even lead to poor guanxi as it is generally considered very rude to interrupt a Chinese negotiator in the middle of his speech or verbal remarks in China. Generally, it is recommended that the international negotiators reserve all their questions and comments until after the Chinese negotiators have stopped talking.

During negotiations, it important for the international negotiator to observe the appropriate Chinese cultural sensitivities. In particular, the negotiators should avoid any gestures or non-verbal communications which may be considered as rude.

One simple negotiation technique in China is to avoid eye fixing or staring at a Chinese negotiator. Some Western negotiators might like to look straight into the eyes of the negotiators on the other side during negotiations especially when they are stressing a key negotiation point. This may be regarded as a good, direct behaviour in Western conflicts or negotiations, i.e. staring down your opponent during conflict. However, the international negotiators should realize that this might be regarded as impolite and lacking respect in China.

Another rude gesture that Western negotiators should avoid doing during negotiations would be not to thumb the negotiation table during negotiations. Some inexperienced Western negotiators have done this to emphasize some of their key points during negotiations. However, they need to remember that this would be considered as very rude in China. In some extreme cases, the Chinese negotiator could consider this to be a serious personal insult which could result in them walking away from the negotiation table.

During long negotiations, it is also recommended that the international negotiators do not push the Chinese negotiators too hard for a clear 'yes' or 'no' answer unless it is absolutely necessary. In most Chinese and Asian cultures, they normally do not say no directly, as a direct 'no' can be seen as a failure and might result in some loss of face. As such most Chinese and Asian negotiators tend to express their refusal in many different verbal and non-verbal ways. It is important for the international negotiator to actively listen and observe the non-verbal communications and body language of the Chinese negotiators to fully understand their real meaning.

In many negotiation situations, it is important for the international negotiators to use specific 'investigate negotiation' techniques to find out more in-depth information on key negotiation issues from the opposing negotiators whilst maintaining good guanxi. Useful investigative negotiation techniques involve reformulating their questions with different approaches to confirm the real meaning or get the real answer from the Chinese negotiators. Details of investigative negotiation techniques will be described in more detail later in this chapter.

During long negotiations in China, the translator and observer on the international negotiation team can play important roles. They should help the international negotiators to more thoroughly understand the real meaning of the Chinese negotiators' words and non-verbal behaviours. They should provide accurate, factual translations of what the Chinese negotiator has said. They should also help to interpret the subtle meanings behind the words of the Chinese negotiators, based on both verbal and non-verbal communication, as most Western negotiators often find these helpful.

Chinese business negotiation tactics and techniques

During long negotiations in China, the negotiators on both sides normally negotiate hard and try to push their own negotiation positions. They employ various negotiation tactics and techniques during their negotiations in China. Analysis of business negotiation cases in China shows that some of the most commonly applied negotiation tactics include time pressurizing, multiple negotiation issues, reopening issues, etc. These negotiation techniques and tactics will be described in more detail below.

A common but useful negotiation tactic which experienced negotiators often use during negotiations in China and globally is to concede the obvious during a negotiation. This is a simple but effective negotiation tactic. If applied well, these easy wins can also help to build guanxi and trust with the opposing negotiators. However, this negotiation tactic needs to be applied well by experienced negotiators in such a way that the opposing negotiators do not feel they are being treated badly.

Very good advice on the negotiation tactic of conceding the obvious was given by Mark Katz who was the former White House speech writer to US President Clinton. He said, "If you concede the obvious you're conceding nothing, but you gain back credibility. That's a trade you should make every time." What he had said over thirty years ago is still very true regarding business negotiations today.

A common but dangerous negotiation tactic that negotiators commonly use during negotiations in China is to apply artificially tight negotiation deadlines. A good business example for this negotiation tactic is that the negotiators might agree to set an artificial target date for a big signing ceremony for their agreements after the negotiations. The Chinese and international chief negotiators often use the limited availabilities of their top management as levers to set these target dates. The international negotiators often use the availability of senior company directors from their overseas corporate head offices to travel to China to attend the signing ceremony as an excuse to get some specific dates. The Chinese negotiator might also use the availability of senior Chinese government officials and top Chinese company executives to attend the proposed signing ceremony as excuses to set some very tight target dates.

Normally the target dates set by both parties at the start of negotiations would be sufficiently far ahead to ensure that both parties are negotiating in good faith and it would reasonably be expected that they reach agreement by the prearranged dates. Then during actual negotiations, the negotiators on either side might employ various negotiation tactics to ensure that negotiation progress is slower than expected. The various time-delaying negotiation tactics could include refusal to concede on key points, renegotiating different key issues or employing other delaying tactics. So as time drew closer to the pre-agreed target signing dates, the negotiators would then try to force the opposing negotiators to agree to their demands quickly or they would threaten to delay the agreed signing ceremony so as to force for more concessions.

The successfulness of this time pressurising negotiation tactic is dependent on whether the impending signing ceremony would put sufficient pressures on the negotiators on the other side to agree to some crucial concessions so that the signing ceremony could go on as planned.

These negotiation tactics may be ineffective against experienced negotiators as beforehand they would have the necessary support from their senior management – not to be bound by artificial signing ceremony dates in China. Experienced negotiators would normally not agree to a fixed signing date at the start of negotiations in China. They normally make it very clear to the negotiators on the other side that the signing ceremony is scheduled only after the completion of negotiations and after both sides have agreed to all the final contracts. Experienced negotiators would not allow the negotiators on the other side to set an unrealistic target date in their negotiations and then use it as an artificial deadline to force concessions.

Very good advice on negotiation target dates and delaying tactics was given by former US President Abraham Lincoln many years ago. He said, "If I had nine hours to chop down a tree, I'd spend the first six sharpening my axe." What he had said so many years ago is still very valid regarding negotiation deadlines and negotiation delaying tactics in modern business negotiations today.

One of the most common negotiation tactics during business negotiations is for the negotiators to attempt to wear the other side down by relentlessly raising new negotiation issues as soon as the old ones have been resolved. This will often result in long, endless negotiations which are very exhausting for both sides. Another common negotiation tactic is for the negotiators to make some wildly unreasonable demands and also to increasingly resist the counter proposals of the other side. Both of these negotiation tactics are designed to wear down the negotiators on the other side until they become exhausted. Then they might capitulate and accept some concessions during negotiations.

However, the successfulness of these pressurizing negotiation tactics are normally heavily dependent on the time availability and constraints of the negotiators on the opposite side. If the opposing negotiators are under pressure from their senior management to come up with an early agreement, then they might be more susceptible to give into different demands under pressure. However, if the negotiators on the other side are experienced and have obtained realistic negotiation timelines and targets from their management, then these pressurizing negotiation tactics are unlikely to be effective and have little chance of being successful in negotiations in China.

Another common negotiation technique is for the negotiators to reopen or revisit different key negotiation issues after initial verbal agreements during negotiations. This can be a particularly effective negotiation technique if the negotiators see that the other side, normally the foreign negotiators, have moved their key negotiators and lawyers onto other projects after feeling that they have secured the necessary key agreements in their negotiations in China. If the local negotiators reopen key negotiation issues, then they might be able to pressurize the remaining negotiators on the other side to give some concessions.

However, the successfulness of this negotiation tactic is heavily dependent on whether the foreign negotiators allow themselves to be pressurized by these techniques. Normally experienced international negotiators can resist pressures from local negotiators to reopen issues which they have agreed after long negotiations. This also brings into question the integrity of the opposing negotiators on trying to reopen issues that have already been agreed. This could then cause the local negotiator to suffer serious loss of face if they want to press on with their demands. Alternatively, the international negotiator could also apply the same technique and threaten to reopen other key negotiation issues. Finally, the international negotiators could firmly restate their negotiation positions and refuse to bend until the local negotiators agree not to return to issues already agreed.

It is important for international company's top management to continue to maintain their international negotiation team together in China not only after completing all the negotiations but also until all the contracts have been finally prepared, agreed and signed. Some international companies start to move some of their key negotiators away from China after what they thought was the completion of the negotiations. They may have some nasty surprises if the opposing negotiators reopen different negotiation issues to try to force the remaining negotiators to give some concessions.

Good advice on the application of the different negotiation strategies and tactics was given by the famous Chinese military strategist Sun Tzu in his famous historical book, *The Art of War*, many years ago. He said that the successful general, or chief negotiator, should wait and prepare well before charging headlong into battle or negotiation. He said that they should spend their time observing and cultivating change in the strategic landscape. He said that they should study the other side's preparations and resources, then choose the opportune moment to strike, or deliver their arguments during negotiations. Sun Tzu wrote this many years ago; however, some of his advice, especially on preparations and tactics, is still very relevant for modern business negotiations in China between the Chinese and international negotiators.

Investigative negotiations techniques

Analysis of multiple business negotiations in China have shown that it is useful for both Chinese and international negotiators to apply the 'investigative negotiation' tactics and techniques during their negotiations to get more relevant, valuable information from the opposing negotiators. The key objective of investigative negotiations is to probe the opposing negotiators with various open questioning tactics to find out as much additional information as possible on the ongoing negotiations. These could include questions on their real negotiation motives, negotiating positions, plus details of their negotiation proposals. This sensitive information is normally very difficult to get during the intensive negotiations in China as the negotiators would be reluctant to share their real negotiation motives and negotiation positions. Hence the negotiators normally need to ask the opposing negotiators lots of good, investigative questions and then undertake rigorous analysis of different aspects of the negotiations to unearth the required information.

During investigative negotiations, negotiators use various investigative questioning techniques, to ask the negotiators on the other side not only what they want, but also why they want what they proposed during negotiations. Analysis of multiple business negotiation cases in China shows that when a negotiator asks "why?" during intensive investigative negotiations then the negotiators on the other side are more likely to share with them some additional information as this will give them more face. Therefore they might provide more useful information on their negotiation drivers and their negotiation proposals.

An advanced investigative negotiation tactic is for the chief negotiator to arrange for several different negotiators to ask, as part of their overall investigative strategy, various investigative questions from different angles on the proposal from the opposing negotiators. This investigative approach by various pre-selected negotiators can help to increase pressure on the opposing negotiators to yield more relevant information which can be helpful for later analysis.

After an investigative negotiation round, the negotiators undertake rigorous analysis of the different pieces of information they have gathered through their investigative negotiation tactics. In many cases, it is like trying to place together different pieces of a giant jigsaw puzzle. The combination of investigative negotiation with good rigorous analysis should help the negotiators to put together a bigger picture of the negotiation. This will then help them to uncover the real, deep interests and motivations behind their opposing negotiator's proposals and arguments. These should then help the negotiators to identify appropriate counter arguments and develop suitable counter offers.

An example of an interesting business negotiation in China is that during intensive negotiations in China on an important Sino-foreign marketing contract, the Chinese and international negotiators were able to agree on the difficult key pricing and marketing arrangements after long negotiations. However, the Chinese negotiators then refused to grant the international negotiator's company exclusive marketing rights in one of the key provinces in China. This province was one of the key target markets for the international company. The international negotiators tried their best to push their negotiation demands but the Chinese negotiators were insistent. The negotiations were long and intensive, but both sides had their entrenched positions and refused to give in. To try to overcome their negotiation stalemate, the international chief negotiator then tried to solve the major negotiation hurdle by applying investigative negotiation tactics. He asked the Chinese chief negotiator open, investigate questions including, "Why would the Chinese company refuse to grant marketing exclusivity in the key province?" With the good trust and guanxi that developed during their negotiations, the Chinese chief negotiator explained confidentially that their company had previously already agreed with another leading Chinese State-Owned Enterprise to cooperate on the marketing for five years in that particular province in China. The Chinese chief negotiator said that they could not go back on their promise with the other Chinese company as this would then cause them to lose a lot of face in the Chinese system. This was a very simple but important new piece of marketing information for the international chief negotiator and his team. After discussions with his overseas head office, the international chief negotiator was then able to offer the Chinese chief negotiator a revised win–win negotiation offer. The new negotiation offer allowed the Chinese company to keep their promise to the other Chinese company for five years in the particular province concerned. However, after that period they would have to commit to offering full marketing exclusivity to the international company. This new negotiation solution, developed with the aid of investigative negotiation tactics, allowed the Chinese and international negotiators to overcome a major key hurdle in their negotiations. They were able to quickly wrap up their negotiations on the marketing agreement which became a win–win agreement for both sides.

The key learning from this important business negotiation case in China is that 'investigate negotiation' with its various open questioning techniques can help negotiators to gain valuable information during intensive negotiations in China and globally. This additional information can then help the negotiators to develop innovative negotiation solutions which could help both sides to overcome serious hurdles during negotiations. This in turn will help them to reach an agreement quicker on win–win contracts which are mutually acceptable for both sides.

Negotiation assertiveness tactics

During business negotiations in China, it is an important for an international negotiator to be able to strike an effective balance between being keqi, displaying empathy and being assertive in his different negotiation approaches and responses.

'Keqi' requires a negotiator to appear courteous and humble in China. Empathy requires a negotiator to effectively understand the opposing negotiator's perspectives and negotiation drivers. Assertiveness requires the negotiator to clearly express and advocate their own negotiation interests and perspectives. The ability to combine these three important qualities effectively during negotiations in China is an important and valuable negotiation skill for international negotiators.

Different negotiation tactics for negotiators to balance keqi and empathy with assertiveness in their ongoing negotiations in China will be discussed in the next section.

Analysis of different business negotiation cases in China has identified a simple but effective empathy negotiation tactic which can be applied easily across the negotiation table. This will involve the international negotiator showing respect to the Chinese negotiators and asking the Chinese negotiator to present their views and arguments first as this will help to give them face. Then during the Chinese negotiator's deliveries, the international negotiators should show interest and undertake active listening. The international negotiators could also ask various clarification questions to the Chinese negotiator after his delivery. However, these questions should be factual and without judgement. This will help the Chinese negotiators to feel that the international negotiators are empathetic and actively listening to their views. These will help to provide a better atmosphere for the negotiations and build better guanxi.

A simple but proven assertive negotiation tactic for a negotiator to actively prepare for assertive negotiations is by practising their negotiation storytelling in front of their negotiation team members. They should practise saying aloud what they want to say during negotiation. They should ensure that their verbal delivery is clear and as if they are telling a story to their friends. The negotiator should try to rehearse and improve their verbal negotiation responses and storytelling so that these appear more assertive and may be more persuasive. Then the negotiator should make a list of the key points prior to the negotiation meeting so that he or she is able to recall them and deliver them effectively to the opposing negotiators during his assertive negotiation session.

A useful negotiation analysis technique is for a negotiator to objectively analyze their own or the opposing negotiators' likely approaches and responses to the negotiation and any areas of potential conflict. In particular, the negotiators should analyze if these negotiations draw different reactions from each negotiator. This includes tendencies towards compromise, competition, accommodation, or avoidance in the ongoing negotiation. By analyzing and thinking about how the opposing negotiators are likely to respond, this could help the negotiator to improve their negotiating strategies and be more assertive during negotiations.

Negotiation offers and counter offer tactics

Long business negotiations in China normally involve the negotiators on both sides making some initial negotiation offers and responding with various negotiation counter offers. It is a key part of negotiation planning and strategy development for a chief negotiator to decide if they should make the first negotiation offer or wait for the opposing chief negotiator to make the first offer instead.

It would be very rare during business negotiations that the first offer tabled by your opponent might be close to one's ideal negotiation targets. If this occurs during negotiations, then it is very important for the negotiators to use the appropriate negotiation strategy to deal with the near perfect offer.

One possible negotiation option would be to accept the offer and finalize the negotiations quickly. An alternative negotiation strategy would be to make some counter offers and keep on negotiating for some time before finally accepting the offer.

It is interesting to note that a lot of research on global negotiations has shown that if the first offer from a negotiator is immediately accepted by an opposing negotiator, then this can result in the negotiator who made the first offer feeling that their first offer was too good. In many business negotiations, most negotiators often voice many 'if only' concerns. These concerns can range from, 'I should have made a tougher first offer', to 'maybe I have overlooked some important aspects in my first offer.' In extreme cases, some negotiators might even feel that they have under-performed in their negotiations. Then they might try very hard to reopen the negotiations again or try to repeat their first offer.

Hence it is generally recommended that a negotiator should still try to demand some concessions from the opposite negotiator, even if the first offer is very close to one's ideal negotiating position. There is some possibility that the opposite negotiator might offer further concessions. If not, then it is always possible for the negotiator to accept the initial first offer after some hard negotiations. Then the negotiator who made the first offer will likely feel more satisfied. They often feel that they have had good tough negotiations with their first offer and that they have not given away too much in their first offer.

In addition, analysis of many business negotiation cases in China and globally has shown that the negotiators on both sides are more likely to live up to their agreements if these agreements have been reached after tough negotiations. They would be less likely to want to reopen negotiations or seek further concessions in case these would trigger further negotiations or reopening of issues by the opposing negotiators.

In most business negotiation situations, the first offer from the opposing negotiators is very unlikely to be acceptable. In these negotiating situations, then, the negotiator would have to protect themselves from the anchoring effects of the opposite negotiator's first offer. To develop a suitable counter offer, it is important that the negotiators use various negotiation tactics, including to first gather additional information on the opponents' negotiation positions, alternatives and reserve positions. The negotiators might apply 'investigative negotiation' techniques to fish for more valuable information to help their negotiation analysis before reverting with a suitable counter offer. Details of various possible investigative negotiation techniques have been described earlier in this chapter.

In business negotiations in China, it is a useful negotiation technique for the negotiators to try to combine an aggressive counter offer with a joke. Experienced negotiators often apply this technique as this helps to lighten the mood of the negotiation and also helps to preserve face for both sides during the subsequent difficult negotiations on the tough offer. In addition, this negotiation tactic could also help to reduce the anchoring effects of the opposite negotiator's first offer.

In most negotiations in China, the negotiation of offers and counter offers are likely to take many rounds with long, complex negotiations. During these long, complex negotiations, it is important to be continuously aware of the aspirations of the opposite negotiators against one's own negotiation limits and objectives. These long, hard negotiations also help to make the negotiators on both sides feel more satisfied that they have had good negotiations and that they have not given away too much. Hence the negotiators on both sides are then more likely to support and live up to the joint agreements which they have reached after tough negotiations. They are then much less likely to want to reopen negotiation issues or seek future concessions as they realize that this could result in some more tough negotiations between the two sides.

8 Chinese business negotiation

The final stages

船到桥头自然直
Chuán Dào Qiáo Tóu Zì Rán Zhí
As the ship reaches the bridge, it has to align with the bridge to berth.
Cross the bridge when we come to it.

Executive overview

The final stages of business negotiations in China need to be managed well to ensure successful closure of the different key business principles after long negotiations by both the Chinese and international negotiators. Then the negotiators and lawyers need to work together to develop the various written agreements and contracts in line with all the key business principles negotiated. The agreed contracts are normally signed at a big, high-level signing ceremony involving senior Chinese government leaders plus top management from both the Chinese and international companies. This requires careful planning by both the Chinese and international negotiators. Suitable systems should also be established to ensure smooth post-negotiation implementation of all the agreed contracts.

Final stages of Chinese business negotiations

High-level business negotiations in China with leading Chinese companies are normally very complex and take a long period of time. The business negotiations between the Chinese and international negotiator are normally a combination of 'win-loss distributive negotiations' and 'win-win integrative negotiations'.

High-level business negotiations in China normally involve multiple parties involving Chinese SOEs, local companies and international companies. In some complex international deals, there might also be involvement in the negotiations by relevant central and local government authorities. These negotiations would be complicated involving multi-phases of negotiations and multiple partners.

Business negotiations in China typically start with the formal negotiation opening meeting. This is followed by a long mid-negotiation stage involving many rounds of negotiation on different key business negotiation issues. When both sides have negotiated and agreed many of the key business principles, then the negotiations move into the negotiation finalization and closure stages.

Throughout all the business negotiations in China, the Chinese negotiators would normally stress the important key negotiation principle of 'equity and mutual benefits' for all the negotiations. There are often many complex business issues at stake which would make it very difficult for the Chinese and international negotiators to be able to agree them straight away. Many rounds of negotiations are often required over long periods to reach mutually acceptable and beneficial agreements on all the key business principles.

The high-level business negotiations between the Chinese and international negotiators can last several years involving many rounds of negotiations in China and overseas. After each round of negotiations all the new concessions gained plus the new demands tabled need to be evaluated by both the Chinese and international negotiation teams. Detailed analysis is undertaken and discussed with the relevant businesses and corporate sponsors. After detailed analysis and internal discussions, suitable new negotiation approaches should be developed. Then the chief negotiator and his team should present these to their corporate sponsors for support and to gain appropriate new negotiation mandates. After gaining the international top management support, the international chief negotiator and the negotiators can then implement these for the next round of negotiations in China.

In the meantime, the Chinese partners' negotiators will also undertake similar analysis and discussions with their corporate sponsors and businesses leaders. The Chinese chief negotiator might also have to seek support from relevant Chinese government authorities if the negotiations involve sensitive international trade issues or strategic investment areas in China.

The complex, complicated negotiation process in China can continue over a period of several years until the Chinese and international negotiators have negotiated and agreed all the key business principles which both parties consider to be win–win and mutually beneficial. Then the negotiators and their lawyers can begin to prepare and develop the required written agreements and contracts, within the frameworks of the agreed key business principles, for final review and signing.

To celebrate the signing of the final agreements and contracts, a big signing ceremony is normally held in China. The formal signing ceremony for important high-level agreements might be held in the government state guest house in Beijing or provincial guest houses. The signing ceremony is normally attended by senior government representatives together with the top management of the foreign and Chinese partners. There are usually media announcements and media events which have to be managed well by both the Chinese and international parties.

Chinese business negotiation finalization process

In Chinese business negotiations, it is important to realize that the finalization of negotiations can also involve different negotiation rounds and requires careful management by the negotiators. The Chinese and international chief negotiators and their teams should discuss and agree a joint negotiation finalization process at the start of their negotiations. The negotiators should agree clear arrangements for the finalization and closure of the various negotiations. These normally involve negotiating and agreeing all the key business principles plus developing final written agreements acceptable to both parties.

Most important business negotiations in China involve many rounds of negotiations which can take place over several years. After each major negotiation rounds, the Chinese and international negotiators should prepare a joint negotiation minutes to confirm their mutual understanding of the negotiation progress, key issues agreed, plus outstanding issues to be negotiated.

This stage-wise negotiation finalization approach should help both the Chinese and international negotiators to confirm and capture all the key business principles agreed during each of their negotiation rounds. This should help the Chinese and international negotiator to achieve smoother negotiation finalizations.

In addition, these written joint minutes should help the Chinese and international negotiators to better honour the various commitments and agreements that they have already made during each of the negotiation sessions. It should also minimize the chances of negotiators on either side trying to reopen negotiations issues at the end of negotiations and trying to gain some additional concessions from the opposite negotiators.

After completion of negotiations, it is important for both the Chinese and international negotiators to discuss and agree a suitable post-negotiation implementation plan. This should include how the final agreements and contracts are to be implemented in both companies together with suitable progress monitoring.

In addition, the Chinese and international negotiators need to work with relevant communication and training staff in their respective companies to ensure that all the finalized agreements and contracts are communicated well to the relevant divisions of the Chinese and international companies. Clear and good communication of the finalized agreements is important to get the buy-ins and support for the various agreements from different divisions in the Chinese and international companies. In addition, there are requirements to train relevant company staff on the details of the finalized agreements and contracts. These are all important elements in ensuring smooth implementation of the agreed contracts in both the Chinese and international companies.

In addition, it also important for the Chinese and international negotiators to agree how to jointly communicate their joint negotiation progress and finalized agreements externally. This would normally include preparing suitable joint media releases to the outside world and external media. The Chinese and international negotiators should also work with relevant public relations staff from their respective companies to plan the signing ceremony plus to prepare relevant announcements in China and globally.

If the Chinese and international negotiator overlooked the various important negotiation finalization and implementation requirements, then these could seriously undermine the smooth implementation of the finalized agreements and contracts. In the worst case, this might lead to disagreements and disputes between the Chinese and international parties and the re-opening of some key negotiation issues.

Hence it would be important to be quite specific in enumerating and describing both the Chinese and international party's obligations and commitments in the post-negotiation implementation. The Chinese and international negotiators should also consider what could go wrong during the implementation of their different agreements. They should then address these possibilities with suitable frameworks for future post implementation discussions and remedial actions. It is also useful to consider suitable provisions for non-compliance and non-performances including appropriate penalties for both parties.

Taking the different important aspects into consideration, many leading Chinese and international companies have found it useful to establish a high-level post-negotiation steering committee, with top management representatives from both the Chinese and international companies. They would be responsible for reviewing the implementation progress post negotiation and ensuring that all the finalized agreements and contracts are implemented smoothly in both companies with minimum disagreement.

Negotiation finalization and closing tactics

At the final stages of business negotiations in China, the Chinese and international negotiators should focus on finalizing the negotiations and closing the major deal. They need to negotiate all the different key business principles and negotiation issues plus develop mutually acceptable and agreed solutions for each of them. After agreeing all the key business principles, the Chinese and international negotiators should work together with their lawyers to formalize the various agreed key business principles into new written agreements and contracts which are acceptable to both sides.

In business negotiations in China, finalizing and closing negotiations normally involves a process of gaining validation and acceptance by both sides rather than one side forcing agreement upon the other side. Some aggressive negotiators try to close agreements quickly by pushing really hard. This might sometimes lead to gains in the short-term but are most likely to be unsustainable and likely to create losses in the longer term. In negotiations in China, the Chinese and international negotiators normally agree to use the collaborative, win–win approach which helps to create win–win agreements which are more sustainable on a longer-term basis.

A simple but effective negotiation closure tactic which could be used to close deals under the collaborative approach normally involves the negotiator asking the opposite negotiator simple but important questions such as, "What makes this agreement or solution especially attractive to you?" Other useful questions to ask the negotiators on the other side could include "Do you think this approach would work?" or "Would you agree we should do it this way?" These open-ended questions should help the negotiators on both sides to finalize their negotiations on a win–win collaborative basis faster.

To successfully close deals in China, it is very important to consider the possible key barriers to finalizing and closing the negotiations. Negotiation research at leading US business schools has shown that the most common barriers to closing negotiations in China and globally include negotiation reactive devaluation, strategic behaviour and authority issues. Each of these major negotiation hurdles will be described in more detail in the next section together with possible remedial solutions.

A common behavioural barrier to the closure of many business negotiations, particularly during offer-making and reacting with counter offers, involves the quite common 'reactive devaluation' behaviour amongst both experienced and inexperienced negotiators. Negotiation research at leading US business schools has demonstrated that there are some strong human tendencies to reactively devalue the offers from the opposing negotiators. It is quite normal for negotiators to question the offer from opposing negotiators in a negative manner. A common doubt that many negotiators raise to a reasonable offer from the opposing negotiators is to question if the negotiation issue is truly important to the other side, then why should the opposing negotiators be making any concessions during negotiations. These quite common 'reactive devaluation' behaviours during negotiations can prevent both sides reaching reasonable agreements on key business issues during negotiation.

Hence it would be important for negotiators to look at the negotiation offer from the opposite negotiators objectively. They should try to control their normal reactive devaluation tendencies by evaluating the pros and cons of the negotiation offer more objectively. Then they can develop a suitable counter offer which might help them to finalize a reasonable win–win deal with the negotiators on the other side quicker.

Another common negotiation behavioural barrier to deal closures is the 'over cautious strategic negotiation' behaviour of both experienced and inexperienced negotiators. This can be caused by negotiators on one or both sides being unwilling or afraid to table their best negotiation offer to the other side for fear of possible rejections by the opposing negotiators.

This common strategic negotiation barrier can be overcome by several negotiation tactics. One simple but effective negotiation tactic is for negotiators on both sides to build sufficient trust with each other so they feel comfortable to table their best negotiation offers to each other during negotiations. Then the negotiators on both sides can discuss these offers objectively and quickly come to agreement. Alternatively, the negotiators could enlist a trusted, unbiased, independent third-party to help the negotiators on both sides hammer out a deal quickly.

One useful negotiation tactic to promote deal closures during business negotiations is for the negotiators on both sides to discuss their potential 'zones of possible agreement' (ZOPA). The Chinese and international negotiators, after building good guanxi and trust in each other, can try to discuss their potential ranges of agreement for the different key negotiation issues. This is just the potential range of compromise within which the negotiators from both sides could reach agreement on the key business principles being negotiated. The Chinese and international negotiators would not have to reveal to each other their real negotiation bottom lines which they could continue to keep confidential. Then the negotiators on both sides could try to negotiate and make offers and counter offers to each other within their possible ZOPA ranges. This negotiation tactic and approach could help the negotiators to find win–win agreements which are acceptable to both sides quicker.

Another common negotiation closure tactic is to apply suitable deadlines or time limits to the negotiations. Some negotiators try to impose a deadline or time limit at the start of negotiations. However, the proposed timelines should be realistic and practical, otherwise it will be seriously challenged by the opposing negotiators. The negotiators should also beware of the risks of possible negotiation time-delaying tactics which may be applied later in the negotiations by some tough opposing negotiators. This could create more pressure on the negotiators to give some early concessions within artificially tight negotiation time limits.

High-level negotiation tag team closure tactics

Complex high-level negotiation tag team approaches have been used successfully in various actual high-level business negotiations in China to quickly achieve final major deal closures by the Chinese and international chief negotiators involving their top management. This is normally a very complex tactical arrangement which needs to be handled by very experienced chief negotiators with full support from their top management. However, if these are managed and executed well, then the high-level negotiation tag-team approach can be very effective in helping to resolve the outstanding deal breakers quickly and helping to accelerate final negotiation closures on major deals in China and globally.

It is also worth noting that the high-level negotiation tag team approaches have also been applied successfully in high-level international diplomatic negotiations and many bilateral country-to-country negotiations. In these international diplomatic negotiations, the appointed ambassadors and their senior foreign-service specialists negotiate and prepare much of the groundwork for the draft bilateral agreement before the Ministers from both countries meet to discuss and resolve any remaining high-level issues. After closures and drawing up of the relevant bilateral agreements, then the Heads of States of the two countries witness the signing of the high-level bilateral agreements by their respective senior government representatives with wide international media coverage.

The Chinese and international chief negotiators and their negotiation teams need to understand that the high-level negotiation tag team approaches involve very complex high-level negotiation arrangements. These normally require very careful, meticulous planning and faultless execution by both Chinese and international parties. It could be very disruptive if these were not managed and executed well.

Both the Chinese and international chief negotiator should agree all the detailed arrangements in advance with their respective corporate sponsors and top management. Then the Chinese and international chief negotiators discuss and agree all the details of the management tag team arrangement with each other. If this is not done well, then it could cause significant disruption to the negotiation process. In the worst case, it could result in serious loss of face and confidence in the chief negotiators by their senior management.

The negotiation tag team approach needs to be managed very well by experienced chief negotiators but it can be very effective for high-level business negotiations in China. In the specialized, high-level negotiation team approach, the appointed Chinese and international chief negotiators and their team would first try to negotiate all the key business principles and negotiation issues. They would have to try to negotiate hard and come to agreements on most of the key issues. There would normally still be a few remaining outstanding high-level key negotiation issues which might also be the key deal breakers. In that case, both the international and Chinese chief negotiators should fully brief their corporate sponsors and top management on the key negotiation progress and outstanding deal breakers. Each of the chief negotiators should discuss and agree with their respective top management the appropriate negotiation strategies to resolve these deal breakers with the other side. Then the two chief negotiators should discuss and agree a mutually convenient date for a high-level meeting at which the actual top decision makers from both sides could meet to discuss and resolve these key deal breakers, with the support of the two chief negotiators and their negotiation teams.

At the pre-arranged, executive meeting, the top decision makers from both sides, together with their chief negotiator and negotiation team, meet to negotiate and resolve the few remaining key deal breakers. They would normally discuss various potential concessions from both sides on a holistic basis to try to find win–win compromises for the various deal breakers. This should help both sides to reach mutually acceptable solutions to the key deal breakers with acceptable concessions on both sides.

After reaching agreement on all the key deal breakers and making suitable compromises, the top decision makers on both sides should also discuss and agree the process for both parties to finalize the various agreements and contracts for final signing. Then they normally discuss and agree all the important arrangements for the final signing ceremony in China. The key details would normally include the right date for the ceremony, which senior government officials to invite and which senior corporate executives would attend and which top Chinese and international executive should speak at the ceremony.

The key negotiation lesson is that high-level business experiences in China have shown that the high-level executive tag team negotiation approach is a very effective negotiation approach for final deal closures for major joint ventures and projects in China. However, it involves very complex negotiation arrangements which would need to be managed very well by experienced chief negotiators. The chief negotiators on both sides would have to pre-discuss and agree all the arrangements for the high-level meeting well in advance. The chief negotiators would also need to get full support and endorsement from their corporate sponsors and top management. If these arrangements were not done well, then it could cause significant disruption to the final negotiation process plus serious loss of face to the chief negotiators.

An example of a successful case in China which used the high-level negotiation tag team approach involved a leading international company and a top Chinese SOE to achieve successful closure on their negotiations for a major multi-billion joint venture in China. The international chief negotiator and his negotiation team first discussed and negotiated all the key business principles and negotiation issues with the Chinese chief negotiator and his negotiators. At the end of over three years of hard negotiations, there were still a few remaining negotiation issues which were also the key deal breakers for both sides. Both sides had been negotiating long and hard on these outstanding issues, but they reached a stalemate in their negotiations. Then the international and Chinese chief negotiators both discussed and agreed to use the high-level negotiation tag team arrangement to resolve these final issues. Both the chief negotiators briefed their respective corporate sponsors and top management on the key negotiation progress and outstanding deal breakers. Each of the chief negotiators then agreed with their top management the appropriate negotiation strategies to resolve these deal breakers during the high-level meeting in China. Then the two chief negotiators discussed and agreed a mutually convenient date and venue for the high-level meeting at which the true top decision makers from both sides would meet to discuss and resolve these key deal breakers, with the support of the negotiation teams.

At the pre-arranged high-level meeting, the top decision makers from both the Chinese and international companies, together with their chief negotiator and negotiation team, met to have intensive negotiations to resolve the few remaining key deal breakers. The Chinese and international top decision makers negotiated and discussed various possible compromises on a holistic basis taking into account the bigger picture. These high-level negotiation approaches help both sides to reach mutually acceptable solutions to the key deal breakers after making acceptable compromises.

After reaching agreement on all the deal breakers, the top management on both sides also agreed the process for finalizing the various agreements and contracts through their negotiation teams and lawyers. In addition, they also discuss and agree the key arrangements for the important signing ceremony in China, including the dates, which state leader and senior government officials to invite, and which senior corporate executives should attend from overseas, etc.

After the high-level meeting, the Chinese and international chief negotiators and their teams work with the lawyers to quickly develop all the required contracts within the frameworks of the agreed key business principles. The Chinese and international partners then sign all the contracts at a big signing ceremony in Beijing attended by key state leaders. The Chinese and international partners then establish their new joint venture in China in line with their agreements.

Negotiation finalization risks and mitigation tactics

During the final stages of negotiations in China, there are many potential risks which the chief negotiator and the negotiation team need to be aware of in order to manage them well. They should also have suitable risk mitigation measures to deal with these in their negotiations with the Chinese negotiators. Analysis of Chinese business negotiation cases shows the major finalization risks include business licence and scope, disputes, foreign law, Chinese contract norms, etc. The details of each of these important negotiation finalization risks will be described in the next section together with potential mitigation measures and negotiation tactics.

One of the key negotiation finalization risks in China and globally is for the negotiators to ensure they really know the identity of the other contracting party and who they really represent. The negotiators and their lawyers should undertake the necessary due diligence and company searches to check the registered company data and public records in China and worldwide. In addition, the negotiators and their lawyers should clearly confirm the ownership structure of the Chinese company and the identity of the real shareholders. This might take a lot of in-depth investigation utilizing different reliable sources. However, it is important to guard against the potential risks of being cheated by criminals who would set up bogus companies to trick foreign companies into deals and remitting forex contributions into the fake accounts of criminals in China and overseas.

Another major risk for negotiation finalization in China could be unclear Chinese company ownership and shareholder structures. The international negotiators and their lawyers must undertake the required investigations to clarify and understand the Chinese company's ownership structure and confirm the real shareholders. The ownership and shareholder information might be difficult to obtain as there may be many layers to the ownership structure involving Chinese and BVI company entities. To mitigate these risks, it is very important for the international negotiators and their lawyers to work with relevant authorized and reputable Chinese agencies to confirm and clarify this important ownership and shareholder information.

Analysis of business negotiations and contracts in China shows that a simple but effective negotiation tactic for international negotiators to minimize and mitigate against the risks of unclear corporate entities in China is to ensure that international companies should only deal with a legally registered company in China. It would be even more desirable if the Chinese company have also been listed in a stock exchange in China or overseas, such as Hong Kong, New York or London. These listed companies would normally include the top Chinese SOEs and leading Chinese private companies which have been properly registered and listed.

The international negotiators and their lawyers should also undertake their own investigations to include reviewing the Chinese company's business licence to ensure its validity. They should also confirm its official Chinese name plus its address and legal representatives. Prior to contract signing, it is important for the international negotiators and their lawyers to request that the Chinese company's legal representative or deputy initial each page of the agreement separately, together with the international company legal representative, to safeguard against the risk of pages in the contracts being replaced at a later date.

Then at the contract signing, all the agreements and contracts should be signed by the legal representative of the legally registered company in China. The negotiators and lawyers must ensure all the signed agreements and contracts signed in China are also stamped with the authorized company chops of both the Chinese and international companies to ensure that the contracts are legally valid and enforceable in China. There are strict legal requirements and controls on the issue and use of authorized company chops by registered companies in China. The Chinese company's official chop is registered with the China Public Security Bureau (PSB).

Another significant risk for negotiation finalization in China would be the Chinese company's business scope and its limitations. In China, a company's business scope is authorized and granted by relevant government authorities. Each Chinese company would have an approved and registered business scope issued by the Chinese government. The Chinese company's business scope would determine the business activities the Chinese company can and cannot engage in. It is not legal for a Chinese company to exceed their authorized business scope and be involved in unauthorized business activities.

The international negotiators should also realize that the various agreements and contracts that they have negotiated with their Chinese partner might become invalid if the business activities of the negotiated deals falls outside the authorized business scope of the Chinese company. If the Chinese partner knowingly engages in business activities not permitted under its authorized business scope, then they could become liable to prosecution and sanction by the Chinese authorities. Hence the international negotiators and their lawyers must fully investigate and validate the authorized business scope of their Chinese partner company to ensure that they are negotiating within the Chinese company's valid business licence and business scope. The Chinese company's business licence and scope must also have been authorized and granted by the Chinese State Administration for Industry and Commerce (SAIC) plus other relevant Chinese government authorities.

Another major negotiation finalization risk for the international negotiators to manage in China would be to ensure that the Chinese representatives signing the various agreements and contracts negotiated actually have the relevant authorization to sign the various contracts. In China, there are strict legal requirements that commercial agreements and contracts must be signed by the authorized Chinese company's legal representative. In China, the chairman of a Chinese company would normally be the authorized legal representative of the company under Chinese law. If someone other than the Chinese company's legal representative has been nominated to sign the agreements, then proper written authorization must be obtained to verify the signer's authority.

Another noteworthy contract finalization risk in China is that many international companies and negotiators have tried to push the Chinese company and their negotiators to accept standard international contract norms and forms in the business negotiations. There are potentially a lot of risks in trying to do this as Chinese negotiators would normally resist this strongly. In the worst case, the Chinese negotiators would counter propose that the international negotiators should accept the Chinese government contract norms and forms. Most international companies and their negotiators would find this very hard to accept.

To mitigate against the risk of deadlocks in the contract norm negotiations, an effective proven negotiation tactic is for the international and Chinese chief negotiators to agree that they would try to negotiate and agree new joint agreements with specific terms and clauses in a form which would be acceptable to both Chinese and international parties. The negotiators should not try to force each other to use the Chinese or international contract standard forms as this would lead to difficult negotiations with entrenched positions on both sides.

Another finalization risk in China is that many international legal negotiators and lawyers have tried to push their Chinese legal negotiators to accept the application of foreign law in their agreement which can create serious disagreement and tough negotiations. High-level business negotiation experiences in China have shown that this would be a hotly debated issue in business negotiations in China. The Chinese negotiators would be very reluctant to submit themselves and the Chinese company to foreign laws. In addition, the Chinese courts would normally not have significant experience in applying foreign laws. Chinese law normally prevails by default in the law courts in China.

On the important issues of applicable law for key Sino-foreign contracts, a proven and effective negotiation tactic in China is for the international and Chinese chief negotiators to mutually agree to apply Chinese laws together with strong suitable boiler plate clauses on arbitration, dispute management, termination, etc.

Another finalization risk in China is that some international negotiators have tried to push for referring disputes from their future Sino-foreign joint venture to a foreign court which could create difficult negotiations with the Chinese negotiators. The Chinese negotiators would be very reluctant to accept these. The international negotiators need to carefully consider the pro and cons of referring different disputes from their joint venture in China to a foreign court. Whilst foreign courts might provide a more international and familiar environment with internationally accepted fairness and impartiality, the negotiators have to also carefully consider whether it would be practical to resolve all the issues from the future Sino-foreign joint venture in a foreign court overseas. A proven and effective negotiation tactic in China is for the international and Chinese negotiators to agree to resolve their disputes in a mutually acceptable arbitrary court.

One important contract finalization risk in China and globally is that some negotiators go back on or reopen the agreed terms of the deals and contracts. Analysis of business negotiations in China has shown that in some cases negotiators have reopened some of the negotiation issues near to contract signing to force some concessions from the other side. One proven and effective mitigation measure is for negotiators to stand firmly against late reopening of agreed negotiation issues by the opposing negotiators. If these were really serious issues, then they could be escalated to the highest level of both the Chinese and international company to resolve before contract signing. This is normally a good deterrent against some negotiators trying a fast trick of reopening issues to try to get some concessions just before signing.

One major negotiation finalization risk for international negotiators in China is that their negotiated agreements and contracts could be considered invalid in

China if they do not comply with the Chinese laws or regulations. Hence it would be very important for the international negotiators and their legal representatives to get the relevant expert legal opinions to confirm that all the agreed terms and clauses in all their negotiated agreements and contracts are considered lawful in China and overseas.

In China, the accurate and consistent translations of the agreed joint venture agreement and contracts in both Chinese and English could be one of the biggest negotiation contract finalization risks. Some inexperienced negotiators may leave the translators to get on with the translation of the final contracts and agreements without supervision and checks at the end of the negotiations. This is undesirable as poor translations can often lead to future disputes.

Hence it is highly recommended that the international negotiators and their lawyers pay special attention to the translation of all the joint written agreements and contracts. They should have qualified bilingual lawyers prepare all the agreements to ensure that the contracts are identical in both English and Chinese. They should also have the Chinese translation reviewed by an independent qualified Chinese translation agency to ensure that both English and Chinese translations are consistent. It is not uncommon for contract disputes to occur in China due to poor or inconsistent translations between the English and Chinese contract versions.

Another major negotiation and finalization risk is potential breaches to agreements in China. If a breach of the agreements results in damages, then the parties can claim for compensation in China. The normal methods for compensation calculations in China are based on the losses suffered as decided in a Chinese court. A lot of international companies and negotiators find this difficult to accept. Hence the international negotiators should include in their negotiations with the Chinese negotiators suitable boiler plate clauses that specify ways that the parties will calculate potential future damages in case of disputes and also agreed arbitration procedures. These boiler plate clauses should be transparent, fair and reasonable so that they are acceptable to both the international and Chinese negotiators. Then these clauses must be included in all the relevant agreements and contracts after negotiations in China to ensure that they are valid and enforceable.

Chinese negotiation partnership risks and tactics

Joint venture negotiations in China involve in-depth negotiations between the Chinese and international negotiation teams. For joint ventures to be successful in China, it is critical that the Chinese and international partners complement and match each other well. In the joint venture negotiations, the Chinese and international negotiators should consider all the different business and partnership issues required to contribute to the successful operations of the future joint venture. These normally include board composition and governance, management nomination and structure, organizational structure and effectiveness, corporate governance, codes of ethics, key business principles, key staff nomination, management position rotations, etc.

In addition, the Chinese and international negotiators should also consider during their joint venture agreement negotiations the possibility of future partnership disputes and how to resolve them. As such, the Chinese and international negotiators should include in the joint venture agreement the potential risks of the negotiated business partnership in China going wrong in the future for a wide range of reasons. These could include the serious risks that the business agreements and arrangements being negotiated before might become no longer suitable for the international and Chinese partner in the future. Hence it would be important for the negotiators to include well thought out fair exit or divorce clauses in the joint venture agreement to cater for these remote future possibilities and to avoid expensive legal proceedings in the future.

A famous example of a previously successful business case which broke up is the international and Chinese partnership between the Groupe Danone of France and Wahaha of China. The Chinese and French partners had a very serious dispute in China lasting over two years involving public rallies, nasty personal attacks, serious accusations, plus an expensive legal dispute and proceedings. They finally agreed in 2009 to resolve their dispute after two years of nasty disputes. The foreign partner, Danone, agreed to exit the joint venture and sold its 51 per cent stake in the Wahaha Group, one of China's largest beverage companies. In their joint statement, Danone and Wahaha said that they had finally agreed to an amicable split after the long disputes, with Wahaha agreeing to pay cash to acquire Danone's 51 per cent share, which would then gave Wahaha control of their existing joint venture in China. The two companies also agreed to drop their various legal proceedings against each other. This resulted in the ending and termination of a previously successful joint venture between the French food company Danone and its Chinese partner Wahaha.

The Chinese and French joint venture was initially very successful and had grown into a major US $2 billion beverage conglomerate, one of the largest in China. The joint venture also developed and owned one of China's best-known drinks and food brands. The terms of the divestment sale were not disclosed publicly but it was generally estimated that Danone received more than US $500 million for the sale of its 51 per cent share in the joint venture to Wahaha.

The disputes between the French and Chinese partners started in 2007 and dragged on for over two years before final resolution in 2009. In 2007, Danone accused Wahaha of secretly establishing and operating a set of parallel companies in China that mirrored their joint venture's operations. Danone accused Wahaha of using these mirrored Chinese companies to produce virtually identical products to their joint venture. Danone estimated that these would have caused losses of up to US $100 million from their joint venture in China. Danone also accused the Wahaha chairman, Zong Qinghou, of leading the fraudulent companies in China with the help of various senior collaborators with various non-transparent Chinese and offshore entities.

Wahaha chairman Mr Zong retaliated strongly against the various accusations from Danone. He organized top Wahaha executives to hold public rallies and news conferences denouncing their French partner. Wahaha argued that Danone had known all along about the various Chinese ventures but had become jealous at their eventual success and profitability in China. Wahaha also said Danone had been trying to purchase these Chinese ventures cheaply but were rebuffed. Wahaha claimed that Danone had been investing in other Chinese competitors across China, and these were serious violations of their joint venture agreement which contained agreed partnership exclusivity clauses. Wahaha officials refused to allow Danone executives to enter their joint venture buildings and headquarters in China.

There were also serious personal attacks on both sides. Danone launched an investigation into Mr Zong and his family. During the dispute, Wahaha chairman Mr Zong also accused Danone of harassment and of organizing a smear campaign against him and his family. Wahaha also publicly denounced various Danone executives by name and said that these French executives had not played any worthwhile operating roles in their Sino-foreign joint venture in China.

The dispute dragged on for over two years with bitter, public disputes and legal proceedings. The dispute also escalated to the highest political circles and government levels in both China and France. In late 2007, the dispute and its associated tensions had grown so serious that the then French President, Nicholas Sarkozy, brought up the dispute in a high-level state meeting with the then Chinese President, Hu Jintao.

After two years of bitter disputes and legal proceedings, both sides finally announced that they had reached an 'amicable' settlement in 2009. Both companies claimed that the settlement had been the outcome of renewed efforts of both parties to put an end to their dispute. They said that they had productive negotiations which took place in the spirit of mutual respect. They also said that they received good support from both the Chinese and French governments in resolving their dispute.

After the settlement, Mr Zong Qinghou, the chairman of Wahaha, said that Chinese companies would be willing to cooperate and grow with the world's leading companies on the basis of equality and reciprocal benefit. Danone's chairman and chief executive, Franck Riboud, said that the Danone and Wahaha partnership had helped to build a strong and respected brand in the Chinese beverage industry.

The key learnings from this serious partnership dispute between these leading French and Chinese companies demonstrate the importance for the Chinese and international negotiators to consider during their joint venture negotiations the possibility of potential future partnership disputes. As such, they should negotiate suitable exit and arbitration clauses in their joint venture agreement to avoid possible future disputes and expensive legal proceedings.

In joint venture agreement negotiations, it is very important that the Chinese and international negotiators negotiate and agree suitable arbitration clauses for their new joint venture agreement and associated contracts. Under Chinese law, the Chinese and international partners are free to choose binding arbitration as a dispute resolution mechanism. Normally arbitrations between the Chinese and international partners are quicker and less expensive than litigation and suing each other in court. To ensure there is proper access to arbitration, the suitable arbitration clauses must be included in the agreed commercial agreements after negotiations.

Specifically, the international and Chinese negotiators should ensure that the agreed arbitration clause, in their joint venture agreement plus all their other associated contracts, should state that both sides will agree to arbitration in case of serious disputes. The clause should also stipulate which future disputes will be subjected to arbitration in the future. It is also very important to negotiate and agree the appropriate arbitration commission that would be acceptable to both the Chinese and international companies. China is a party to the New York Convention on the Recognition and Enforcement of Arbitral Awards (New York Convention). This means that most foreign awards obtained in arbitration can be enforced in China as long as the arbitration clause is compliant with Chinese legal requirements.

For arbitration within China, the China International Economic and Trade Arbitration Commission (CIETAC) has been one of the most frequently selected arbitration forums. Foreign or international arbitration forums can be used by the Chinese and international companies for arbitration. However, this would have to be first negotiated and agreed by the international and Chinese negotiators. Then the mutually agreed international arbitration body must be included and stipulated in the arbitration clause in the final signed agreements for this to be legal and enforceable.

Business negotiations are never 'over'

In China, and also in any other country, it is essential that negotiators are aware that negotiators on the opposite side may try to reopen issues or to renegotiate agreed issues at the final stages of negotiations to gain some more concessions. In the worst cases, some negotiators might even try to reopen negotiation issues just moments before the planned contract signing ceremony to force some last-minute concessions.

Hence, it is very important when negotiators are finalizing and closing negotiations and agreements that they first confirm that the key provisions have been agreed so that there are no surprises. At this stage, negotiators on both sides will still need to discuss and sell their agreed deal to their corporate sponsors and senior management. These internal management and stakeholder discussions on the various proposed contracts could indeed result in the Chinese or international negotiators having to come back with some further requests for negotiations, if there were any last-minute requests from their senior management or powerful internal stakeholders.

If the negotiators from one party do have to come back to renegotiate some key business principles or terms after initial agreements, then it would be important for the negotiators to confirm if this was a genuine request from their top management. It would often be very difficult for the negotiators on the other side to know whether they were being misled and if the need for renegotiations and revisions were legitimate. It would be important for the negotiators to resist being pressurized into granting any last-minute, unreciprocated concessions during the final stages of negotiations. They should also highlight the important key Chinese negotiation principle of 'equity and mutual benefit' to ensure that any last-minute concessions would apply equally to both parties. Generally, it is strongly recommended that negotiators should be very firm in dealing with any requests from the opposing negotiator for last-minute changes made during contract finalization or just before contract signing. If the negotiators from one side would be reopening some issues and asking for major new concessions, then the negotiators on the other side should always ask them to fully justify these requests with comprehensive reasons. This would help to flush out the true motives and backgrounds for the opposing negotiators wanting to reopen negotiations and getting last minute concessions. In addition, the tough response would also help to discourage further requests to reopen other issues.

In this situation, the negotiators should say they want to consider making similar requests to get equally favourable adjustments based on the key Chinese principle of mutual equality and win–win negotiations. This will help to flush out the true motives of the opposing negotiators wanting to reopen negotiations and getting last minute concessions. In addition, this tough response will also help to discourage further requests to reopen negotiations.

Generally, these last-minute revisions and negotiations lead to tough and difficult negotiations between the negotiators on both sides. In addition, it could also lead to poor guanxi and lowering of trust between the sides which would not be good for the future joint venture. In these difficult circumstances, experienced negotiators often use humour to diffuse the tension and to maintain the good guanxi that had been built over the long negotiations.

Very good advice on humour was given by the famous US author Mark Twain in the early twentieth century. He said: "The human race has only one really effective weapon and that is laughter." What he had said many years ago is still very true today. Experienced negotiators often use humour and laughter as part of their negotiation tactics to diffuse tense negotiation situations in China. This allows them to maintain good guanxi and to find win–win solutions for very difficult negotiation issues.

Chinese post-negotiation implementation tactics

After completing the extended negotiations in China and agreeing all the key contracts, the negotiators on both sides should discuss and agree suitable post-negotiation implementation systems and processes to ensure that all their final agreed contracts can be implemented smoothly and not fail due to lack of attention.

Analysis of high-level negotiations in China and globally suggests that there are proven best practices which can be useful to apply to negotiations in China. A very useful negotiation best practice is that the Chinese and international negotiators discuss and develop suitable joint 'post-negotiation action checklists' which contain all the required post-negotiation implementation action items. The negotiators should also assign suitable action parties for the various important action items. This post-negotiation checklist is an important internal document between the two partners as they can use it for post-negotiation implementation monitoring.

The negotiators should also discuss and draft a post-negotiation implementation schedule which clearly delineates the agreed implementation timeline and schedule for the key agreed action items, with defined target dates.

In addition, the Chinese and international negotiators should discuss what will happen in cases where there is any non-compliance by either party in completing their agreed actions. They would also need to formulate a jointly agreed process to implement remedial actions for any non-compliance by either party.

High-level business negotiation experience suggested that the Chinese and international negotiators should also develop a jointly agreed timetable for the planned implementation review meetings. These meetings should involve the senior management from both sides and also the senior management from the new joint venture. The key purposes of these high-level post negotiation management meetings would be to review the progress of the various agreed actions and to discuss suitable remedial actions for any non-compliance.

These regular meetings and discussions will then allow both parties and the new joint venture to allocate sufficient resources with appropriate time and money to attend to the proper implementation of the negotiated contracts and agreements. In addition, suitable resources on both sides must be made available for monitoring the progress and compliance by both parties on the various agreements.

Analysis of best post-negotiation implementation practices by some leading companies has shown that it is useful for the international and Chinese companies to put in place some formal consultative process for post-negotiation implementation. This could include a 'hotline' between the top executives of the Chinese and international partner companies. This would then help to support a process by which the two parties could communicate directly with each other whenever the need arises in the future in addition to their regular meetings.

Another good post-negotiation practice worth considering would be that many leading international and Chinese companies have agreed to form a 'joint, high-level, post-negotiation implementation steering committee'. This joint committee would normally include the top corporate sponsors for the joint venture from both the international and Chinese companies plus their respective chief negotiators and senior managers. They should meet regularly to discuss and review the post-negotiation implementation progress. They could also discuss suitable remedial action for areas that were not progressing as planned and agreed remedial action for both parties.

Negotiation agreements and contracts finalization

At the end of negotiations in China, it is very important for the international and Chinese negotiators to commit all the key business principles agreed in their negotiations into formal written agreements. These agreements should capture all the key points agreed in the various rounds of negotiations. The agreements should contain clearly written clauses for all the key agreed business principles which have to be agreed by the negotiators on both sides so that these agreements are ready for signing.

Business negotiation experiences in China and globally show that a large percentage of business disputes have arisen after negotiations because of a misunderstanding between parties. A well proven negotiation best practice is that clearly written agreements would help to prevent future misunderstandings and disputes. Furthermore, the process of writing the agreements would often force the negotiators from both parties to focus and confirm all the key agreed negotiation points. Finalizing the written agreements is an important step in making them legally enforceable after completion of the negotiations.

Analysis of high-level negotiations and contract preparation experiences in China and globally has shown that it would usually be advantageous for the international negotiators to try to assume responsibility for preparing the initial draft agreements. This would normally be a better negotiating position than letting the Chinese negotiation team prepare the drafts and then the international negotiation team being put in a position of having to review and comment on the draft translated agreements from the Chinese negotiators and lawyers.

The final written draft agreements should cover all the key agreed negotiated business principles, terms and clauses. The agreements should be clearly written, well organized and simple, as many agreements have failed due to being too complicated. The legal clauses should be written in an objective and non-partisan manner.

If possible, the agreements should also include some aspirational language about the new joint venture and the future cooperation. A good negotiation example would be that the agreements should contain some clauses clearly expressing the goals and aspiration of both the Chinese and international parties in their new future joint venture. In addition, it should highlight the key purposes of the agreement and the spirit in which the agreements would be made.

The final agreements should also include all the key agreed issues which the negotiators on both sides have specifically agreed not to be covered by the agreements. These exclusions would be particularly important to be included to avoid potential future disputes and misunderstandings between the two parties.

The agreements should also contain a clear timeline with key milestones for implementation plus key performance targets. There should be clear focal points on both sides responsible for compliance, monitoring and enforcing performance.

The legal clauses in the final agreements should be clear and concise with no ambiguous wordings which could be misinterpreted. It is important for the technical and language experts to review all the drafts to ensure that the written agreements accurately reflect the parties' negotiated outcomes and agreements.

In China, business negotiation experience has shown that the agreements would normally have to be in both Chinese and English, or in the language of the international party. Accurate translations of the agreements is critical. It is very important that the translators on both the negotiation teams should review all the agreements to ensure that the final documents accurately reflect the parties' negotiation outcomes in both the English and Chinese translations.

In addition, when an agreement is written both in Chinese and English, then it would be necessary to specify which language would be the official language of the contract or whether both languages enjoy equal effect. In China, it would be common practice that the Chinese language is agreed to be the official language. However, some leading international companies have also succeeded in agreeing with their Chinese partners that both Chinese and English have equal effect. In addition, Chinese courts and international arbitral bodies might also deem the English language agreement to be valid if the contracts were to be presented to the courts in the future.

It is also important for the international negotiators to discuss and pre-agree with the Chinese negotiators the acceptable written formats for the agreements. It is important to note that the acceptable signed agreement formats often vary greatly between the West and the East. For most European and international companies, a PDF containing a signed contract, scanned and sent via email, would often be acceptable. However, Chinese companies would normally require a hard copy of the signed and sealed agreement to be physically delivered to them to lodge in their company safes.

Prior to the final signing of the contracts, it is highly recommended that the negotiators and lawyers on both sides should review all the relevant documents of the other company to ensure all these would be in order. They should verify both companies' registered names, addresses and their legal representatives. In addition, both parties should confirm who are the compaies' legal representatives and that they have been empowered to sign the agreements by the boards. It would also be important to have clear written evidence on the explicit decisions from the boards of both the international and Chinese companies approving all the contracts to be signed and authorizing their legal representatives to sign them.

In China, each registered company would have a specific legal representative for the company together with an authorized company seal. It is customary in China that both the Chinese and international chief negotiators are mandated by the top management of each of their companies to initial each page of final agreements to certify that the agreements are ready for final signing. At the formal signing, the legal representatives from both the Chinese and international companies should both signed the final agreements and contracts.

At the official signing of the agreements in China, it would be important that after all the required signatures, all the agreements and contract should also be sealed with the authorized company chops. Many foreign and international companies do not normally use company chops. However, for most Chinese companies, the authorized company chop would still be considered to be the most important requirement for the agreements to become valid. In China, the common practice would be to always keep the authorized company chop in the company safe for safe keeping. There would be formal control procedures for authorized persons to take the company chop out of the company safe for the contract signing and sealing. After signing and sealing the contracts, the authorized company chop would normally be put straight back into the company safe and locked up by authorized persons.

In China, all official contracts should normally have been stamped with both the company chops or seals and bear both the legal representative's signatures. In some rare situations, a contract sealed with a company chop but not signed could also be consider valid too if both sides have agreed to this. Historically in China, a seal would be considered more binding whilst a signature is normally less significant. However, the modern Chinese Contract Law has now stipulated that a written contract could be considered legally binding when it has been signed or sealed by the legal persons from each party.

Chinese contract-signing ceremony

In China, to celebrate the signing of major agreements and contracts, the international and Chinese partners would normally hold a big signing ceremony at a special venue in China. They would normally invited state leaders, central and local government leaders plus senior executives from both the international and Chinese companies to attend. After the signing ceremony, there would normally be a big Chinese banquet to celebrate the signing.

These signing ceremonies would normally require detailed discussions and planning by both the international and Chinese partners. Key arrangements that would need to be discussed and agreed by both sides would normally include what would be the right venue for the signing ceremony, which state leader to invite, which key central and local government representatives to invite, which senior executives from both the Chinese and international companies should attend, who should speak, plus what should be the gifts for the guests and what would be Chinese Banquet after the signing ceremony, etc.

The formal signing ceremony for important high-level agreements in Beijing would normally be held in the Government State Guest House in Beijing or in leading hotels in Beijing. If the signing ceremony were to be held in the provinces, then it could be held in the Provincial Guest Houses or leading hotels in the province concerned.

The signing ceremony would normally be attended by senior central and local government representatives together with the top management of the foreign and Chinese Partners. If the agreements were of sufficient high level interests, then an appropriate state leader might be invited to attend to witness the signing.

Prior to the signing ceremony, there would normally be a lot of formal work that the negotiators from both sides should undertake. It would be very important that the negotiators and lawyers on both sides should check each company's business licence, especially the name and business scope, to ensure that all would be in order. In addition, both companies must confirm that their legal representatives have been empowered by their boards to sign the final agreements and contracts. There should be suitable board resolutions from both the international and Chinese company's boards approving all the contracts for signing and authorizing the legal representatives to sign them.

Prior to the formal signing ceremony, the chief negotiators from both the Chinese and international partners should confirm in writing to their respective legal representative and top management that all the agreements and contracts would be in order and would be ready for their signing. Then the legal representatives from both the Chinese and international companies should examine all the contracts and sign their initials on each page of the agreed contracts to ensure that they would be ready for final signing and chop. In many cases, the legal representatives will empower the chief negotiators on both sides to initial all the contracts for them as these could involve initialling hundreds of pages of contracts. These initialized contracts would then be locked up in an authorized company safe. These initialled contracts would only be taken out of the company safe by authorized persons just before the signing ceremony so that they are ready for the final signing and stamping by the authorized company chops at the signing ceremony.

At the official signing ceremony of the agreements in China, designated masters normally briefly introduce the key state leaders and VIPs in attendance. The state leader would witness the signing of the key joint venture agreement in front of the guests and media. After signing, all the agreements and contract should be sealed with the authorized company chops by authorized personnel from both sides. After the signing and sealing of all the contracts, the company chops and the signed contracts would normally be taken back into the company safe for safe storage.

A good example of a successful Sino-foreign joint venture signing ceremony was held in 2000 by the CNOOC Shell Petrochemical Joint venture Limited CSPCL. It was the largest Sino-foreign joint venture in China with US \$4.2 billion of investment from Shell and CNOOC. The Chinese and international partners jointly prepared their Feasibility Report and submitted it in 1996 for central government approval. After reviews by the relevant central government department, it was approved in 1997. Then after over three years of hard and complex negotiations by the Chinese and international negotiators, the joint venture agreement plus associated supplementary contracts and local contracts were signed in two large separate signing ceremonies. The joint venture contract and associated contracts were signed first in a major signing ceremony held in the state guest house in Beijing. It was attended by the then Chinese Premier, Li Peng, who witnessed the signing of the joint venture agreement by top executives from CNOOC and Shell Chemicals. Then a second signing ceremony for the key local contracts was held in Huizhou attended by leading local government leaders and officials plus senior Chinese and international company executives. After each of the signing ceremonies, there were large Chinese banquets with accompanying performances.

After the signing ceremony in 2000, the new CSPCL joint venture was then successfully established in Huizhou Municipality, Guangdong Province to build the mega US \$4.2 billion Nanhai Petrochemical Project. The new petrochemical complex included various advanced chemical plants compromising of a new ethylene cracker with downstream chemical and derivative plants. It was a 50/50 joint venture with CNOOC and Shell each holding a 50 per cent share in the new joint venture.

In 2002, the final investment decision was taken by both CNOOC and Shell to go ahead with the mega US \$4.2 billion Nanhai petrochemical project. The mega complex was completed successfully and commissioned on schedule in 2006.

The CSPCL joint venture has been working successfully. Their major petro-chemical and chemical complexes have been operating well. The complex compromised a 950 KTPA Ethylene Cracker, 165 KTPA Butadiene unit, 250 KTPA Low Density Polyethylene (LDPE), 260 KTPA High Density Polyethylene (HDPE), 260 KTPA Polypropylene (PP), 350 KTPA Mono-Ethylene Glycol (MEG), 640 KTPA Styrene Monomer, 290 KTPA Propylene Oxide (PO), 170 KTPA of Polyols and 60 KTPA Propylene Glycol. The Chinese and international partners have been discussing and planning further expansions for the successful joint venture in China.

Chinese contract-signing banquets and tactics

After important signing ceremonies in China, the Chinese and international partners normally hold a big Chinese banquet to celebrate the signing. It is an important occasion for the top executives from both the Chinese and international company to attend. There would also be good opportunities to build good guanxi with senior leaders and VIPs.

The seating in the Chinese banquet would generally be all pre-arranged. It would normally be an honour to be invited to be seated at the top table. The most important guests would be seated on the right or left side of the Chinese host on the top table. The Chinese host would normally start the banquet with toasts to the VIPs and leaders.

During the banquet, it would be normal for all guests to take a wine glass and walk around the room toasting other important guests and VIPs. For important VIPs, it would be quite normal to have long queues of guests waiting to toast and ganbei with them.

It is also a good time for the international and Chinese negotiators and partners to compliment each other on the successful negotiations and contract signing. It would be important to take the time and effort to compliment the other negotiators on the successful negotiation outcomes after the hard negotiations. This would help to maintain better long-term relations and guanxi, which could help with resolving future difficulties in the implementation of the various agreements post negotiation.

Analysis of high-level negotiation cases in China has shown that creating goodwill and guanxi during the concluding steps of negotiations is of great value, as it can help the negotiators and management in the setup of the new joint venture plus resolving various post-negotiation implementation issues. In addition, the successful negotiations and signing of the agreements, might also path the way for senior executives to consider more future cooperation between the Chinese and international partners.

After a few rounds of toasts, the VIPs and guests would normally sit down to start eating and to enjoy some of the performances. It would also be a good time for them to engage the other VIPs and guests at their table on various informal discussions, small talks and further toasts.

At the end of the banquet, the Chinese host would normally make the final toast. It usually includes good wishes such as 万事如意 (wanshi ruyi), which literally means to hope all the guests will get all they have been wishing for, or 一路顺风 (yilu shunfeng), which literally means bon voyage or safe travels for all the guests.

Then it would be customary for the top foreign executive from the international company to thank their Chinese host for the excellent banquet and to wish both parties successful cooperation in their future joint venture and cooperation.

Agreements communication, announcement and engagement

At the end of successful negotiations and for the signing ceremony in China, it would also be important for the international and Chinese parties to jointly prepare and agree on some joint public media messages and engagements. The Chinese and international negotiators should work together with their public relations and external relations staff from the two companies to agree on how they would like to communicate their negotiation progress and the key non-confidential points of their agreements to their key constituencies, important stakeholders and the public at large.

Their joint public message should normally identify the international and Chinese companies involved in the new joint venture. It should provide a concise but accurate summary of the various agreements and contracts negotiated and agreed. The public message should also include the key goals to be realized by the new joint venture. It would be important that the Chinese and international companies compliment each other on reaching their joint accord after tough negotiations. The joint announcement should also give a clear public message that both parties see a very positive future for their future joint venture and cooperation as a result of the agreements successfully completed.

It is recommended that the international and Chinese parties should take extreme care on considering the possible different views and interests of the public audience who would be receiving the joint public messages. Both companies should also take into account relevant regulatory or oversight obligations on their joint public messages.

The international and Chinese parties might also like to consider organizing a joint public information campaign on the agreements and the planned future joint venture. These will help the companies and the future joint venture to engage with their key stakeholders, constituencies, local community leaders and residents. The Chinese and international partners would normally use appropriate professional PR agencies to organize and support their planned media and PR campaign for the new joint venture in China and globally.

Part IV
Chinese joint venture negotiations and establishment

9 Chinese joint venture agreement negotiations

美名胜过美貌

měi míng shèng guò měi mào

A respected brand name is always better than just beautiful packaging.
Good reputation lasts forever.

Executive overview

An understanding of the relevant policies and legal requirements in China is important for new joint ventures and foreign investments. The Chinese government has been implementing extensive policies to attract Foreign Direct Investments (FDIs) into China and to establish different Sino-foreign joint ventures. These have resulted in high amounts of foreign investment flowing into China over the last few decades. These investments have in turn led to extensive negotiations between Chinese and international partners negotiation teams on the establishment of many Sino-foreign Joint ventures and Foreign Invested Enterprises (FIEs) in China. Joint venture negotiations are usually long, complex, and involve a lot of difficult negotiations. The final agreements need to meet the extensive requirements of the different permitted joint venture and FIE contract forms and models stipulated by the Chinese government and laws. The various joint venture requirements plus the specific contract forms and models will be reviewed and analyzed in this chapter together with relevant business negotiation case examples.

China's foreign investment policy, laws and regulation overview

The Chinese government has been introducing an extensive framework of foreign investment laws and regulations in order to encourage foreign investments into China. China has implemented these regulations at the central, provincial and municipal levels to meet their high-level strategic policy objective of attracting and promoting foreign investments in China.

These Chinese joint venture laws and regulations have also been evolving and changing in response to business requirements and changes. Hence the foreign companies doing business or investing in China need to closely observe the new foreign investment laws and regulations in China most likely to affect them. The main laws and regulations for foreign investments in China and establishing Sino-foreign joint ventures in China currently include the following:

- The law of PRC on Chinese-Foreign Equity joint ventures and its implementation regulations.
- The law of PRC on Chinese-Foreign Contractual Joint Ventures and its implementation regulations.
- The law of PRC on Wholly Foreign-Owned Enterprise and its implementation regulations.
- The law of PRC on Foreign-Invested Enterprises, the income tax and its implementation regulations.
- Industrial Catalogue for Foreign Investment.
- Regulations for Guiding the Direction of Foreign Investment (Guiding Regulations).
- Provisions on Guiding Foreign Investment Direction.
- Catalogue of Advantageous Sectors for Foreign Investment in Central and Western Regions.
- The law of PRC on the Protection of Taiwan Compatriots' Investment.

The above key laws and regulations stipulated by the PRC Government also apply to the various investments from Hong Kong, Macao and Taiwan into China mainland.

One of the Chinese government's top policy objectives would be to encourage FDI into certain encouraged priority industrial sectors. There would also be specific restrictions on FDIs into some specific sensitive and strategic sectors in China that foreign investors must be aware of. These normally include proposed new investments into sensitive and strategic areas covering military or national security.

The key national regulations for foreign investments in China include the 'Regulations for Guiding the Direction of Foreign Investment. (Guiding Regulations). The Guiding Regulations have categorized all the foreign investment projects into one of the four types of projects, which include 'encouraged projects, permitted projects, restricted projects and prohibited projects'.

The four different key project classifications under the Chinese government's 'Guiding Regulations' have major impacts on the feasibility of all proposed new foreign investments and projects in China. Two of the most important classes of projects are the 'encouraged' and 'permitted' projects. The key differences between 'encouraged and permitted projects' in China would be that 'encouraged projects' include projects or investments that the PRC Government would be encouraging a foreign investor to invest in with Chinese partners. These encouraged projects are normally also entitled to preferential China tax treatment on the import of capital goods if certain conditions are met under the existing foreign investment promotion policies. However, 'permitted projects' is not normally eligible for these preferential tax relief incentives.

In addition, foreign investors should realize that any proposed foreign investments in the 'restricted projects' class normally have to undergo extensive studies and reviews by the various state government and provincial-level departments. These reviews normally take a long time, and there must be very good justification for these new proposals before they would be approved by relevant China government authorities.

In addition, two Chinese government 'Investment Catalogues' published under the 'Guiding Regulations' are important and relevant for foreign companies or investors to consider. These two catalogues, together with the 'Guiding Regulations', formed the main legal policy framework for applicable government policies, laws and regulations used in the review, examination and approval of foreign investment projects and FIE.

The 'Catalogue for Guiding Foreign Investment in Industries' (Foreign Investment Catalogue) has been regularly updated by the PRC Government, including major reviews in 2011 and 2015. This catalogue listed the specific industries in China for which foreign investment would be 'encouraged, restricted or prohibited'. The projects that were not included in this catalogue would normally fall under the category of permitted projects for foreign investments.

On 7 December 2016, China's National Development and Reform Commission and Ministry of Commerce jointly released a draft new version of the 'Catalogue for the Guidance of Foreign Investment Industries' for public comment. They issued the new draft catalogue following the recent reforms of the FIE approval regime in China. The 'Negative List' or the special administrative measures on access of foreign investments section of the catalogue would determine whether foreign investments in specific industries would be subject to the approval of MOFCOM and NDRC. The new draft catalogue indicated the potential opening of a significant number of sectors, which were previously restricted and prohibited to foreign investors. Comparing the new draft catalogue to the current catalogue, issued on 10 March 2015, it was found that the new draft catalogue reduced the number of restrictive measures from 93 to 62. These restrictive measures covered limitations on ownership of shares, restricted items plus prohibited areas and items for foreign investment in China.

The 'Catalogue of Priority Industries for Foreign Investment in the Central and Western Regions' (Central and Western Region Catalogue) was published by the PRC Government to promote investment in the Central and Western regions of China. This catalogue listed the various industries in the Central and Western regions of China for which foreign investment would be specifically encouraged as part of the Chinese government's 'Go West Policy'. It was recently updated in March 2017, which repealed the previous catalogue issued in 2013.

On 20 March 2017, the National Development and Reform Commission and Ministry of Commerce released the revised Catalogue of Advantageous Sectors for Foreign Investment in Central and Western Regions 2017 (Revised). This new catalogue would repeal the last Catalogue of Advantageous Sectors for Foreign Investment in Central and Western Regions issued in 2013.

The revision of the catalogue is a major move to open up the economic systems and attract foreign investments to the central and western regions of China. The new catalogue is in line with the Circular of the State Council on Expanding Opening-up and Positively Utilizing Foreign Investment, which was issued by the State Council in 2017. The new 2017 catalogue supports Central and Western regions to undertake industrial transformation with foreign investments and to improve open economic developments in various regions. The revised catalogue contained 639 items, which was an increase of 139 compared with the previous version. The new catalogue promoted investments in traditional industries, such as agricultural and green farming. It also promoted investments in high-tech industrial development, such as LCD, integrated circuit manufacturing, smart phone, laptop and biological medicine. The catalogue also encouraged the acceleration of service sector development, such as partial producer services and life services. In provinces with good labour force availability, the catalogue also promoted new export-oriented industry clusters. New infrastructure developments were also encouraged.

The Chinese government has also introduced equal corporate tax treatment to all foreign and domestic enterprises in line with China's WTO commitments. In order to encourage technology transfers by foreign companies into China, the government has introduced various tax concessions for foreign investments and projects which would qualify as 'advanced technology projects or high technology industrial investments'. These advanced technology projects would enjoy special tax holidays plus capital goods import tax exemptions which could provide significant fiscal attractions for the Chinese and international partners investing in new advanced technology joint ventures.

In the past, the majority of foreign investment projects would have to be approved by NDRC and relevant China central government authorities. With the new Chinese government reforms, new major foreign investments in selected strategic industries in China with total investment values of above US $300 million would still require the approval of NDRC and relevant central government departments. These include detailed Chinese expert reviews of the proposed joint project Feasibility Study Report (FSR), plus approvals by the National Development and Reform Commission (NDRC) and the Ministry of Commerce (MOFCOM).

In addition, major new proposed projects in China would also have to prepare the required Environmental Impact Assessment Reports (EIA) as part of their submissions. The EIA would have to be reviewed by relevant Chinese environmental experts as part of its approval by the Chinese Ministry of Environment (MOE).

For foreign invested projects in non-strategic industries with project values of less than US $300 million, the provincial and municipal governments have been delegated with the appropriate authority to approve these new local projects or enterprises, as part of the recent government reforms in China. These would normally enable the Chinese and international companies investing in these local projects to gain government approval faster.

Overview of foreign investments in China

In the late 1980s, China implemented several regulations and policies for Sino-foreign joint ventures. China also established special economic zones (SEZs) and special industrial zones with good infrastructure to promote foreign investments in different regions of China.

In June 1995, the 'Provisional Guidelines for Foreign Investment Projects' was introduced by the PRC Government. A key highlight of these guidelines was that the energy sector in China was categorized as a priority sector for foreign investments to China. As a result of these special measures, China has attracted high foreign investments and FDI inflows over the years into China's oil and gas sectors. In 2012, China attracted Foreign Direct Investment inflows of over US $253 billion, which was 37 per cent higher than the FDI of US $185 billion in 2011.

In 2016, FDI in China continued its steady growth with strong foreign investments in the service industry. The China Ministry of Commerce reported that total FDI in 2016 rose 4.1 per cent, year-on-year, to reach US $118 billion. The 2016 FDI growth was lower than the 2015 FDI growth of 6.4 per cent. However, foreign investment in the service industry in China rose 8.3 per cent year-on year-to some US $84 billion and it accounted for 70.3 per cent of all FDI into China in 2016. The 2016 FDI into high-tech services was particularly strong and it rose by over 86 per cent from a year earlier to reach US $14 billion. The FDI to the FTZs in Shanghai, Guangdong, Tianjin and Fujian also rose strongly in 2016 by over 81 per cent to US $13 billion. The FDI from the United States into China rose by over 52 per cent, whilst the FDI from the European Union into China rose by over 41 per cent.

An important example of the opening up of the foreign investment market in China was that, in December 2004, the Chinese government lifted the restrictions on foreign companies investing in wholesale, retail and distribution enterprises in China. This was in line with China's WTO commitments which they agreed to in 2000. As a result, many international oil companies (IOC) have entered the Chinese downstream oil product retail markets. Some of the leading multinationals oil companies have established significant oil products retail joint ventures with leading Chinese NOCs, such as Sinopec, PetroChina, CNOOC and Sinochem, in the different major regional oil retail markets of China.

A successful example of a Sino-foreign oil retail joint venture is the Shell Sinopec oil retail joint venture. Shell and Sinopec negotiated and agreed to establish their new joint venture in Jiangsu after China entered the WTO and the Chinese government opened the downstream oil retail market for international and Chinese company to form joint ventures. After hard negotiations by the Chinese and international negotiators, they agreed that Sinopec would hold 60 per cent of the joint venture shareholding and Shell would hold 40 per cent. The joint venture was established in Jiangsu Province and has been successfully operating 2000 oil fuel retail stations in different regions of the province.

Chinese Sino-foreign joint ventures models

To attract foreign investment, China has been offering a range of different permitted FIE business models to facilitate foreign investments in China. These include Sino-Foreign Equity Joint Ventures, Sino-Foreign Contractual Joint Ventures or Wholly Owned Foreign Enterprises (WOFEs). Other possible foreign investment models include Share Company with Foreign Investment, Foreign Invested Holding Company, etc. To date, the Sino-Foreign Equity Joint Ventures, Contractual Joint Ventures, WOFEs and Holding Companies models have emerged as the most popular business forms for foreign investments in China. The different company forms in China will be described in more detail in the next section.

Sino-foreign Equity Joint Ventures (EJVs) in China

Equity Joint Ventures or EJVs are also known as 'Share Company with Foreign Investment'. These are Sino-foreign enterprises jointly established and operated by both the Chinese and international partners and are basically limited liability companies set up for a specific business purpose. A good business example is the establishment of a new major manufacturing facility in China. After approval and establishment, it would acquire the status of an independent Chinese legal entity. The foreign investor would normally be required to hold a minimum shareholding of 25 per cent in the EJV.

The rewards, risks and benefits of the EJV are normally shared between the Chinese and international partners in proportion to their respective shareholdings. The international partner could negotiate to make their investment in cash or in kind, such as capital investment, advanced management systems or technologies, advanced machineries and intellectual property rights. The Chinese partner could also negotiate and provide land, buildings, labour and facilities as part of their equity contributions into the joint venture for its future operations. The international partner could negotiate their share of profits and other legal interests arising from such joint venture. They could also negotiate whether they plan to remit their profits overseas in line with the latest PRC Government forex requirements, or to reinvest the profits into the joint venture on further future expansions or into their other projects in China via a separate permitted Chinese holding company structure.

Sino-foreign Contractual Joint Ventures (CJVs) in China

Contractual Joint Venture or CJVs are Sino-foreign enterprises that are jointly established according to their cooperative conditions. In these establishments, both the foreign and the Chinese partners would negotiate and agree in their joint venture contract the various key business principles and cooperation conditions. These would normally include negotiating key partners' rights, obligations, incomes distribution, risks and debts, company management and negotiations on the property transaction when the contract expires.

In China, a CJV could operate without a legal entity status or as a limited liability company with a legal person status. If the CJV operates without legal entity status, then the international and Chinese partners in the CJV are liable for all the civil liabilities in proportion to their assets. In CJVs with legal person status, the foreign partner should have a minimum invested capital of 25 per cent in the CJV's registered capital. On the other hand, in CJVs without legal person status, the minimum shareholding and invested capital for the international investor in the EJV would be determined by China's Ministry of Commerce (MOFCOM) regulations.

Sino-foreign Wholly Owned Foreign Enterprises (WOFEs) in China

Wholly Owned Foreign Enterprises or WOFEs are permitted legal entities in China that would be wholly owned by one or more foreign investors. In WOFEs, the foreign investors can make all the investments without any Chinese partners. They then receive all the revenues and profits of the WOFE, but they would also be required to bear all the risks.

In China, WOFEs are usually structured as limited liability companies with legal person status. However, they might also take other legal forms, such as a company limited by shares or partnership. If the foreign company do want to change in the future from being a WOFE to another joint venture legal model in China, then they would need to apply for new approval from MOFCOM.

In the WOFEs, the foreign company and management have full independence and power to manage their WOFE company in China. Some foreign companies would prefer to set up a WOFE in China as they believe it would better protect their intellectual property rights, advanced technologies and specialized processes.

It should also be noted that foreign investors are not allowed to set up WOFEs in selected strategic industrial sectors in China. If an international company want to invest in these strategic sectors in China, then they would have to form a new joint venture with an approved Chinese partner. These restrictions might be relaxed in the future as China would like to promote more foreign investment. However, it will still be highly likely that some of the very strategic sectors remain tightly controlled. Good business examples of strategic sectors in China include the military, arms and armament sectors which have significant national security implications and linkages.

Foreign invested holding companies in China

China has also allowed multinational companies to establish foreign-invested holding companies in China. These are similar to the 'Holding Company' structure in Western countries, but there are a couple of key differences.

Multinational companies might use a 'Holding Company' structure in China in order to increase their investments and/or facilitate re-investments in China. Multinationals can also put all their various investment projects and Sino-foreign joint ventures, already established in China, under one corporate business umbrella. These should help international companies to improve the management coordination and control of their various business ventures and investments across China with different Chinese partners.

A foreign invested Holding Company in China might also invest in various business areas such as industrial, agriculture, infrastructure and energy. However, these business areas must be listed in the encouraged sectors classification for foreign investments in China in the 'NDRC Guiding Regulations'.

A Foreign Invested Holding Company in China could also undertake most of the normal typical business activities and operations in China. These might include purchasing, procurement, distribution and provision of after sales service, etc.

China's Provisional Regulations also stipulate that a Foreign Invested Holding Company in China might enjoy the preferential treatment applicable to an FIE. They can apply for an FIE certificate and licence from the relevant government ministries and agencies in China.

China Sino-foreign investment contracts overview

Sino-foreign economic contracts in China are governed by the 'PRC Government Contract Law', which was first implemented in October 1999 and has been updated regularly by the PRC Government.

The PRC law on 'Sino-Foreign Cooperative Joint Ventures' was first adopted on 13 April 1988 at the first session of the 7th National People's Congress by the Chinese government. Then it was revised on 31 October 2000 at the 18th meeting of the Standing Committee of the National People's Congress.

All foreign companies investing in China must prepare and negotiate their various contracts and Joint Venture Agreements (JVAs) with their Chinese partners in accordance with the relevant PRC laws and regulations. In addition, the Chinese partners would normally highlight to their foreign Partners the importance of complying with the basic key principle of 'equality and mutual benefit' in all their contracts and joint venture negotiations in China.

In line with international business negotiation best practices, the negotiators appointed by the Chinese and international companies should keep extensive, detailed records of their negotiations and contractual documentations in China. These will be useful in updating their management on the negotiation progress in China as well as being good references in case of any future disputes or disagreements. All agreed Sino-foreign contracts and joint venture agreements in China must be submitted to the Ministry of Commerce (MOFCOM) for their final review, approval and record.

When a new Sino-foreign joint venture or enterprise is being established, the Chinese and Foreign partners should negotiate an extensive JVA together with relevant associated contracts. These would normally include the supplementary contracts, for example licensing, trademark and marketing. For large manufacturing joint ventures in key provinces, additional key local contracts would have to be negotiated, such as utility supply, land grant, etc.

The international and Chinese negotiators should negotiate and agree all the key business principles and contractual requirements essential for the future operations of the proposed joint venture. These would normally include shareholding ratio, partners' rights and control, nomination rights for key staff and positions, financing and equity injections, distribution of earnings and dividends, product lifting and marking, sharing of risks and losses, etc.

Analysis of key JVAs in China highlights the key requirements that the Chinese and international negotiators should also negotiate and agree the so-called 'boiler plate clauses' in the JVA. These boiler plate clauses normally cover future dispute management, arbitration, mediation, termination and ownership of property on the termination of the contract term.

The joint venture, when it has been approved and registered in China, would then acquire an 'independent Chinese legal entity status'. It would have its own legal representative which would normally be the Chairman of the Board, as stipulated under Chinese laws. Hence the Chinese and international negotiators should also discuss and agree the board composition, number of directors for each side, board authorities and corporate governance issues, etc., in their JVA negotiations.

There is also increased recognition of the importance of including a good arbitration clause in the JVA between foreign and Chinese companies. This is because arbitration would help to provide an effective framework for foreign companies and their local Chinese partners to resolve their possible future differences and disputes, whilst allowing them to continue to work together on their business ventures in China. This would in turn help to prevent or minimize expensive and damaging litigations between the foreign and Chinese companies.

International companies can choose to refer any disputes in China to the 'China International Economic and Trade Arbitration Commission' (CIETAC), which is the permanent arbitration body of the 'China International Chamber of Commerce', or other international arbitration bodies accepted by the Chinese partner. These should be negotiated and agreed by the Chinese and international negotiators as part of their JVA negotiations.

China Sino-foreign joint venture negotiation and registration

The Chinese government law on 'Sino-Foreign Cooperative Joint Ventures' was first adopted on 13 April 1988 at the first session of the 7th National People's Congress by the Chinese government. It was then revised on 31 October 2000 at the 18th Meeting of the Standing Committee of the National People's Congress.

The law has been developed to promote and increase economic cooperation and technological exchanges with foreign, international companies in China. It also encourages foreign partners and investors to form Sino-foreign joint venture or cooperative enterprises in China with suitable Chinese partners. These new Sino-foreign joint ventures between the Chinese and foreign partners normally need to be negotiated and established based on the key principle of 'equality and mutual benefit' in China.

When the international and Chinese partners are negotiating to establish a new Sino-foreign joint venture, they would normally have to negotiate and agree a comprehensive JVA together with the relevant key sub-contracts covering service, licence, technology transfer, management, land use, utility supplies, etc. Analysis of high-level joint venture business negotiation cases in China shows that these negotiations can take two to four years involving hundreds of contracts covering all the essential services required by the future joint venture.

In the main JVA negotiations, the Chinese and international negotiators should negotiate and agree all the key contractual terms which are essential for the normal operation of the new joint venture. Analysis of high-level joint venture business negotiations in China indicates that these should include the key topics of board composition, numbers of directors from each partner, board governance, shareholding ratio, management organization and control, nomination rights for key managers and staff by each partner, financing and equity injections, future principles for distribution of earnings and dividends, product lifting rights by each partner, pre-marketing and marketing arrangements, and sharing of risks and losses.

In addition, the Chinese and international negotiators should also negotiate and agree the relevant boiler plate clauses covering potential future areas of disputes between the partners. Analysis of joint venture business negotiation experiences shows that these should cover dispute management between partners, mediation arrangements, international arbitrations, joint venture termination conditions, ownership of properties, liquidation of the joint venture, etc.

It is very important for the negotiators to understand that the joint venture, after approval in China, would be granted and acquired an independent Chinese legal entity status. Hence the Chinese and international negotiators must negotiate, discuss and agree the board, number of directors for each side, board authorities and corporate governance issues before joint venture establishment. The chairman of the future joint venture would then become the legal representative of the joint venture under Chinese law.

Joint venture business negotiation experiences in China show that a good arbitration clause should be included in the joint venture contract. This should be negotiated by the foreign and Chinese negotiators as part of their joint venture negotiations. Arbitration will help to provide a framework for foreign and Chinese partners to resolve their disputes, whilst working together on their business ventures. This will also help both parties to minimize future expensive litigations. The Chinese and international negotiators should also negotiate and agree if future arbitrations should take place at the China International Economic and Trade Arbitration Commission (CIETAC), which is the permanent arbitration body of the China International Chamber of Commerce, or at other international arbitration bodies. In addition, the negotiators must debate and agree whether arbitration should be done under Chinese law or under a suitable international legal system.

After completion of business negotiations, the Chinese and international partner must submit their agreed JVA with the Articles of Association, plus other key sub-contracts and documents, for review and approval by the China Ministry of

Commerce MOFCOM and other relevant state council departments responsible for foreign economic relations and trade. These government bodies then review the agreements and contracts in detail. They can then decide to approve or reject the application within 45 days of its receipt, which would be in line with the latest Chinese government system and procedures.

After approval of the JVA and associated contracts by the relevant government authorities, then the Chinese and international partners can make applications for registration and business licence to the State Administration for Industry and Commerce (SAIC) within 30 days of receiving the approval certificate. The joint venture or cooperative enterprise can become formally established once the business licence has been issued by the Chinese government authority. Then, the joint venture should register itself with the China State Administration of Taxation within 30 days of its establishment.

After approval and during the cooperation period of the joint venture, if the international and Chinese partners find it necessary to amend their approved JVA, then these amendments must be re-submitted to MOFCOM and other relevant examining and approving bodies in the Chinese government for their new approvals. If the amendments affect the official industrial or commercial registrations or tax registrations of the joint venture, then these new amendments should also be registered with the State Administration for Industry and Commerce or the China State Administration of Taxation.

After joint venture establishment, the international and Chinese partners should both invest and inject their agreed assets into the new joint venture. These equity and asset injections into the joint venture by the Chinese and international partners must be done strictly in line with the JVA. These injections could be in the forms of cash, land-use rights, industrial property rights, non-patented technology or other property rights, etc.

In China, it is normal practice for both foreign and Chinese partners to use independent assessors who have been authorized and registered in China, to independently assess and evaluate the values of each partner's equity contributions, which could be in the form of land, buildings, technologies or processes. After detailed reviews and assessments by the authorized assessor, they will issue valuation certificates to the Chinese and international partners plus to the joint venture.

Both the foreign and Chinese partners are obliged to provide their agreed 'equity injections' on schedule, as per the provisions agreed in the JVA and in accordance with the provisions of the Chinese regulations. If such obligations are not met within the agreed schedule, then the State Administration for Industry and Commerce in China could specify a deadline for fulfillment by the partners. If the obligations are still not fulfilled by the specified deadline, then the case is escalated to the relevant examining and approving body in the PR China government who would then, together with the State Administration for Industry and Commerce, review and deal with the non-complying case as per relevant Chinese laws and regulations.

High-level business negotiation experience shows that the duration of the future joint venture must be negotiated and agreed by the international and

Chinese negotiators as part of the JVA. In China, the JV's duration would normally be between 15 to 30 years depending on negotiations between the Chinese and international negotiators. The agreed JV duration must also be specified in the JV contract for approval by the government authorities in China. After approval, if both the Chinese and international partners agree to extend the cooperation duration and terms, then a new application would have to be submitted to the relevant China government approving body 180 days before the expiry of the JV co-operation term. After receipt of the application, the Chinese government authority normally takes 30 days to decide if they agree to grant approval to the JV's extension application.

A good example of successful Sino-foreign joint venture business negotiations is that of BP and Sinopec in their SECCO joint venture. The Shanghai SECCO Petrochemical Company Limited involved three partners, including China Petroleum and Chemical Corporation (Sinopec Corp.), Shanghai Petrochemical Company Limited (SPC) and BP East China Investment Company Limited. They negotiated and agreed to form a new major joint venture in Shanghai with a total investment of about US $2.7 billion with agreed shareholding ratios of 30 per cent, 20 per cent and 50 per cent between the Chinese and international partners respectively. It was one of the largest petrochemical joint ventures in China. The complex included a 1.09 million TPA Ethylene Cracker and eight major chemicals production plants. SECCO has been successfully producing different petrochemical and chemicals, including ethylene, propylene, polyethylene, polypropylene, styrene, polystyrene, acrylonitrile, butadiene, benzene, toluene and byproducts. It has been producing more than 3.2 million tonnes per year of petrochemical and chemical products for the Chinese and international petrochemical markets.

In 2017, BP agreed to sell its shares in the SECCO joint venture in China to Sinopec for US $1.68 billion. This was in line with BP's strategy to raise up to US $5.5 billion from their global asset divestments in 2017 to help pay for their settlement for the 2010 Deepwater Horizon disaster in the US. As part of the deal, BP agreed to sell its 50 per cent stake in the Shanghai SECCO Petrochemical company to China Petroleum & Chemical Corporation, a wholly owned subsidiary of the Hong Kong-listed Sinopec and BP's partner in the joint venture in Shanghai.

Sino-foreign joint venture supplementary contract negotiations

When international and Chinese partners agree in principle to establish a new Sino-foreign joint venture in China, they need to appoint Chinese and international negotiation teams to negotiate and agree a new comprehensive JVA between the two parties. In parallel, the Chinese and international partners also need to appoint negotiators from both sides to negotiate and agree all the relevant key supplementary contracts required to support effective operations of the new joint venture in the future. These would normally include the key licence contracts, technology transfer contracts, management service contracts and marketing services contracts.

As part of the supplementary contract negotiations, the Chinese and international negotiators need to negotiate all the required licensing contracts between the parent companies with the joint venture. These normally include the licensing of advanced technologies or manufacturing processes which the Chinese partner would like the international partner to bring or transfer into the new joint venture in China as part of their investment in the future joint venture. These negotiations are often difficult and tough as they involve sensitive areas, such as the protection of confidentiality of the advanced technologies from the international company. Normally international companies have many concerns about leakages of confidential design information of their advanced technologies and processes in China. The negotiators should negotiate and agree suitable arrangements for intellectual property right sharing and protection in China. In addition, they would have to negotiate and agree arrangement of suitable transfer of technology from the international partner to the Chinese company. On the other hand, the Chinese negotiators may stress the valuable assistance that the Chinese company would give the joint venture by providing competent Chinese engineers and operators who would help the joint venture to implement and operate these advanced technology processes in China.

The Chinese and international negotiators would also need to negotiate all the required management services contracts between the parent companies with the joint venture. These negotiations would normally cover the joint venture being able to enjoy or draw on advanced management services, management processes and international systems which the Chinese partner would like the international partner to bring into the joint venture as part of the international partner's investment in the new joint venture. These negotiations would normally be difficult as it would involve tough negotiation on sensitive areas such as the levels of protection of confidentiality of the advanced management systems plus the intellectual property rights of the advanced management systems and processes in China. On the other hand, the Chinese negotiators would stress the valuable assistance that the Chinese company would provide to the joint venture by providing sufficient high quality, competent Chinese managers and staff which would help the international company to implement and operate these advanced management systems and services successfully in the joint venture.

The Chinese and international negotiators also need to negotiate all the required marketing and sales services contracts between the two parent companies with the joint venture. These negotiations normally cover the joint venture being able to enjoy the latest marketing systems, new customer base and customer sales management systems which the Joint Venture would use to maximize sales and marketing results in China. These negotiations would normally be difficult as it would involve negotiating sensitive areas such as protecting the confidentiality of these advanced marketing and sales systems in China. In addition, the negotiators need to negotiate suitable arrangements and fees for the transfer of advanced international marketing and sales knowhow from the international partner to the Chinese partner. As a counter argument to lower the marketing knowhow fees to be charged by the international company, the Chinese negotiators would argue strongly for the valuable help that the Chinese company would be giving to the international company for them to gain access to the vast Chinese market.

China Sino-foreign joint venture local contracts negotiations

In addition to the JVA and supplementary contract negotiations, the Chinese and international companies also need to nominate suitable negotiators from both the Chinese and international companies to form a separate joint local contracts negotiation team. The joint local contracts negotiation team would then negotiate all the required local contracts with senior government officials from the relevant local and provincial government authorities on behalf of the Chinese and international companies and the future joint venture. The new key local contracts would typically include the appropriate land grant and use contract, resettlement contract, electricity supply contract and water supply contract.

It should be noted that the local contract negotiation team often negotiate with very senior local government officials, such as mayors of local Chinese cities plus the heads of important Chinese local companies, etc. Hence the senior management of the Chinese and international companies should select suitable senior negotiators who also have a good understanding of Chinese local government systems and procedures. It would also be important that these senior negotiators have a good understanding of Chinese negotiation culture and customs and can speak Chinese.

In addition, the Chinese and international company management should appoint an experienced Chinese government relationship manager to join the local contracts negotiation team so he or she can help the local contract negotiation team to liaise effectively with senior local government officials and authorities in line with the Chinese government regulations and requirements.

In addition, the Chinese and international senior management should appoint suitable experts in each of the technical and process areas relevant to the key local contract negotiations. These normally include site design, electricity supply, utilities supply, water experts, etc.

The joint Chinese and international partners local contracts negotiation team would need to negotiate the key Land Grant and Use Contract between the future joint venture with the key local and provincial government land authorities. These normally include negotiating the granting of the required plot of industrial land by the local government to the future joint venture, allowing them to build the planned new plants and manufacturing facilities and office buildings. A Chinese partner and local company may also bring suitable plots of land and buildings into the new joint venture as part of their investment in the future joint venture. These negotiations would be difficult and tough as they involve sensitive negotiations on the land valuation and land grant fees that the future joint venture would need to pay to the local government in China. The international and Chinese partners must also ensure that the local government handle all the required discussions and application to the central government on any requirements to convert any farming land to industrial land as this would be strictly controlled.

If there are any resettlement requirements from the land, then the joint Chinese and international partners' local contract negotiation team need to negotiate the resettlement contract between the future joint venture with the key local and provincial government land authorities. This would normally include negotiating the required compensation that the joint venture would pay to the local government for requirements to resettle residents from the land designated for the new joint venture's industrial site to other suitable residential areas. The compensation would normally cover building new residential houses and schools for the children of the resettled residents and compensation for loss of livelihood of the residents. These negotiations can be tough as it involves difficult negotiation on the appropriate compensation fees and compensation that the future joint venture will need to pay to local government and residents. The international and Chinese partners must also ensure that in their negotiations with the local government that the relevant local government authorities will handle all the required resettlement discussions and arrangements with the local residents, as there are strict legal requirements and control for resettlement in China. If the resettlements were not handled well, then this could lead to strikes and demonstrations by the affected residents in China. This could then lead to adverse local and international media coverage which could be very bad for the public image of the Chinese and international companies.

The joint Chinese and international partners local contract negotiation team would also need to negotiate the various utilities supply contract, especially electricity supplies and water supplies, between the future joint venture with the key Chinese local utilities supply company and relevant local government authorities. These would normally include negotiating the amounts of local electricity, water and other required utilities that the local utilities companies would be able to supply and guarantee to the future joint venture. In addition, they would need to negotiate the fees for these utilities plus any capital investment contributions for any new utilities supply infrastructures, such as electricity substations and water supply lines. These negotiations can often be difficult as they involve reaching agreement on the appropriate fees and compensation that the future joint venture would be willing to pay to the local companies and local government authorities. The international and Chinese partners must also ensure that the local government will help in coordinating the various local utilities companies to ensure that they would be able to meet all the utilities requirements of the future joint venture to ensure its smooth operations without unplanned power outages.

10 Chinese joint venture post-negotiation implementation

善有善报，
Shàn yǒu shàn bào,
Kind deeds will normally generate good rewards.
What goes around comes around.

Executive overview

To establish a new joint venture in China, the Chinese and international negotiators need to negotiate and agree the required new joint venture agreement, new supplementary contracts and local contracts. After approval of these agreements by the Chinese government authorities, the Chinese and international partners need to work together to establish the new joint venture successfully in China. They need to complete the formalities of proper joint venture registration with Chinese authorities and establish new joint venture bank accounts and a company chop. In addition, the joint venture board needs to be established with suitable directors nominated by the Chinese and international partners. Details of joint venture establishment and management will be described in more detail in this chapter.

Sino-foreign joint venture approval and registration in China

Once the Chinese and international negotiators have successfully completed their negotiations of the required joint venture contracts, supplementary contracts and local contracts, then the Chinese and international partners begin preparation for formal approval and registration of their proposed new joint venture in China. In China, the joint venture approval and registration process normally takes place at the same time as the joint venture's registration and trademark registration.

The joint venture establishment process in China normally starts with the reservation of the chosen joint venture company name with the State Administration for Industry and Commerce (SAIC). Trademark registration in China can take over six to twelve months. Hence it would be advisable that the Chinese and international partners should initiate their Company name and Trademark registration processes as soon as the Chinese and international negotiators have reached agreement on the name of the joint venture and prior to completing the negotiation of all the required agreements and contracts to formally establish their Sino-foreign joint venture.

The Chinese and international negotiators normally first negotiate and agree a relevant Memorandum of Understanding (MOU) or Letter of Intent (LOI) which would outline the key business principles of the future joint venture. The Chinese and international partner should also prepare an initial project proposal which they need to submit to the China National Development Reform Commission (NDRC) and China Ministry of Commerce (MOFCOM) for review.

If the proposed initial project proposal is accepted, then the NDRC grants a 'Lu-tiao', which literally means giving the go ahead to the Chinese and international partners to develop further details of their proposed joint venture. The Chinese and international joint venture partners can then go on to develop the required details of their project and prepare their joint Project Feasibility Study Report (FSR) for approval. The Chinese and international partners would normally jointly select and hire qualified design institutes in China to help them prepare the detailed joint FSR together with the required Environmental Impact Assessment Reports (EIA). These should then be submitted for review and approval by the relevant Chinese departments and authorities, which would normally include the NDRC and MOFCOM. The EIA report also needs to be submitted to the Environmental Protection Bureau and Ministry of Environment for review and approval.

After approval of the FSR and EIA by the Chinese government, the international and Chinese negotiators can then negotiate the joint venture agreement and the supplementary agreements and local contracts. After completion of all the contract negotiations, then the Chinese and international joint venture partners should prepare and submit a joint investment application to MOFCOM and other relevant China government approval authorities. The investment application should be supported with the agreed joint venture contract, articles of association, supplementary contracts, local contracts, FSR and other relevant documents.

Prior to making their investment application to MOFCOM, the joint venture partners need to have negotiated, agreed and acquired suitable lands or buildings for the joint venture. The key investment terms and shareholder ratios have also to be negotiated and agreed by the international and Chinese negotiators. If the Chinese partner were contributing land or building to the future joint venture as part of their equity contributions, then the relevant land use rights certificate plus a board resolution allowing the joint venture the use of the designated land and buildings is required. The valuation of the land and buildings should be independently assessed in China by independent authorized assessors. Then the final valuations need to be negotiated and agreed between the international and Chinese negotiators as part of their joint venture negotiations.

MOFCOM review the negotiated joint venture agreement, supplementary contracts and local contracts to ensure that they are all in line with Chinese law and regulations with no precedents. MOFCOM involve various Chinese law experts in the review of the proposed agreements and contracts to ensure that all comply with Chinese laws and regulations. These experts would normally raise some detailed questions which the Chinese and international companies would have to answer first. Only after all the experts have confirmed that they are satisfied with all the contracts after their review, then MOFCOM would grant their approval for the new joint venture. MOFCOM also issue a formal approval certificate for the new joint venture.

On receipt of the formal joint venture approval certificate from MOFCOM, the Chinese and international joint venture partners can then apply for the new joint venture business licence from the State Administration of Industry and Commerce (SAIC) in China. Once the business licence has been issued by SAIC, then the new joint venture would become a separate legal entity in China under Chinese law and could then operate independently.

The joint venture partners should then prepare and make the new, authorized company chops for the new joint venture. In China, the authorized company chops should be used to stamp all the various joint venture contracts and important documents so that they can become legally valid and enforceable. The authorized company chops normally need to be stored securely in the company safe. The new joint venture management would also have to develop a suitable, stringent procedure on the use of the company chops by the authorized joint venture personnel. The joint venture also needs to register their new company chops with the relevant public security bureau in China.

The new joint venture should also apply for an organization code certificate from relevant government authorities. Then the joint venture management should open new bank accounts in both US $ and RMB with a reputable bank in China. They should also register the new joint venture with the relevant Chinese government authorities including the State Administration for Foreign Exchange (SAFE), State Administration for Taxation (SAT), Customs Office Statistics Bureau, etc.

The total joint venture application, review and registration process, depending on the size and complexity of the new joint venture in China, generally takes from six months to one years for the small, simple joint ventures. For the larger, more complex joint ventures the time period for application, review and registration in China can be longer.

Sino-foreign joint ventures operation and management in China

After the new joint venture has been formally established and registered in China, then the new joint venture management should ensure that the joint venture should carry out its business management activities as per the approved JVA and the agreed articles of association. The joint venture, should first form a board of directors which would have the highest authorities to make important decisions with respect to major business issues. The nomination of the directors by the Chinese and international company should be in line with the provisions of the approved JVA and agreed articles of association.

The board chairman and vice chairman should each be nominated by the foreign and Chinese partners, as agreed in the JVA. In addition, the foreign and Chinese partners should then each nominate their agreed number of directors in line with their shareholding ratios and the JVA provisions. If the joint venture has a 50/50 shareholding ratio, then it would be normal for the Chinese and international companies to both nominate equal numbers of directors to the JV board. This would normally involve three or four directors, each to be nominated by the Chinese and international partners. However, it should be noted that in China, the board chairman would be recognized as the official legal representative for the whole joint venture entity, under Chinese law. The board should also appoint suitable board secretaries to assist the board. Normally the Chinese and international companies would each nominate a board secretary so they would work together as joint board secretaries for the JV board. The joint board secretary roles are normally also in line with Chinese customs and practice. It is important for them to work together to negotiate and prepare suitable board agenda for the board chairman and directors to approve prior to board meetings. After board meetings, the joint board secretaries should negotiate and prepare the draft board minutes for the board chairman and directors to approve.

The board should also appoint a general manager (GM) together with the senior JV management team so they can undertake the day-to-day management and operation of the joint venture. In Sino-foreign joint ventures in China, it is normal practice if one partner has the nomination right for the board chairman, then the other partner should have the nomination right for the general manager of the joint venture. The key purpose of this arrangement is to ensure the proper check and balance in the new joint venture management team. This should also help to improve the corporate governance of the new joint venture. Joint venture contract negotiation experience in China has shown that the nomination rights of key staff is always an important issue for the international and Chinese negotiators to debate and agree during joint venture negotiations.

The GM and his senior management team would also have to build up the new JV management team with key management staff, as agreed in the JVA. The nomination rights for key management positions would have been negotiated and agreed during the JVA negotiations and included in the final agreed JVA. The key management positions to be nominated by Chinese or international partners would normally include GM, CFO, CTO and COO. For all the key joint venture staff and nominees, they should have suitable new employment contracts with the JV. These new employment contracts should stipulate their employment terms, remuneration, welfare benefits, labour, insurance, etc.

In addition, the new JV employees in China should form a trade union inside the JV as per Chinese legal provisions. The JV would be legally and mandatorily required, under PRC Law, to provide its agreed employee trade unions with the required, essential facilities to conduct its normal activities.

If any disagreements occur in the future between the international and Chinese partners in their new joint venture, then this should first be resolved through mutual consultation or mediation. If both the international and Chinese partners still cannot agree after mediation, then the dispute may be presented to a suitable Chinese arbitral body or an international arbitration body for arbitration. This should be undertaken as per the arbitration provisions as agreed in the JV contract. If the Chinese and international partners and their negotiators have not included any arbitration provisions in their JV contract and they also failed to conclude a written arbitral agreement after a dispute has arisen, then ultimately a law suit might be filed in a Chinese court by the partners against each other.

Joint venture financial management

Proper financial management is one of the most important functions of the JV management team. One of the key duties of the new GM, together with the chief finance officer (CFO), would be to ensure that the JV set up and maintain the appropriate books of accounts for the JV in China. They should also provide the required accurate accounting statements as required by the board and in line with the regulations and requirements of the financial and taxation authorities in China. If the JV cannot meet or comply with these requirements, then the relevant Chinese financial authorities could fine the new JV. The State Administration for Industry and Commerce could also order the temporary closure of the JV business operations. In serious cases, they might suspend or cancel the business licence of the JV until the new JV management have introduced suitable remedial actions to the requirements and satisfaction of the Chinese authorities.

The GM and CFO of the JV would be required to open suitable RMB and foreign exchange accounts with a reputable Chinese bank or a financial institute in China authorized by the State Administration of Foreign Exchange (SAFE). These accounts would be required for the JV to conduct RMB and foreign exchange dealings and payments, as per the relevant foreign exchange control regulations and procedures in China.

One of the most important joint venture forex transactions is the decision by the joint venture board on whether it should distribute dividends to its shareholders. In particular, they should discuss if they need to remit the dividends for the international partner abroad to the international company's overseas accounts. If the JV board agree to remit dividends overseas, then the joint venture would have to get approval from relevant Chinese government authorities in line with latest Chinese forex control regulations. In addition, the wages of some foreign JV employees might also need to be remitted abroad, after paying the required individual income tax in China.

If the JV requires additional financing or loans in addition to the foreign and Chinese partners' equity injections, then the JV board and management might choose to raise these with Chinese banks in China or from overseas banks. In China, the foreign and Chinese partners must meet the minimum debt and equity ratios as stipulated in the latest Chinese regulations. The joint venture plus its partners could also choose to raise additional RMB loans from leading banks or financial institutions in China to refinance its forex loans from international banks. The various types of insurance required by the JV should also be provided by an authorized insurance company in China.

To support the JV's manufacturing operations, the JV needs to import the required raw materials and export their finished manufactured products. These must be undertaken in line with the agreed JV operational scope and business licence, as approved by the PRC Government. The JV might also purchase the required raw materials, feedstocks and fuel from the domestic or international markets as per their approved operational scope. The JV management should ensure that they have sufficient forex to meet these specific requirements.

The JV might also enjoy special preferential corporate tax treatment if their investment project would qualify as an 'advanced technology' project in China. The JV management would have to make special applications to the relevant Chinese authorities together with relevant supporting evidence. The JV might also enjoy preferential import duty treatment on imported capital goods for the construction of the JV manufacturing plants, as per China's preferential foreign investment treatments.

On termination of the joint venture, its assets, claims and debts should be liquidated as per the termination clause in the JV contract. The joint venture partners must also complete the required joint venture registration cancellation processes with the China State Administration for Industry and Commerce SAIC and the Chinese Taxation Authority.

Sino-foreign joint venture partners selection and negotiations

Analysis of successful joint ventures in China shows that one of the key success criterion for Sino-foreign joint ventures in China is the quality and commitment of both the Chinese and foreign partners. The negotiation and alignment of interests for both the foreign and Chinese partners' interests in a Sino-foreign joint venture can be very complex and usually take a lot of detailed analysis, discussion and negotiations.

During partnership selection and negotiations, the international and Chinese companies should take into account the potential future partners' possible complementarity match, strength and weaknesses, strategic fitness, commitments, codes of ethics, etc. Key factors to consider when choosing a suitable Chinese partner in China should include government relations, market leadership and networks in China, partnership goals, synergies, capabilities and skills. In addition, both the Chinese and international companies should consider what added values that they could each bring to the future joint venture.

On partnership goals, it would be important to analyze and understand what each of the partners want from the future joint venture and their strategic goals? This would include detailed competitor profiling and analysis plus strategic needs analysis. The past records of each partner's previous joint ventures with other companies should be reviewed to see if there were any major partnership disputes and how have these been resolved.

One of the key and sensitive areas of collaborative business relationships in China is for international companies to appreciate the true worth of having a Chinese partner's good guanxi and relationship with the central and local government as well as other important stakeholders in China. These are very important and sensitive questions which would normally take a lot of in-depth research to answer. Normally the good guanxi and relationships of the partners with the

Chinese government and key stakeholders is a key success factor for the future joint venture. This is normally one of most important and sensitive considerations for the international partner in their choice of a suitable partner in China, especially if they are new to China and need a strong Chinese partner to help them with establishing the right guanxi and government relationships. It is also important for the international company to check and find out if the potential Chinese partner might have any hidden guanxi baggage or burdens from their past dealings which would negatively influence the proper functioning of the future joint venture.

In addition, the international company should try to find out the identity of the real shareholders and ultimate sponsors in the Chinese system for their Chinese partner company. This sensitive data would often not be easy to find in China. The international company could consider hiring one of the reputable authorized Chinese agencies to assist them in undertaking the relevant company searches and checks in China. The international company should also ensure that all their partnership arrangements and relationships in China are legal and transparent.

Analysis of multiple Sino-foreign joint venture partnerships in China shows that one of the key partnership concern areas regards confidential knowhow transfer. It is important to identify at the start of the Sino-foreign partnership negotiations whether the Chinese partner wants the international company to provide and transfer advanced technologies and international management systems to the future joint venture. Many international companies have many concerns about advanced technology knowhow transfers in China, especially on the leakage of confidential design data to other Chinese competitors. These would often lead to difficult and intensive negotiations during the partnership and licensing negotiations. Suitable provisions for these advanced technologies transfers and international management systems knowhow transfers should be negotiated and included in the joint venture agreement and appropriate supplementary contracts. It is important to identify these key partnership aspirations and requirements early as these could raise sensitive confidentiality and intellectual property rights issues for the Chinese and international negotiators to include in their negotiations of the JVA and supplementary contracts.

Many leading international companies also undertake detailed competitor analysis and investigations to find out if their Chinese Partners have future ambitions to grow their strategic business operations and market positions in China and to expand in key overseas markets globally. This could then raise future competition issues between the Chinese and international companies, both in China and overseas markets. The international and Chinese negotiators must discuss and negotiate these potential future market competitions in their joint venture negotiations. They should negotiate and agree their future marketing and marketing service arrangements as part of their JVA, marketing contract and marketing service contract negotiations. Their negotiated market arrangements should also be in line with the requirements of WTO and local and international competition stipulations. The development of the Chinese market and its demand dynamics and possible future growth potentials must also be considered by the Chinese and international partners in their marketing discussions and negotiations.

It would also be very important for negotiators from the Chinese and foreign partners to discuss and agree the required business scope and rationale of the JV during their partnership negotiations and the JVA negotiations. The project's business scope should be clearly defined by discussing and agreeing all the possible business activities that the future joint venture might want to conduct. The Chinese and international partners must then prepare a clear list of the aspired business activities of the proposed new joint venture for approval by the relevant Chinese government authorities. After approval, these business activities must be included in the approved business scope of the joint venture. Any future changes or proposed expansions in the business scope of the joint venture in the future would then require the Chinese and international partners to apply to relevant Chinese government authorities for additional approvals.

The joint venture's future resources, utilities and energy supplies, plus feedstock requirements should also be carefully considered and identified in the joint project Feasibility Study Report to be submitted to the central and local government for approval. These are key areas for the government review and approval by relevant central and local government authorities. The Chinese and international partners should discuss and agree the sourcing of key feedstocks, utilities and energy supplies resources as well as the human resources required for the future joint venture. The Chinese and international partners should establish a joint local contract negotiation team to negotiate the various utilities supply contracts and land use contract with the relevant local and provincial government authorities and local companies.

The Chinese and international partners must also negotiate and discuss the desired tenure and duration of the proposed joint venture in China. There are standard government guidelines on the joint venture periods, but they can also ask for extensions. The Chinese and international negotiators should negotiate and agree these periods as part of their joint venture agreement negotiations. Various joint venture agreement business form options should also be considered and evaluated financially by the partners.

Partnership synergy negotiations and tactics

Analysis of different Sino-foreign partnership negotiations shows that it is very important to consider the potential synergies and strategic fits between the future Chinese and international companies during partnership discussions and negotiations. The three key areas of partnership synergies normally include financial synergy, market synergy, plus technical and operational synergy. The Chinese and international negotiators should negotiate and agree detailed arrangements for optimizing each of these three important partnership synergies, in order to maximize their value contributions to the future joint venture during their negotiations. In addition, the alignment of different partners' strategic interests and aspirations, including cultural and management compatibility, should also be evaluated.

On financial synergies, the Chinese and international negotiators should negotiate and agree the appropriate arrangements by the Chinese and international partners for financial support and equity injections into the future joint venture. Analysis of different Sino-foreign joint ventures in China have shown that many Chinese partners would be injecting land and buildings as part of their equity contributions to the future joint venture. In China, the valuations of the land and buildings contribution could be done by independent authorized assessors, to be chosen by both partners. Then the Chinese and international negotiators should review these valuations so that they can then negotiate and agree the final valuations for these equity injections in the final joint venture contract.

On market synergies, the Chinese and international negotiators should negotiate and agree the appropriate arrangements by the Chinese and international partners for market network support and provision of international marketing systems for the future joint venture. Analysis of different Sino-foreign joint ventures in China has shown that many Chinese partners negotiate with a perceived value of introducing the international companies to local key markets in China in which the Chinese partner has good networks or a dominant market position. On the other hand, the international negotiator may be negotiating based on their perceived values of their advanced international sales and marketing systems that they would bring into the joint venture and China. The Chinese and international companies can both ask independent assessors to provide suitable valuations of each of their proposed market synergy contributions. The Chinese and international negotiators would review these valuations but they would need to negotiate and agree the final valuations of each of these proposed market contributions to agree mutually beneficial arrangements for both the Chinese and international companies in the final JVA.

On technology and operational synergies, the Chinese and international negotiators should negotiate and agree the appropriate arrangements by the Chinese and international partners for advanced technology transfer and provision of competent operational support for the future joint venture in China. Analysis of different Sino-foreign joint ventures in China has shown that many Chinese partners and their negotiators would be negotiating based on their ability to provide a sufficient number of suitably trained and competent Chinese staff and operators for the future joint venture. They would argue that these human resources would contribute to supporting the various operations and functions of the future joint venture in China. On the other hand, the international company and its negotiators would be negotiating based on the value of the advanced technologies and international manufacturing systems that they would be bringing into the future joint venture in China. The Chinese and international companies could ask independent assessors to provide suitable valuations of each of their proposed technology and operational synergy contributions. Then the Chinese and international negotiators would have to review these valuations carefully as they may be estimations. The negotiators also need to negotiate and agree the final valuations of these proposed technology and operational contributions by each of the Chinese and international partners so as to agree mutually beneficial arrangements for both companies in the final joint venture agreement, final technology licensing contracts and technology service contracts.

Very good advice on partnership selection was given by the famous Italian diplomat and political philosopher Niccolo Machiavelli in his famous book, *The Prince*, in the sixteenth century. He said, "The forces of a powerful ally can be useful and good to those who have recourse to them [...] but are perilous to those who become dependent on them." Although the saying was given several hundred years ago, it is still very relevant for creating a strong joint venture partnership.

Key Sino-foreign joint ventures with leading Chinese national oil companies

In China, many successful Sino-foreign joint ventures and partnerships have been established by Chinese and international companies. These include joint ventures between leading Chinese SOEs and multinational companies in the oil and gas, petrochemical and chemical sectors in China. These major joint ventures normally require long and difficult negotiations by the Chinese and international negotiators. After they have successfully completed the required negotiations of the joint venture agreements, supplementary contracts and local contracts, then these agreement and contracts are reviewed and approved by the relevant Chinese government authorities. After approval, these new joint ventures then become fully established in China by the Chinese and international partners. Some examples of the key, leading Sino-foreign joint venture business negotiation cases in China are summarized in the next section.

In 1950, the Chinese and Soviet governments both agreed and entered into their first oil and petroleum joint venture in China to jointly develop Xinjiang's Dushanzi oil fields. The Sino-Russian Petroleum Co. Ltd was established and launched on 27 March 1950.

Post 1979, China entered into various oil, gas, petrochemical and chemical joint ventures with leading multinational corporations, such as Shell, BP, Total, Saudi Aramco and SABIC.

A good example of a Sino-foreign joint venture and successful business negotiation is the major CNOOC Shell Petrochemical Joint venture Limited CSPCL. The new CSPCL joint venture was established by Shell and CNOOC in Huizhou Municipality, Guangdong Province to build the mega US \$4.2 billion Nanhai Petrochemical Project. The new petrochemical and chemical plants included a new ethylene cracker with downstream chemical and derivative plants. It was agreed to be a 50/50 JV with CNOOC and Shell each holding a 50 per cent share in the JV. In 2000, the Nanhai petrochemical project joint venture contract was signed after over three years of tough negotiations. In 2002, a final investment decision was taken by both CNOOC and Shell to go ahead with the US \$4.2 billion Nanhai petrochemical project. The mega complex was completed and commissioned on schedule in 2006. The petrochemical and chemical complexes are working well. It is comprised of 950 KTPA Ethylene Cracker, 165 KTPA Butadiene unit, 250 KTPA Low Density Polyethylene (LDPE), 260 KTPA High

Density Polyethylene (HDPE), 260 KTPA Polypropylene (PP), 350 KTPA Mono-Ethylene Glycol (MEG), 640 KTPA Styrene Monomer, 290 KTPA Propylene Oxide (PO), 170 KTPA of Polyols and 60 KTPA Propylene Glycol.

Shanghai SECCO Petrochemical Company Limited was founded by China Petroleum and Chemical Corporation (Sinopec Corp.), Shanghai Petrochemical Company Limited (SPC) and BP East China Investment Company Limited. They agreed a joint investment of about US $2.7 billion with shareholding ratios of 30 per cent, 20 per cent and 50 per cent respectively. It was one of the largest petrochemical joint ventures in China. These included a 1.09 million TPA Ethylene Cracker and eight major chemicals production plants. SECCO produces ethylene, propylene, polyethylene, polypropylene, styrene, polystyrene, acrylonitrile, butadiene, benzene, toluene and byproducts. It produces more than 3.2 million tonnes per year of petrochemical and chemical products for the Chinese petrochemical market.

Sinopec Fujian Refining & Chemical Company Limited is a large-scale, integrated, petrochemical enterprise jointly invested by Fujian Petrochemical Company Limited (FPCL), ExxonMobil China Petroleum & Petrochemical Company Limited (EMCP&P) and Saudi Aramco Sino Company Limited (SASC). They jointly made a total investment of US $4,963 million with an agreed shareholding ratio of 50 per cent, 25 per cent and 25 per cent between FPCL, EMCP&P and SASC respectively after their negotiations. The refining capacity is 12 million TPA (240,000 barrels per day) and it mainly processes Saudi Arabian sour crude oil. It also has an 800 thousand TPA Ethylene Cracker, an 800 KTPA Polyethylene Unit, a 400 KTPA Polypropylene Unit and a 700 KTPA PX Complex, as well as the first integrated POX/COGEN (IGCC) Unit in China to generate hydrogen, steam and electricity.

Sinopec SABIC Tianjin Petrochemical Company (SSTPC) Limited is a successful JV between Sinopec and SABIC with an agreed 50/50 shareholding ratio. The petrochemical complex, which was established with a joint investment of US $2.7 billion, has a one million TPA Ethylene Cracker. It produces over three million tonnes of petrochemical products per annum including Ethylene, Polyethylene, Ethylene Glycol, Polypropylene, Butadiene, Phenol and Butene-1.

BASF-YPC Company Limited is a major joint venture between Sinopec and BASF with a negotiated shareholding ratio of 50/50. The construction of their mega petrochemical complex started in September 2001 and commercial operation started in June 2005. The joint investment for the first phase amounted to US $2.9 billion. It comprised ten world-scale petrochemical processing plants including an ethylene cracker. The downstream units comprised a 250/300 KTPA EO/EG plant, 400 KTPA LDPE plant, 250 KTPA Oxo-C4-Alcohols plant, 160 KTPA Acrylic Acid and 215 KTPA Acrylic Esters plant, 30 KTPA Propionic Acid plant, 50 KTPA Formic Acid plant, 36 KTPA Methylamine plant and 40 KTPA Dimethylformamide plant. BASF and Sinopec have also signed a MOU for the further expansion of BASF-YPC, with new investments of about US $1 billion. The expansion includes nine main chemical production plants including NIS, butadiene, IB, PIB, 2-PH plant, BG and SAP.

Sinopec and Shell also agreed to form a new Sino-Foreign JV at Yueyang in Henan Province in 2001 to build the first coal gasification plant in China. Shell agreed to license their advanced Shell Coal Gasification Technology to Sinopec. The joint venture has an agreed shareholding ratio of 50/50 between Shell and Sinopec. The board is comprised of equal numbers of Shell and Sinopec directors, who have been working well together. The coal gasification plant has been working well and the syngas produced have been used by Sinopec for urea fertilizer production in their downstream chemical plants in Henan.

Sinopec and Shell have also established a major oil retail joint venture in Jiangsu for 2000 oil retail stations. Sinopec and Shell negotiated and agreed the establishment of the joint venture after China entered the WTO and the Chinese government opened the downstream oil retail market for international and Chinese companies to form joint ventures. After negotiations, the joint venture agreed that Sinopec would hold 60 per cent of the joint venture shares and Shell would hold 40 per cent.

BP has also established joint venture agreements with both PetroChina and Sinopec to build and operate over 800 dual-branded, oil retail stations in the Guangdong and Zhejiang Provinces in China. These new downstream oil retail joint ventures were established in line with China's WTO entry and the opening up of the downstream oil retail market by the Chinese government.

Chevron has also negotiated and agreed a major production-sharing contract with CNPC for the joint development of the Chuandongbei natural gas area in Sichuan Basin in Central China. Chevron is also working with CNOOC to develop offshore oil resources in the South China Sea and in Bohai Bay.

PetroChina, Shell and Qatar Petroleum Co QPC have recently established a new Sino-foreign joint venture to construct a major new oil refinery with ethylene cracker and downstream petrochemical complex in Zhejiang on the East coast of China. PetroChina would be the majority shareholder with 51 per cent share. Royal Dutch Shell and Qatar Petroleum would each be holding 24.5 per cent shareholdings in the joint venture.

Bibliography

Adair, W., Brett, J. and Okumura, T. (2001). Negotiating Behavior When Cultures Collide: The United States and Japan. *Journal of Applied Psychology*, 86(3), pp. 371–385.

Adler, N. and Gunderson, A. (2008). *International Dimensions of Organizational Behavior*, 5th ed. Eagan, MN: Thomson/South-Western Publishing.

Ambler, T., Witzel, M. and Xi, C. (2000). *Doing Business in China*. London: Routledge.

Baldrige, L. (1993). *Letitia Baldrige's New Complete Guide to Executive Manners*. New York: Macmillan, p. 121.

Barbosa, D. (2009). Danone Exits China Venture after Years of Legal Dispute. *New York Times*. Available at: http://www.nytimes.com/2009/10/01/business/global/01danone.

Barton, D. (2013). China Half a Billion Middle Class Consumers. *The Diplomat*, USA.

Berge, R. and Wang, H. (2009). Clean Coal Technology in China: A Strategy for the Netherlands, Master's thesis, University of Twente, Netherlands.

Blackman, C. (1997). *Negotiating in China: Case Studies & Strategies*. Australia: Allen & Unwin.

Boao Forum for Asia Annual Conference (2014). BFA, Hainan PRC.

Boao Forum for Asia Annual Conference (2015). BFA, Hainan PRC.

Bremmer, I. and Huntsman, J. (2013). How to Play Well with China. *New York Times*. Available at: http://www.nytimes.com/2013/06/02/opinion/sunday/how-to-play-well-with-china.html?mcubz=3.

Chartered Management Institute (2016). Winning Ideas – Top 5 Management Articles of the Year. February 2016, CMI, London, UK.

Confucius (551–479BC). *The First Ten Books* translated by D. C. Lau. New York: Penguin Books, reprinted in 1979.

DuPont (2013). Sustainable Energy for a Growing China [PDF]. Available at: http://www.dupont.com/content/dam/dupont/corporate/our-approach/global-challenges/documents/DuPont_SustainableEnergyforGrowingChina_052013.pdf.

Fenby, J. (2014). *Will China Dominate the 21st Century?* New York: John Wiley & Sons.

Fisher R., Ury, W. and Patton, B. (1991). *Getting to Yes: Negotiating Agreement Without Giving In*. New York: Penguin Books.

Galinsky, A. (2004). When to Make the First Offer in Negotiations. *Working Knowledge*, 8 September.

GPCA and McKinsey (2015). *Thoughts for a New Age in Middle East Petrochemicals*, released at 10th GPCA Forum in Dubai UAE, November 2015.

Graham, J. L., Mintu, A. T. and Rodgers, W. (1994). Explorations of Negotiation Behaviors in Ten Foreign Cultures Using a Model Developed in the United States. *Management Science*, 40(1), pp. 72–95.

Harris, D. (2014). China Joint Ventures: A Warning/*China Law Blog*. China Law Blog. Available at: http://www.chinalawblog.com/2014/08/china-joint-ventures-a-warning.html.

Harvard Business School Publishing (2004). Should You Make the First Offer? *Negotiation*, July 2004.

Hofstede, G. (1980). *Culture's Consequences: International Differences in Work-Related Values*. Newbury Park, CA: Sage Publications.

Huidian Research (2013). *In-Depth Research and Forecast of China Ethylene Industry for 2013–2017*. PRC: Huidian.

Huxley, A. J. (1941). *The Uniqueness of Man*. London: Chatto.

International Energy Agency (2012). *World Oil Market Report 2012*. Paris: IEA.

International Energy Agency (2013). *Report & Roadmap for Energy Conservation & GHG Emission Reductions by Catalytic Processes*. Paris: IEA.

International Energy Agency (2014). *World Energy Outlook 2014*. Paris: IEA.

International Energy Agency (2015). *World Energy Outlook 2015*. Paris: IEA.

International Monetary Fund (2013). *World Economic Outlook Databases*. Washington, DC: IMF.

Kimmel, P. (1994). Cultural Perspectives on International Negotiations. *Journal of Social Issues*, 50(1), pp. 179–196.

KPMG (2012). *Investment in PR China Report*. KPMG.

Lederach, J. P. (1995). *Preparing for Peace*. Syracuse, NY: Syracuse University Press, p. 43.

McCann, D. (1998). *How to Influence Others at Work*, 2nd ed. Oxford, UK: Butterworth Heinemann.

Machiavelli, N. (1513). *The Prince*. Italy: publisher unknown.

Mark, R. (1997). Enron's Rebecca Mark: "You Have to be Pushy and Aggressive". *Bloomberg Business Week*. Available at: https://www.bloomberg.com/amp/news/articles/1997-02-23/enrons-rebecca-mark-you-have-to-be-pushy-and-aggressive.

Matar, W., Murphy, F., Pierru, A. and Rioux, B. (2015). Lowering Saudi Arabia's Fuel Consumption and Energy System Costs Without Increasing End Consumer Prices. *Energy Economics*, 49, pp. 558–569.

Nakanishi, M. and Johnson, K. M. (1993). Implications of Self-Disclosure on Conversational Logics, Perceived Communication Competence, and Social Attraction: A Comparison of Japanese and American Cultures. *Intercultural Communication Competence*, pp. 204–221.

Neidel, B. (2010). Negotiations, Chinese Style. *China Business Review*, 37(6), pp. 32–35.

Novinger, T. (2001). *Intercultural Communication: A Practical Guide*. Austin, TX: University of Texas Press, p. 121.

OECD (2013). MENA Task Force on Energy & Infrastructure 2013 Report on Renewable Energies in the Middle East and North Africa MENA: Policies To Support Private Investment, with Inputs by Henry Wang and other OECD MENA Task Force Team Members, OECD, Paris.

Offiong, D. A. (1997). Conflict Resolution Among the Ibibio of Nigeria. *Journal of Anthropological Research*, 53(4) , pp. 423–442.

OPEC IEA IEF Energy Conference 23 March 2015, IEF, Riyadh, Saudi Arabia.

Plotinus (205–270ACE). The Six Enneads, Rome, 250 ACE.

Pricewaterhouse Coopers (2013). China M&A 2012 Report, May 2013, PWC, UK.

PRC (2014). New FDI Measures: Management Measures for Approval and Filing of Foreign Direct Investment (FDI) 外商投资项目核准和备案管理办法, MOFCOM, Beijing, PRC.

PRC Government (2013). Catalogue of Investment Projects Approved by Government (2013) 政府核准的投资项目目录（2013年本), PRC Government, Beijing, PRC.

PRC Government (2013). The Catalogue of Priority Industries for Foreign Investment in Central and Western China中西部地区外商投资优势产业目录, PRC Government, Beijing, PRC.

Salacuse J. W. (2003). *The Global Negotiator: Making, Managing, and Mending Deals Around the World in the Twenty-First Century*. New York: Palgrave Macmillan.

Salacuse, J. W. (2004). Negotiating: The Top Ten Ways That Culture Can Affect Your Negotiation. *IVEY Business Journal*, 69(1), pp. 1–6.

Schwab, K. (2010). *The Global Competitiveness Report 2010–2011*. Geneva: World Economic Forum.

Secretariat, O.P.E.C., (2013). World Oil Outlook, 2013, Vienna, Austria.

Secretariat, O.P.E.C., (2014). World Oil Outlook, 2014, Vienna, Austria.

The National (2013). China Largest Net Importer of Crude Oil Report, 6 March, USA.

Tian, X. (2007). *Managing International Businesses in China*. Cambridge, UK: Cambridge University Press.

Ury, W. (1993). *Getting Past No: Negotiating Your Way from Confrontation to Cooperation*. New York: Bantam.

Wang, H. (1990). Canada Patent CA2008347: "Removing Hydrogen Cyanide and Carbon Oxy-Sulphide from a Syngas Mixture", Shell Internationale, Amsterdam, Netherlands.

Wang, H. (1995). *Oil & Gas Journal* (*OGJ*) Published Paper on UK Refinery Successful Demonstrations of New Ethyl Benzene Process, 2005, Authored Jointly by Henry Wang together with Mobil USA & Raytheon USA.

Wang, H. (2001). The Prime Minister Office of a Leading Asia Pacific Country Hosted a High-Level China Strategy Meeting for multiple Ministries Senior Directors & Advisors, Speech & Presentation on China Social, Economic and Industrial Developments & China Strategy Developments, Singapore.

Wang, H. (2003). *China Daily* News Interview Report in Beijing on EU Work Group Energy Proposals to Government with Henry Wang, Chairman of EU Energy, Petrochemicals, Oil & Gas Committee, 2003, *China Daily*, Beijing, PRC.

Wang, H. (2003). China Ministry of Commerce & Foreign Trade MOFCOM Transnational Company Forum Speech on New Development Strategy of Transnational Companies in China, MOFCOM, Beijing, PRC.

Wang, H. (2003). China National Development Reform Commission NDRC Energy Research Institute ERI Report on China Medium & Long-Term Energy & Carbon Scenarios Report, 2003, Jointly by China Energy Research Institute of the PRC Government National Development Reform Commission with USA Lawrence Berkeley Lab of USA Government Department of Energy & Shell Group Planning with Contributions from Henry Wang, NDRC ERI, Beijing, PRC.

Wang, H. (2004). China Economics Round Table in Beijing Speech & Paper on China Clean Energy Sustainable Developments, China Economics Roundtable, Beijing, PRC.

Wang, H. (2004). China Ministry of Foreign Affairs & Institute of International Cooperation Meeting in Beijing in 2004, Speech and Paper on China Energy Business Outlooks & International Co-operations, MOFCOM, Beijing.

Wang, H. (2004). China SASAC Minister Meeting in Beijing China in 2004, Speech and Paper on China Energy Scenarios & Challenges, SASAC, Beijing.

Wang, H. (2004). London School of Economics Lecture & Paper on China, Outlooks & Opportunities, London School of Economics (LSE), London, UK.

Wang, H. (2004). UK Prime Minister Climate Change Adviser & DEFRA Director General Ministerial Meeting in London UK in 2004, Presentation and Paper on China Energy & Climate Change Outlook, DEFRA, London, UK.

Wang, H. (2004). USA and UK Counsel Generals Meetings in Shanghai, China, Presentation and Paper on China Energy Outlooks, 2004, UK Embassy, Shanghai, PRC.

Wang, H. (2004). Wharton Shell Group Business Leadership Program Business Case Inputs, Wharton Business School, Pennsylvania, USA.

Wang, H. (2005). Board Meeting of a leading International Chemical Company & a TOP Middle East Company Joint Venture, presentation on China Economic & Energy Outlooks, 2005, Singapore.

Wang, H. (2005). China Daily CEO Corporate Social Responsibilities Round Table, *China Daily*, Beijing, PRC.

Wang, H. (2005). China Economic Summit at Great Hall of People in Beijing in 2005, Paper on China Energy Outlooks & Scenarios, *China Cajing Economic Magazine*, Beijing, PRC.

Wang, H. (2005). China Energy and Strategy Seminar for a Leading Asia Government Prime Minister Office (PMO) and Key Ministries Presentations & Papers on Chia Energy Planning & Developments, Market Access & Cooperation Strategies & Challenges, Shell Asia.

Wang, H. (2005). China Global Economic & Leadership Summit, Speech on Energy Economic Developments by Henry Wang with USA Nobel Economists at the Grand Hyatt Hotel in Beijing, Organized by China Cajing Economic Publishing Group, Beijing, PRC.

Wang, H. (2005). China Ministry of Foreign & Economic Cooperation [MOFCOM] Summit in China in 2005, Speech and Paper on Multinational Co Co-operations & Sustainable Developments in China, MOFCOM, Beijing, PRC.

Wang, H. (2005). China State Council Development Research Council (DRC) in Beijing in 2005 Presentation on Global & China Energy Scenarios, DRC Beijing.

Wang, H. (2005). International Advanced Management Seminar for Top Multinational Executives, Presentations and Papers on Global and China Business Issues, Energy Planning in China, Government Structures in China & New Business Development in China, New York Bar Association HQ, New York, USA.

Wang, H. (2005). Lecture & Paper on Multinational Cos Operations in China, 2005, Tsinghua University, Beijing, PRC.

Wang, H. (2005). Netherlands Energy Minister Meeting in Beijing in 2005, Presentation on China Energy Developments, Netherlands Embassy, Beijing, PRC.

Wang, H. (2005). UK China Bilateral Energy Strategic Cooperations Paper with UK China Bilateral Energy Work Group, UK Embassy, Beijing, PRC.

Wang, H. (2006). China Advanced Management Seminar in Beijing China for Top International Executives, Presentations & Papers on China Business Issues, China Energy Planning & China Business Developments, 2006, Shell, Beijing, PRC.

Wang, H. (2006). *China Daily* CEO Climate Change Round Table Interview on Climate Change Outlooks by Henry Wang, 2006, *China Daily*, Beijing, PRC.

Wang, H. (2006). Climate Change & Sustainable Development Seminar for PRC Government Senior Officials Presentation & Paper on International Sustainable Development, Climate Change, Carbon Technologies & Management, 2006, Tsinghua University, Beijing, PRC.

Wang, H. (2006). Energy Seminar for PRC Government Top Officials at Joint Tsinghua Harvard MPA Course Presentation & Paper on Global Energy Planning, Advanced Technologies & Management to Vice Ministers/Governors, 2006, Tsinghua University, Beijing, PRC.

Wang, H. (2007). EU Chamber of Commerce China, Presentation on Clean Energy Developments & Opportunities, 2007, EUCCC, Beijing, PRC.

Wang, H. (2008). China Netherlands Prime Ministerial Energy Summit, paper on Integrated Energy Management, Clean Energy & Sustainable Development, November 2008, Tsinghua University, Beijing, PRC.

Wang, H. (2008). China State Council Development Research Council Presentation on Clean Energy & Coal Developments in China & Globally, November 2008, DRC Beijing, PRC.

Wang, H. (2008). Remin University and China Carbon Forum Conference in 2008, Speech and Paper on Clean Coal Developments and Copenhagen Negotiations, Remin University, Beijing, PRC.

Wang, H. (2008). UCL Distinguished Speaker Lecture on China Advanced Coal Technology & Successful Project Developments at University College London.

Wang, H. (2009). Argus Carbon Report Interview in London UK in Oct 2009 on China Carbon & Climate Change Trends, by Henry Wang with Argus Carbon (ed.), Argus, London, UK.

Wang, H. (2009). *Bloomberg* News Interview in Singapore in Oct 2009 on China Climate Change Policies Outlooks by *Bloomberg* Asia Editor with Henry Wang, *Bloomberg*, Singapore.

Wang, H. (2009). Carbon Forum Asia in Singapore, Keynote Speech & Paper on China Climate Change & Sustainable Development Policies, October 2009, Singapore.

Wang, H. (2009). Carbon Forum Asia in Singapore, Paper on China Carbon Market Management and Outlook, March 2009, Singapore.

Wang, H. (2009). China Carbon Forum Government Round Table keynote speech on China Clean Energy & Carbon Developments, June 2009, Remin University, Beijing, PRC.

Wang, H. (2009). China International Radio interview in Beijing China in April 2010 on World Bank Six Asia Country Energy Report, China Radio, Beijing.

Wang, H. (2009). UK China Chemicals CEO Working Group Forum in Shanghai, Paper and Presentation on Integrated Energy Management, Clean Energy Technologies & Sustainable Developments in China, November 2009, UK Embassy, Shanghai, China.

Wang, H. (2009). UK Embassy China in Beijing presentation on China Clean Energy & Sustainable Development, UK Embassy, Beijing.

Wang, H. (2010). Asia Pacific Offshore Support Forum in Singapore in April 2010, Paper on China Offshore Support Industry Developments, Singapore.

Wang, H. (2010). China International & Beijing State Radio Interview in Beijing on International Earth Day in April 2010 on Green Energy, Renewables, Chemicals, Coal Gasification, Energy Efficiency & Sustainable Developments, China Radio, Beijing.

Wang, H. (2010). Deep-water Drilling Outlook Summit in Singapore in July 2010, Paper on China Upstream Offshore Developments, Singapore.

Wang, H. (2010). Speech and Presentation on Shale Gas Business Growth, Commercialisation and Developments in China, to the First China International Shale Gas Conference, 26–27 October 2010 in Shanghai, organized by IBC Asia, China.

Wang, H. (2011). Keynote Speech to First International Four Kingdom Carbon International Conference Organized by Saudi Ministry of Petroleum, 2011, Saudi Arabia.

Wang, H. (2012). China Market Developments & Marketing Lecture in April 2012 to EMBA class at University of Colorado Denver Business School, Denver, USA.

Wang, H. (2012). Global & Middle East Petrochemical Growth & Developments at University of Colorado Energy Conference, Boulder, Colorado, USA.

Wang, H. (2012). India Oil IOC Chairman Petrochemical Conclave presentation "Opportunities & Challenges in Industries Winning Strategies", March 2012, IOC, Delhi, India.

Wang, H. (2012). International Energy & Renewables Strategic Co-Development Lecture in April 2012 at University of Colorado Denver Business School, Denver, USA.

Wang, H. (2013). IEA, OPEC and IEF International Energy Conference, January 2013, IEF HQ in Riyadh Saudi Arabia.

Wang, H. (2013). International Energy Agency IEA Energy Efficiency EE Manual review commentary to OECD BIAC and IEA EE Team, August 2013, IEA, Paris, France.

Wang, H. (2013). International Energy Agency World Energy Outlook Peer Review Panel – Global Energy Competitiveness inputs to the IEA WEO Team, April 2013, IEA, Paris, France.

Wang, H. (2013). Presentation to China Ministry of Commerce & China National Oil Companies Delegation Visit to Saudi Arabia, May 2013, SABIC, Riyadh, Saudi Arabia.

Wang, H. (2013). *Successful Business Dealings and Management with China Oil, Gas and Chemical Giants.* London and New York: Routledge.

Wang, H. (2014). Brunei Government Energy White Paper consultations, May 2014, Brunei.

Wang, H. (2014). China Ministry of Foreign Commerce call for comments on new China Administration Measures for Overseas Investment consultations, MOFCOM, Beijing, PRC.

Wang, H. (2014). China State Administration of Taxes SAT Administrative Approval Directory Call for Comments Consultation Inputs, February 2013, China SAT, Beijing, PRC.

Wang, H. (2014). China State Council Legislative Affairs Office SCLAO call for comments on the draft Law of Promoting Transformation of Science and Technology Achievements in the PRC Consultation Inputs, February 2013, China SCLAO, Beijing, PRC.

Wang, H. (2014). China State Council SCLAO Call for Comments on New China Regulations for Information Disclosure Consultation Inputs, May 2014, SCLAO, Beijing, PRC.

Wang, H. (2014). Fourth International Energy Forum & International Energy Authority & OPEC Symposium on Energy Outlooks speech on "Petrochemicals & Chemicals Growth Outlooks & Strategic Developments", 22 January 2014, IEF HQ in Riyadh, Saudi Arabia.

Wang, H. (2014). International Energy Agency World Energy Outlook (IEA WEO) Peer Review Panel Global Energy & Petrochemical Investment Cost Reviews commentaries to the IEA WEO Team, January 2014 in IEA HQ, Paris, France.

Wang, H. (2014). Japan Ministry Economic Trade Industry METI Presentation on Saudi Arabia Downstream Industrial Cluster Development Program, June 2014, SABIC, Riyadh, Saudi Arabia.

Wang, H. (2014). KAPSARC Paper on Energy Productivity Aligning Global Agenda Peer Review comments, April 2014, KAPSARC HQ in Riyadh, Saudi Arabia.

Wang, H. (2014). King Abdullah Petroleum Studies & Research Centre KAPSARC First International Seminar on China Keynote Speech and Presentation on "Sustainable Growth Scenarios & Strategies", 10 March 2014, KAPSARC HQ in Riyadh, Saudi Arabia, March 2014.

Wang, H. (2014). OECD BIAC China Task Force Paper on Priorities for OECD China Cooperations Consultation Inputs, OECD BIAC, Paris, France, September 2014.

Wang, H. (2014). OECD BIAC China Task Force Presentation to OECD China Reflection Group & OECD Ambassadors consultation inputs, 23–24 June 2014, OECD BIAC, Paris, France.

Wang, H. (2014). Presentation on Sustainable Petrochemical & Chemicals Outlooks to OECD Energy & Environmental Committee Meetings on 26 February 2014, OECD BIAC, Paris, France.

Wang, H. (2014). Presentation on Sustainable Petrochemical & Chemicals Outlooks to the 2nd IEA Unconventional Gas Forum, 26 March 2014, Calgary, Canada.

Wang, H. (2014). UK CBI White Paper on Business Energy and Climate Change Priorities for the 2015–2020 UK Parliament consultation inputs, August 2014, CBI, London, UK.

Wang, H. (2014). UK Chartered Management Institute Management Paper of Year 2014: "Business Negotiation Strategy & Planning in China", CMI, London, UK.

Wang, H. (2015). China MOFCOM PRC Foreign Investment Law Consultation Inputs, February 2015, MOFCOM, Beijing, China.

Wang, H. (2015). ICIS 9th Asia Base Oil and Lubricant Conference Keynote Speech on "China Demand Growth & Sustainable Growth Strategies", 10 June 2015, Singapore.

Wang, H. (2015). OECD BIAC Statement for Consultation with OECD Secretary General and Ambassadors, November 2015, OECD BIAC, Paris, France.

Wang, H. (2015). OECD BIAC Statement to OECD Council Ministerial Meeting MCM White paper consultation inputs, April 2015, OECD BIAC, Paris, France.

Wang, H. (2015). OPEC IEA IEF Energy Conference & IEF KAPSARC Energy Roundtable, 23–24 March 2015, Discussion Inputs, IEF, Riyadh, Saudi Arabia.

Wang, H. (2015). PRC State Council Invitation to Consult on the "Suggestions of the CPC Central Committee on Drafting the 13th Five Year Plan of National Economic and Social Development for China" Consultation Inputs, PRC Xinhua News Agency, Beijing, December 2015.

Wang, H. (2015). Singapore Energy Week Asia Downstream Conference: "Global Supply Chain Management, Risk Minimisation, Resource and Cost Optimisation Strategies", 28 October, Singapore.

Wang, H. (2016). China Academy of Science Dalin Institute: "Energy Growth Strategies", November 2016, Dalin, PRC.

Wang, H. (2016). *Energy Markets in Emerging Economies: Strategies for Growth*. London: Routledge.

Wang, H. (2016). EU Chamber of Commerce China Energy Panel: "Energy Markets in Emerging Economies", August 2016, Beijing, PRC.

Wang, H. (2016). OECD Integrity Forum Paper: "Global and MENA SOE Governance and Integrity", April 2016, Paris, France.

Wang, H. (2016). Transparency International SOE Integrity Forum Paper: "Global SOE Management and Governance Improvements", June 2016, Berlin, Germany.

Wang, H. (2016). UK Chartered Management Institute Top Five Management Paper of Year 2015: "China Business Negotiation Strategy", February 2016, CMI, London, UK.

Wang, H. (2017). Cambridge University China Russia NE Asia International Forum Presentation: "Belt & Road Strategic Outlooks", 25 May, Cambridge, UK.

Wang, H. (2017). Chinese University of Hong Kong: "Energy, Environment and Climate Change", March 2017, Hong Kong.

Wang, H. (2017). City of London China Green Financing Speech, 27 June 2017, London, UK.

Wang, H. (2017). *Energy and Environment Growth Strategies*. London: Imperial College.

Wang, H. (2017). Hong Kong Science Tech Association: "Energy, Environment and Climate Change Innovations", Hong Kong.

Wang, H. (2017). Hong Kong University: "Energy, Environment and Climate Change Action Plans", 9 April 2017, Hong Kong.

Wang, H. (2017). House of Lords Cyber Security Panel Speech, 28 June 2017, London, UK.

Wang, H. (2017). Institut d'Etudes Politiques Meeting Speech on "Global Corporate Digital Future Transformation Strategies", 16–18 June 2017, Liechtenstein.

Wang, H. (2017). *International Energy and Environment Growth Strategies*. London: Kings College.

Weldon, E. and Jehn, K. A. (1995). Examining Cross-Cultural Differences in Conflict Management Behavior: A Strategy for Future Research. *The International Journal of Conflict Management*, 6(4), pp. 387–403.

Wiseman, R. L. and Koester, J. (1993). *Intercultural Communication Competence*. Newbury Park, CA: Sage Publications, p. 207.

World Bank, Developing East Asia Pacific Growth, 13 April 2015, World Bank, USA.

World Scientific (2013). *Industrial Map of China's Energy*. Hackensack, NJ: World Scientific.

Xinhua (2013). China M&A 2012 Highlights, 22 May, Beijing, PRC.

Xinhua (2013). PRC President Xi Jinping Joint Written Interview to the Media of Trinidad and Tobago, Costa Rica and Mexico, 31 May 2013, Xinhua News Agency, Beijing, PRC.

Yuen, L. (2011). *Enterprising China*. Oxford, UK: Oxford University Press.

Yuen, L. (2013). *China Growth*. Oxford, UK: Oxford University Press.

Glossary

ACFTU	All-China Federation of Trade Unions
ACIA	ASEAN Comprehensive Investment Agreement
ADB	Asian Development Bank
AIIB	Asia Infrastructure Investment Bank
ASEAN	Association of South East Asia Nations
ASW	ASEAN Single Window
BATNA	Best Alternative to a Negotiated Agreement scenario
BCM	Billion cubic meters
BLNG	Brunei LNG
BP	British Petroleum
BPD	Barrels per day
CAGR	Cumulative annual growth rates
CASS	Chinese Academy of Social Science
CBM	Coal Bed Methane
CBRC	China Banking Regulatory Commission
CAGP	Central Asian Gas Pipelines
CCAA	China Certification & Accreditation Agency (CNCA)
CCPC	Chinese Communist Party Congress
CCR	Continuous Catalytic Reformers
CDM	Clean Development Mechanism
CEO	Chief Executive Officer
CF	Cubic feet
CFO	Chief Finance Officer
CIETAC	China International Economic & Trade Arbitration Commission
CJV	Contractual Joint Venture
CNCA	The Chinese Certification and Accreditation Agency
CNOOC	China National Offshore Oil Corp
CNPC	China National Petroleum Corp
CM	Cubic metres
CMI	Confederation of Management Institute UK
CMPY	Cubic metres per year
CNPC	China National Petroleum Corporation
CO2	Carbon dioxide

CSP	Corporate Strategy and Planning
CSPCL	CNOOC Shell Petrochemical Co Ltd in China
CSR	Corporate Social Responsibility
CSRC	China Securities Regulatory Commission
CTO	Chief Technology Officer
CTCM	Contract Terms amd Clauses Mapping Analysis
E&P	Exploration and Production
ECFA	Economic Cooperation Framework Agreement
EI	Emotional Intelligence
EIA	Environment Impact Assessment
EIA	USA Energy Information Administration of USA
EJV	Equity Joint Venture
EOR	Enhanced Oil Recovery
EPA	Environmental Protection Agency
EPB	Environmental Protection Bureau
EPC	Engineering, Procurement and Construction
FCC	Fluid Catalytic Crackers
FDI	Foreign Direct Investment
FIE	Foreign Invested Enterprise
FIHC	Foreign-invested Holding Company
FSRU	Floating Storage Recovery Unit
FTA	Free Trade Agreement
FTZ	Free Trade Zones
FYP	Five Year Plans of China
GAIL	Gas Authority of India Ltd
GCC	Gulf Cooperation Council
GDP	Gross Domestic Products
GM	General Manager
GOGA	Guangdong Oil & Gas Association
GOM	Gulf of Mexico USA
GTL	Gas to Liquid
GW	Giga watts
HR	Human Resources
IBP	Integrated Business Planning
IAEA	International Energy Authority
IEA	International Energy Agency
IMF	International Monetary Fund
IOC	International Oil Company
IOCL	India Oil Co Ltd
ISO	International Organization for Standardization
JV	Joint Ventures
KPI Key	Performance Indicators
KBPD	Thousand or Kilo barrels per day
KTPA	Thousand or Kilo metric tons per annum
LNG	Liquefied Natural Gas

LPG	Liquefied petroleum gas
LTO	Light tight oil
M&A	Merger and Acquisition
MENA	Middle East and North Africa
MEP	Ministry of Environmental Protection of China
MBPD	Million metric barrels per day
MLR	Ministry of Land and Resources of China
MTJDA	Malaysia Thailand Joint Development Area
MTPA	Million metric tonnes per annum
MNC	Multinational Company
MOFCOM	Ministry of Commerce of China
MOU	Memorandum of Understanding
MTG	Methanol to Gasoline
MTO	Methanol to Olefin
MTO+OCP	Methanol to Olefin + Olefin Cracking Process
NDRC	National Development Reform Commission of China
NELP	New Exploration Licensing Policy of India
NGL	Natural Gas Liquids
NOC	National Oil Company
NPC	National People's Congress of China
NSA	Negotiation Scenario Analysis
NTB	Non-Tariff Barriers
NWS	North West Shelf Australia
OE	Oil equivalent
OECD	Organisation of Economic Cooperation and Development
OPEC	Organization Petroleum Exporting Countries
ORR	Oil reserve ratios
OVL	ONGC Videsh Ltd
PAR	Project Application Report
PDO	Petroleum Development Oman
PE	Poly-ethylene
PMI	Purchasing Managers Index
PNG	Papua New Guinea
PP	Poly-propylene
PRC	People's Republic of China
PSA	Production Sharing Agreement (Upstream)
PTA	Purified Terephthalic Acid
PU	Polyurethane
PX	Para-xylene
Q&A	Questions and answers
QP	Qatar Petroleum
RNP	Relative Negotiation Power Analysis
SAFE	State Administration for Foreign Exchange
SAIC	State Administration for Industry and Commerce
SABIC	Saudi Arabia Basic Industries Co.

SASAC	State Assets Supervision and Administration Commission
SAT	State Administration for Taxation
SCEPC	State Council Environmental Protection Committee
SCS	Sinopec Chemical Sales Co Ltd
SFJV	Sino-Foreign Joint Venture
SG&A	Selling, General and Administrative costs
SIA	Social Impact Assessment
SIPC	Sinopec International Petroleum Exploration & Production Corp.
SME	Small Medium Enterprise
SMTO	Sinopec Methanol to Olefin SMTO
SNG	Synthetic natural gas
SOE	State-Owned Enterprise
SPA	Sale and Purchase Agreements
SPC	Singapore Petroleum Company
SPR	Strategic Petroleum Reserves
SWOT	Strength Weakness Opportunity Threat Analysis
TCF	Trillion cubic feet
TCM	Trillion cubic meters
TPA	Tonnes per annum
TPD	Tonnes per day
UNGC	United Nation Global Compact
WOFE	Wholly Owned Foreign Enterprise
WTO	World Trade Organization
YARACO	Yangtze River Acetyls Company (Yaraco) BP & Sinopec JV
YOY	Year on Year growth
YPC	Yangtze Petrochemical Co of BASF and Sinopec
ZOPA	Zones of Potential Agreement
%	Per cent or Percentage

Index